Kincraft

RELIGIOUS CULTURES OF AFRICAN AND AFRICAN DIASPORA PEOPLE

Series editors: Jacob K. Olupona, *Harvard University*
 Dianne M. Stewart, *Emory University*
 and Terrence L. Johnson, *Georgetown University*

The book series examines the religious, cultural, and political expressions of African, African American, and African Caribbean traditions. Through transnational, cross-cultural, and multidisciplinary approaches to the study of religion, the series investigates the epistemic boundaries of continental and diasporic religious practices and thought and explores the diverse and distinct ways African-derived religions inform culture and politics. The series aims to establish a forum for imagining the centrality of Black religions in the formation of the "New World."

Kincraft   *The Making of Black Evangelical Sociality*

TODNE THOMAS

Duke University Press · *Durham and London* · 2021

© 2021 Duke University Press. All rights reserved
Printed in the United States of America on acid-free paper ∞
Designed by Courtney Leigh Richardson
Typeset in Portrait and Century Schoolbook
by Westchester Publishing Services

Library of Congress Cataloging-in-Publication Data
Names: Thomas, Todne, author.
Title: Kincraft : the making of black evangelical sociality / Todne Thomas.
Other titles: Religious cultures of African and African diaspora people.
Description: Durham : Duke University Press, 2021. | Series: Religious cultures of african and african diaspora people | Includes bibliographical references and index.
Identifiers: LCCN 2020027296 (print) | LCCN 2020027297 (ebook)
ISBN 9781478010654 (hardcover)
ISBN 9781478011781 (paperback)
ISBN 9781478013129 (ebook)
Subjects: LCSH: Black theology. | Evangelicalism—Social aspects—United States. | Race relations—Religious aspects—Christianity.
Classification: LCC BT82.7 .T466 2021 (print) | LCC BT82.7 (ebook) | DDC 280/.4089/96073—dc23
LC record available at https://lccn.loc.gov/2020027296
LC ebook record available at https://lccn.loc.gov/2020027297

Cover art: *Matisse's Chapel*. © 2020 Faith Ringgold / Artists Rights Society (ARS), New York. Courtesy ACA Galleries, New York.

Duke University Press gratefully acknowledges the Harvard Divinity School at Harvard University, which provided funds toward the publication of this book.

This book is dedicated to my mother, father, and son.

To my mother, Doris, who raised me as her daughter without ever clipping my wings. Thank you for being the kind of mother that stays up to keep me company during late-night writing sessions. You have given me the most fundamental lessons in family love. You have taught me that you never regret the love you pour into your kin. I enjoy watching you continue to grow into your gifts and watching you share them with others.

To my departed father, James Thomas Jr., I will always love you. Thank you for being my father from my beginning until your end, for being a type of father you never had, for trying over a course of fits and starts, and persevering. You still inspire me, and I miss you. I will continue to speak your name.

To my son, Tashinga, you have taught me the most lovely, difficult, and enduring lessons about kinship. I love you more and more every day. I thank God for you, and I would do everything over again if it led me to you. Thank you for making me better. I look forward to watching you write your own way and will co-labor to build a world in which your voice can be received for its richness.

Contents

Acknowledgments · ix
Introduction · 1

Part One · Contextualizing the Social Dimensions
of a Black Evangelical Religious Movement

1 · On "Godly Family" and "Family Roots":
Creating Kinship Worlds · 29

2 · Moving against the Grain:
The Evangelism of T. Michael Flowers in the Segregated US South · 57

3 · Black Like Me? Or Christian Like Me?
Black Evangelicals, Ethnicity, and Church Family · 83

Part Two · Scenes of Black Evangelical Spiritual Kinship in Practice

4 · Bible Study, Fraternalism, and the Making
of Interpretive Community · 109

5 · Churchwomen and the Incorporation of Church and Home · 135

6 · Black Evangelicals, "the Family," and Confessional Intimacy · 167

Conclusion · 199   Notes · 213   References · 229   Index · 247

Acknowledgments

The journey to this book has been long. The help I have received is too expansive to describe in a single document. I will do my best to acknowledge the people who have been formative to the completion of this project. If for some reason you do not see your name present, please "charge it to my head and not my heart," as the adage goes.

I would like to thank God for endowing me with life. I would also like to thank my benevolent ancestors for the examples of their lives and for their ongoing protection, encouragement, witness, and wisdom. This includes my Brewster, Davis, Henry, Sheffield, and Thomas ancestors. To my brother, Tim Thomas, it is a sheer delight to watch you grow and evolve. To my niece Madison Thomas, you are love, and you are loved.

To the members of the DBC and CBC communities, thank you for welcoming me into your communities and homes, for sharing your stories, for being kind. I appreciate the conversations, the wisdom, the deep hanging out. I learned a lot about community and life from being within your midst. I remain extremely grateful and humbled by that.

To my Emmanuel United Presbyterian Church family who played such a vital role in my upbringing, spiritual walk, and self-esteem, thank you. Thanks also go to Walter and Gloria Mencer, Barbara Glanz, and Dr. Roberto Benson. You made such a big difference in shaping my life course. I hope to make each of you proud.

To my extended family—my Uncle John and Aunt Janie, my Uncle Joe and Aunt Teralyn, my Aunt Joanne and Uncle Kenneth, my cousins Billy and Alyssa, Jasmine, Tyson, Teia, Casey, Asha, and my other uncles and aunts and cousins—thank you, I love you, and I wish you well.

To my chosen family, the dear people whom I hold and who hold me in their hearts and spirits, thank you, thank you, thank you. I would not have finished without you. The list is long: the University of Virginia sisters of my heart, Z'etoile Imma and Sonya Donaldson. My Vermont family and caregivers and confidants without whom I would not have survived: Cailyne Crowder, Dakota Burr, and Jaydyne Crowder, Bindu Panikkar and Peter Richards, Demethra Bradley, Janice Murikami, Amy Burrell-Cormier and Jesse Cormier, Jinny Huh and David Bond, Wanda Heading-Grant, Maria McGrath, and Kerin Stackpole, Major Jackson, Emily Bernard, John Gennari, Traci Griffith, and the entire Vermont Black Friday Crew. My Boston community who has now become its own diaspora but the love still remains: Marena Lin, Marina Magloire, Brenna Casey, Kathryn and Chris Carr, Samantha Morrison, Kenneth Reaves, Maria Beaute, Valentino Robinson, Imani Uzuri, Courtney Stanley, the members of my Union Church Family, and the list keeps growing.

To my advisor, Susan McKinnon, thank you for mentoring me, for encouraging me not to give up, and for providing me with a model of how to mentor and labor with integrity within my profession. I owe you a debt that I can never repay directly but that I will try to return through my own work as a writer and a teacher. To my dissertation committee members—Ira Bashkow, Cynthia Hoehler-Fatton, George Mentore, and Milton Vickerman—thank you for your support and constructive criticism. To other University of Virginia professors from graduate school who shaped and continue to inspire me— Claudrena Harold, Lisa Woolfork, Marlon Ross, and Ian Grandison—your intellectual and artistic work motivates me.

To my dear anthropologist comrades: Vicki Brennan, Bertin Louis Jr., N. Fadeke Castor, Casey Golumski, Rose Wellman, Asiya Malik, Rhyannon Berkowitz, Arsalan Khan, Clare Terni, Jason Hickel, Brian Howell, Claire Snell-Rood, Aimee Villareal, Alex Chavez, Raja Swamy, Reighan Gillam, Graham Jones, Pensri Ho, and Stanford Carpenter, your support over the years has been immeasurable. I look forward to our future collaborations and anticipate reading your future work as well.

To the faculty of the Religion Department at the University of Vermont— Anne Clark, Kevin Trainor, Ilyse Morgenstein-Fuerst, Tom Borchert, and Erica Andrus—thank you for being such warm and supportive colleagues.

Special thanks are due to the Harvard Divinity School administration who provided book subvention funding to support the publication of the manuscript. Thank you for investing in this work. To the current faculty of Harvard Divinity School (HDS), including Catherine Brekus, David Hempton, David Holland, Dan McKahan, Jacob Olopuna, and Mayra Rivera (to name a few), and the broader Harvard community who are too numerous to name in full here, thank you for your support. Your invitations to present my work, your mentorship, the dynamic examples you set with your own scholarship, and your thirst for learning have propelled me forward. Special thanks to past and current Harvard colleagues Jonathan Walton, Marla Frederick, Laura Nasrallah, Braxton Shelley, Genevieve Clutario, and Jarvis Givens for your mentorship, guidance, and friendship. Thank you to the amazing HDS library staff as well.

Special thanks are also due to the Radcliffe Institute for their award of a Suzanne Young Murray Assistant Professorship, as well as the Radcliffe Institute administration and staff and the 2019–2020 class of Radcliffe fellows and professors. Though our fellowship year was cut short by the coronavirus pandemic, your talent, creativity, and passion will remain a catalyst for my research for years to come. I send each of you my best wishes in your future pursuits and hope our paths will cross again.

To the Tengo Sed writer collective including Natasha Gordon-Chipembere, Alicia Anabel Santos, Vilna Bashi-Treitler, Yndia Lorick-Wilmot, and Michelle Simms, thank you for your encouragement and wisdom.

Humble thanks are also due to the anonymous reviewers who provided two rounds of responses to the manuscript. Your questions and critiques made this work better. I would also like to extend my sincere gratitude to Miriam Angress, Annie Lubinsky, Chad Royal, Donald Pharr, Diane Stewart, Maria Volpe, and the Duke University Press team that helped make this book a reality.

To Shiphrah and the crew at my favorite local coffee shop, thank you for the warm vibes and the caffeine you provide. To Michael Young, our kind building custodian, thank you for helping me with the repeated lockouts that occurred around my writing deadlines. For Kevin, who works at my favorite watering hole, thanks for letting me listen to Emily King on the rough days and for bringing me fries when the kitchen was closed. And for those not named for reasons unwritten, who know who you are: thank you.

Introduction

When describing what it means to be part of a Christian community, Sister Clara Sutton—a sixty-two-year-old Afro-Trinidadian nurse and evangelical church member—concluded that Christians' embodiment of the Holy Spirit fostered a special kinship:

> It's a unique relationship really that you meet people in another country from another place, and you have this one common bond. And they don't really have to know you or know anything about you. But yet the Holy Spirit has made you all kin, and you know it. And that's unique really. It doesn't have to take long to form [a bond with other Christians] at all.

Sutton identified the Holy Spirit as a relating agent that connects Christians across space. This mutual recognition of a shared spiritual relationship tugs them *toward* and ties them *to* one another.

Brother Edward Warrington—an Afro-Jamaican elder—described Christian community as facilitating loving and special relationships grounded in their mutual salvation:

> I'm comfortable with the saints. All of them. Male and female. I love the children. I just think it's a wonderful relationship. I tell people when they're grumbling, "I don't know why you're grumbling, or what you're grumbling about. Look at all the people here who you get to have a relationship with." But uh . . . people of God are very special. They occupy a very special place. You have been brought into the family of God. There's a common acceptance of Jesus Christ.

This book takes Sister Sutton, Brother Warrington, and some of their black evangelical spiritual kin at their word, and digs deep to understand how they conceptualize and enact their spiritual relationships.

Kincraft: The Making of Black Evangelical Sociality is an ethnographic exploration of the community created by the members of a black evangelical church association in the Atlanta metropolitan area. Set in two Afro-Caribbean and African American evangelical congregations named Dixon Bible Chapel (DBC) and Corinthian Bible Chapel (CBC), this project examines church members' spiritual definitions and enactments of family.[1] The black evangelicals of CBC and DBC enjoy a multi-layered religious belonging through spiritual kinship. This they manifest through discourse and practices of relatedness produced as "brothers and sisters in Christ," "spiritual mothers," "spiritual fathers," "spiritual children," and "prayer partners." The study of DBC and CBC evangelicals also reveals that black evangelicals are not the passive subjects of evangelical heteronormative family discourse. Rather, black evangelicals use their spiritual relationships as a mode of *kincraft* that speaks to their religious aspirations for Christian relationships and their lived material experiences with racialization, spatial mobility, and social mobility.

This book is the product of thirteen months of fieldwork in the Atlanta metropolitan area conducted from 2007 to 2008 and subsequent years of data analysis and deliberation. I conducted the majority of my research at DBC, in Lithonia, Georgia, a majority Afro-Caribbean and minority African American congregation. While there I interviewed about a third of the church congregation's membership and engaged in sustained participant observation in institutional and everyday community life. I also conducted a smaller number of interviews with members of CBC: a sister church located in downtown Atlanta, with an African American majority and Afro-Caribbean minority.

In many ways, the process by which I made my way to the DBC and CBC communities mirrors my navigation of the Atlanta metropolitan area's decentralized topography: slow (traffic-laden), roundabout (like the city's infamous circular Interstate 285), and made possible by the guiding voices of local residents. I first heard about the existence of DBC in the summer of 2006 while I was conducting preliminary summer research. Ann Marume, an Afro-Jamaican migrant and social worker who had moved to Atlanta during the 1980s, called it "a local West Indian church." She said that DBC's reputation among local Afro-Caribbean residents was of a church community that sensitively attended to the needs of Caribbean immigrants new to the area. Their quick incorporation of me into their church community as a young, single African American woman with no local relatives verified Marume's claim. I learned about its ethos of community life as both a witness and a subject of local forms of religious belonging. Family was not just something that congregants did away from church in their homes with spouses and children. Family was also a community praxis, a collective spirituality that privileged and made space for Christian connections.

I learned that church members expressed their devotion to their chapel constituency in a variety of ways. Some demonstrated their commitment by regularly gathering with their fellow church members. They frequently attended Sunday church services as well as other weekly church programs such as the Tuesday-night prayer meeting, the Thursday-night Bible study, the Friday-night young adult gathering, or Sunday-evening cell-group meetings. In other instances, church members expressed their devotion to their community by undertaking the nuts-and-bolts leadership and work that kept the chapel running, such as leading Sunday Bible classes and youth educational programs, organizing meals for special events, and developing local and international outreach efforts. Other members conveyed their devotion to their church community by tightening the connections mediating religious fellowship. Through visits and hosting visitors, prayers, Bible studies, and the offering of material aid and advice, these church participants ensured that church membership was not solely a matter of affiliation but also of belonging.

Spiritual kinship was not only a matter of showing up but a conceptual project as well. The CBC and DBC evangelicals cognize their relationships to one another in a number of ways. Congregants expressed the belief that brothers and sisters in Christ should treat one another in the same ways as birth siblings. This was reflected in the common rejoinder to some of my questioning: "Family is family." Through such ethical imaginaries, they closed the gap between the presumably "real" family relationships of biology and those of spiritual kin. The DBC and CBC members also depicted their spiritual family membership in terms of a universal Christian kinship or "family of God." They held the belief that all Christians were sisters and brothers in Christ, regardless of the religious barriers or norms created by racial lines. Both evangelical church communities also understood their spiritual kinship with each other as perforating ethnic boundaries. They knew that familial church belonging bridged or elided the ethnic distinctions between Caribbean Americans and African Americans, and sustained fellowship beyond ethnic conflicts. These members evolved kinship worldviews that modeled alternatives to the racial/ethnic barriers and norms of US congregational life and that added expansive spiritual lexicons of family to a reified heteronormative family grammar.

In the realm of collective religious practices, church members enacted their relationships with one another through biblical, domestic, and reflective practices. Through the common ritual of Bible study, church members produced a shared institutional identity as "Bible believers." As individuals, all church members study the Bible frequently, but church-wide biblical exegesis during worship settings generated a special and exclusionary connection and understanding among churchmen. This institutionalized fraternalism coexisted with everyday spiritual communion among spiritual parents, spiritual children, and prayer partners. Through mundane practices of feeding, kitchen-table talk, prayer, and mentorship, these church members, and especially churchwomen, forged close spiritual connections that deepened and tightened the bonds of congregational life. The black evangelicals of this Atlanta constituency also created confessional intimacies to air their anxieties about marriage and child rearing. They used the close, emotional bonds of spiritual kinship and, in some instances, the context of the interview setting to demonstrate their reflexive engagement with traditional heteronormative family ideals.

This book illustrates that CBC and DBC members were evangelical Christians as a matter of faith but also a matter of relationship, and that they inhabited their evangelicalism thoughtfully. It also demonstrates that religion, kinship, and race descend from genealogical inheritances and collective practices of intention. By documenting the contexts in which black evangelicals reproduced the heteronormative family as well as the instances in which they mobilized spiritual kinship as a counterpoint to nuclear familial and congregational memberships, I illustrate black evangelicals' complex relationship with evangelicalism and evangelical family values. In particular, I illuminate how black evangelicals create sacred solidarities and moralize them in relation to the alienations they associate with the boundaries of ethnicity, race, congregationalism, and the nuclear family in the United States. I illustrate how black evangelicals conscripted spiritual kinship to attend collectively to the moral and pragmatic demands of familial and religious life, as well as the material vulnerabilities that derived from antiblack racism, migration, and neoliberalism. Thus, the stream of evangelicalism they founded might be best considered an institutional and ideological response to popular sensibilities associated with mainstream US evangelicalism, black Church Christianity, urban ethnocongregationalism, and a project of collective spiritual alterity in its own right.

In addition to providing an ethnographic portrait of the social surroundings that constitute an Afro-diasporic evangelical community, this book responds to a double bind that hinders the study of black evangelicalism. The first aspect of this bind is a racial and religious mapping of US Christianity that locates black evangelicals between a white evangelicalism and a "Black Church" Christianity and obscures their unique perspectives. The second is a narrow analytical focus on the heteronormative family, at times reproduced by DBC and CBC members themselves through their subscription to heteronormative family ideals, that obscures the broader social terrain of black evangelical religiosity.

I propose that black evangelical spiritual kinship is best studied as a manifestation of a phenomenon that I identify as *kincraft*: the collective relational ethos and community fashioning that undergirds black evangelical religiosity. Although my perspectives on kincraft emerge from my ethnographic collaborations with black evangelicals, I locate their origins within the broader field of the African Diaspora. This includes the mobilities, intersubjectivities, and sacred imaginaries that have shaped modes of collective black Christian social life and are not wholly reducible to the definitions popularly associated with dominant Anglo-American, bourgeois, and Christian constructs of nuclear kinship and denominationalism.

A Note on Terminology

Definitions and terminology matter. I use the term *Afro-Caribbean* to refer to people, primarily of African descent, born in the countries of the anglophone Caribbean. In general, scholars of ethnicity and race consider Afro-Caribbean immigrants to be a distinctive black ethnic group. I employ the term *African American* to designate people of African descent born in the United States, including the second-generation children of Afro-Caribbean immigrants.[2] I understand African Americans to be a black ethnic group that is distinctive from Afro-Caribbean immigrants. I use the terms *black* and *Afro-diasporic* to refer to Afro-Caribbean and African American evangelical congregants collectively and to denote their shared racial locations in a US political landscape and their overlapping connections to African ancestry and New World histories of slavery and colonialism. Although I use the aforementioned terms, when possible I discuss church members' own use and contestations of ethnic and racial terminology to denote ethno-national and religious identities.

Members of the DBC and CBC most commonly refer to themselves as "Bible-believing" Christians. I use the term *evangelical* rather than *Bible-believing*[3] or *fundamentalist*[4] to locate church members more precisely within US and Caribbean religious landscapes. By *evangelical*, I refer to modes of religious expression that descend from nineteenth-century Anglo-American revivalist Protestant Christianity. In particular, the DBC and CBC communities are influenced by the evangelicalism of Plymouth Brethrenism—a nonconformist religious movement that began in Ireland in the 1820s and emphasized the unity of Christ, anticlericalism, antisectarianism, and the weekly observance of Communion (Hempton 2002). This movement subsequently spread to the anglophone

Caribbean in the late nineteenth and early twentieth centuries (Aymer 2016, 104), and was disseminated to African Americans in the South in the 1950s as a result of Afro-Caribbean evangelism.

Among the key ideas that emerged from this trans-Atlantic context is an emphasis on a born-again conversion experience, a common belief in the Bible as the literal word of God, the belief that spiritual convictions should be manifest in the realm of lived experience (or an attention to moral orthodoxy), and a strong disposition toward the expansion of the Christian community through missionary work (Bebbington 1989; Noll 2001, 13).

I use the term *black evangelical* to identify African American and Afro-Caribbean Christians who hold the key tenets associated with evangelicalism; who have personal or institutional connections with black Bible camps, Bible schools, and conservative churches that emerged in the post–World War II era (Miller 2000); and who differ from mainline African American Protestant Christians and black Pentecostals because of their independence from established black denominational structures (Potter 1979).[5]

I describe neo-evangelicalism in the United States as emerging with the establishment of the National Association of Evangelicals in 1940 and with the rise of the Moral Majority evangelical political coalition that coalesced around conservative family values in the 1970s. It is this strain of neo-evangelicalism that I identify as US mainstream evangelicalism and that I depict as a hegemonic, white religious project. The black evangelicalism in this ethnographic setting illuminates tense distinctions between the civic and religious projects of the "Black Church" and a mainstream white neo-evangelicalism.

The point of this work is not to undermine the historical legacy of the "black Church" (Savage 2008) as a vital institution of African American social life and a site for spiritual, liberatory, and redemptive imaginations; as a theological concept (R. Smith 2014);[6] or even as an important symbolic and material site of black social life in the twenty-first century. Rather, this book illustrates the ways in which blackness and Christianity (and the various means by which people craft affects and affinities in relationship to those constructs), as social facts, cannot be taken for granted in a US religious landscape molded by immigration, ethnic identity politics, "post-racial" racism, and projects of social mobility.

Ideas of family are socially constituted, culturally varied, and made through shared idioms and practices of relatedness (Carsten 2000; Franklin and McKinnon 2002). I use the term *the family* to refer to the heteropatriarchal family that is the dominant definition of family within US religious and secular social milieus. Within US evangelical culture, "the family" refers to an idealized unit that is associated with a hierarchy organized around patriarchal familial leadership, wifely submission to male authority, and children's submission to parental authority, all of which some evangelicals understand to be divinely ordained and ordered (Gallagher 2003). Although my identification of the patriarchal nuclear family as "the family" marks its position as a dominant definition of family in the US, this book does not take "the family" to be the beginning and end of black evangelical reckonings of kinship. Rather, *kincraft* refers to a family beyond "the family" and invites us to the study of spiritually grounded notions of family that should be liberated from a narrower, dominant heteropatriarchal definition of kinship.

Finally, in identifying evangelical traditions I use the term *US* in lieu of *America* or *American* to avoid the imperialist equation of "Americans" as solely those within the United States while erasing the Caribbean, Central American, and South American composition of the Americas (Kaplan and Pease 1993).

Locating Black Evangelicals in the US Religious Landscape

In *American Evangelical Christianity: An Introduction*, Mark Noll writes that "the relationship of African-American churches to evangelical traditions is complex" (2001, 14). There are many reasons that it is difficult to locate black evangelical experiences within the broader landscape of US Christianity. Christianities in the US are multiple, varied, coexistent, and contested.[7] Moreover, the designation *evangelical* can be defined in historical, missiological, soteriological, scriptural, and political terms.[8]

I propose that the challenge of locating black evangelicals within the US congregational landscape is not merely a question of defining what constitutes an evangelical but that it is the result of the racing of religion in the US. Race and religion in the United States are conjoined social phenomena; and in the case of evangelical Christianity, they can even be co-essentialized. Black evangelicalism falls between popular racial and religious models that distinguish a "conservative white evangelicalism" and a "liberal black Church Christianity." To discuss the position of black evangelicals in the religious landscape of the US requires one to address their seeming illegibility as minoritized racial subjects on the one hand or as black Christian outliers on the other.

BLACK EVANGELICALS AND THE RACIAL HEGEMONY OF WHITE EVANGELICALS

Black evangelicals are a diverse group of people who have planted, adapted, critiqued, and reformed evangelical Protestantism in the Americas. They have participated in the religious contexts generated by the First and Second Great

Awakenings, the evangelicalism of the violently antiblack postbellum era, and the neo-evangelicalism that emerged in the post–World War II era.

To trace the history of black evangelicalism, a history that is still under construction, is beyond the scope of this project. Yet there is a need to continue turning North American evangelical studies inside out to denote the nuanced positioning and socioreligious work conducted by black evangelicals. There is also a need to understand the symbiotic relationship of predominantly white evangelical Christian groups to antiblack racism.

The mainstream neo-evangelicalism in the United States that emerged in the mid-twentieth century and that has only more recently been qualified in racial terms has operated as a hegemonic, white religious movement. The 1950s witnessed a neo-evangelicalism that retreated from a previous orientation of social engagement to a deep emphasis on personal conversion, salvation, and an aversion to discussing political matters. By the end of the 1950s and the early 1960s, this white neo-evangelical mainstream began to have conversations about racial equality and rebuked racism as sin (Mullin 2014).

T. Michael Flowers, the Bahamian evangelist who in the 1950s founded the southeastern church network of which CBC and DBC are a part, participated in the changing evangelical landscape of the 1960s by collaborating with black evangelical luminaries such as Tom Skinner to create integrated religious revivals. Flowers also partnered with white evangelicals; inserted himself into a southern, white US evangelicalism; and advocated for a more inclusive evangelical Christianity that included black Christians as religious agents. As an evangelist, Flowers authored theologies of interracialism and universal Christian relatedness. And in imagining transcendent Christian kinship, which included a family of God with black evangelicals, Flowers pushed against the theological and organizational dominance of white framers of neo-evangelicalism.[9] As Flowers founded the southeastern evangelical church association of which CBC and DBC were a part, he also called out white evangelical complicity in racial segregation and fostered contexts of interracial religious collaboration.

The 1960s and 1970s saw progressive and black evangelicals express their disenchantment with anti-systemic approaches to race articulated by mainstream evangelical organizations such as the National Evangelical Association, evangelical periodicals such as *Christianity Today*, and the broader coalescence of the Christian Right. These included an ongoing framing of racism as a matter of individual sinfulness and an aversion to patterns of wealth inequality (Gasaway 2014; Rah 2019). In time, such critiques of a mainstream anti-systemic framing of race gave birth to intra-religious evangelical organizations such as the National Black Evangelical Association in 1963 and the Sojourners community in 1971.

The 1990s witnessed the "religious race bridging project" of the evangelical racial reconciliation movement (Wadsworth 2014, 83). Michael O. Emerson and Christian Smith attribute this movement to black Christian leaders such as John Perkins, Tom Skinner, and the Jamaican minister Samuel Hines. These African American and Afro-Caribbean evangelists were willing to collaborate with white evangelicals and, unlike many of their black Protestant contemporaries, were "all willing to use the term *evangelical*" (Emerson and Smith 2000, 54). Framers of the movement, such as Perkins, Skinner, and Hines, outlined interracial reconciliation as a spiritual and material project. This conciliatory para-church crusade generated a spiritual-relational frame that fostered ritualized scenes of interracial repentance on the part of whites and forgiveness on the part of blacks, and, in some instances, contexts of cross-racial worship and congregationalism (Wadsworth 2014). The racial reconciliation project was also "a radical democratic project" that issued a "call for changing unjust structures of society" through material redistribution, such as the community development and antipoverty work conducted by John Perkins's Christian Community Development Association (Alumkal 2004, 199). The efforts of this reconciliation movement embodied in organizations such as Promise Keepers and the move toward multiracial congregationalism has largely been considered meaningful and symbolic but as having little impact on ameliorating racial inequality in terms of redistributive efforts (Edwards 2014; Wadsworth 2014).

At the beginning of the twenty-first century, the whiteness of US evangelicalism persists. This whiteness is partially demographic in character. According to the Pew Research Center, evangelicals constitute 25 percent of the Christian population in the United States. Within that constituency, whites constitute 76 percent of the total national evangelical community, followed by Latinos at 11 percent, blacks at 6 percent, and Asians at 2 percent.[10] The whiteness of evangelicalism is also a product of racial hegemony. And the workings of that hegemony—the intellectual and moral touchstones that shape the commonsense understandings of a dominant population—is not merely a matter of numbers but of power. The whiteness of US neo-evangelicalism exists as a constellation of interpersonal and corporate notions of race that reproduce white racial and representational privilege and obscure the unique social locations, perspectives, and institutional loci of religious practitioners such as black evangelicals (Blum 2014).[11] Eric Tranby and Douglas Hartmann argue that mainstream US evangelicalism possesses a racialized religious culture and an emphasis on individualism responsible for "normalizing the very cultural practices, beliefs, and norms that privilege white Americans over others" (2008, 342). The effect of centralizing white privilege has been to "marginaliz[e] and exclud[e] the African American experience" within US evangelical settings (Tranby and Hartmann 2008, 347).

Antony Alumkal explains in greater detail contemporary evangelicalism as a white racial project:

> The spread of the mainstream racial project among white Americans could be interpreted as a response to the crisis of white identity. Defining racism as a spiritual problem that is immune to secular solutions gives whites license to oppose affirmative action, welfare, and other divisive government programs. Furthermore, whites who are nostalgic for a sense of ethnic attachment can treat evangelical Christianity as a quasi-ethnic identity, a move that is encouraged by evangelicals' sense of themselves as an embattled religious minority in the United States. Finally, whites can respond to their history as "oppressors" by cathartic acts of repentance, as well as by assertions that Christian identity transcends race, while fully retaining the fruits of white privilege. (2004, 205)

US evangelicalism provides venues for the validation of white moral and material supremacy. White evangelicals tend to deride redistributive efforts to ameliorate the effects of racism as worldly political measures. They diffuse the reality of white privilege through the religious subjection of white identity or claims of moral minoritization. As a result, white evangelical schemas of material and representational privilege remain intact. In such a racio-religious context, "the evangelical" is popularly imagined and studied as white. There is a tendency to typify black evangelicals as tropic outsiders without the means of representational and institutional production to render themselves as insiders.

Nonetheless, this book is neither a reflection on mainstream white evangelicalism nor an effort to use black evangelical religious experiences to deduce the racialization processes of white neo-evangelicalism. Rather, it is an effort to locate black evangelicals at the center of their own religious story. The brief outlines of black evangelicalism's coexistence with white evangelicalism listed above disturb characterizations of black evangelicals as a Christian model minority interested in assimilating white evangelical religious culture. As I will show, black evangelicals not only participate in a white mainstream US evangelicalism but also challenge the racial orientations of its hegemonic whiteness at the level of ideas and independent institutions. In addition to dealing with racial difference within the broader crosscurrents of US evangelicalism, DBC and CBC members also navigate plurality within their own ranks. This book's centering of black evangelicals therefore shows them not only in relation to a metanarrative of US evangelical interracialism but also engaged in the work of building social bridges among themselves and diasporic networks of relatedness that move beyond the racial axis of reconciliation.

BLACK EVANGELICALS AND THE CIVIC RELIGION OF "THE BLACK CHURCH"

Scholars have called for greater attention to the plural institutional, political, theological, and multiethnic strands that make up the "Black Church." An examination of the relationship of black evangelicals to the broader field of African American Christianity tempers some of the institutional orientations ascribed to Black Church Christianity in the United States.

Scholars of African American Christianity have explored how the construct of the "Black Church" led to reductive depictions of African American and Afro-diasporic Christians as a unified racial, religious, and civic block. Curtis J. Evans (2008) notes the irony that it was African American sociologist W. E. B. Du Bois who helped to create the generalizing trope of the Negro Church in employing a methodology that emphasized the significance of local particularities. Evans comments on one of the limitations of the Negro Church construct coined by black social scientists such as Du Bois in the early twentieth century: "The construction of the Negro Church (and its now common appellation, the black Church) has obscured the very real differences among African Americans that Du Bois himself detected, and it has rendered invisible or regressive those black religious groups and practices that do not fit into such categories as progressive or prophetic" (2008, 165).

Evans acknowledges that the invention of the Black Church was a pragmatic move on the part of black social scientists and activists to promote a common agenda for black social reform and political empowerment during a nadir in US race relations. He further argues that the moniker the "Black Church" suggests a uniformity in African American Christian practice that does not hold up when read against historical or contemporary accounts of black religious communities.[12] Anthropologist Marla Frederick also observes that "within the larger corpus of black church studies, we researchers often operate with a bias toward black 'progressive' religion, the tradition of sit-ins, boycotts, and struggles for justice" (2016, 6). The articulation of a black evangelical or conservative politics cannot be equated with deracination, nor does it preclude DBC and CBC members' constructions of significant reflections on blackness and black Christian expressions.

Black evangelicals tend to be understood as ideologues who prioritize separate evangelical religious values over a religious culture of the Black Church, characterized by independent institutions; critical, countercultural theologies; forms of exilic consciousness; charismatic leadership; and civic activism (McGlathery and Griffin 2007). Black evangelicals could be cast as race traitors of sorts who are associated with a conservative, individualistic, values-oriented paradigm that benefits a white evangelical majority over a redistributive political orientation popularly associated with the Black Church and black social progress—as people who value ideology over material conditions.

Such a posture is well illustrated by the ideological leanings of Sister Dolores Regent, a former African American member of DBC who asserted that her vocal support of the Republican candidate George Bush Jr. in the elections of 2000 and 2004 estranged her from family members and other black Christians who questioned her prioritization of moral values over a set of liberal political leanings typically associated with US blacks.

Nonetheless, my research disturbs this reading of black evangelicals as religious subjects who privilege their religious over their racial locations. DBC and CBC members voiced a variety of political leanings during my primary year of fieldwork in 2008, a presidential election year in which the nation elected its first black president. For example, during a Tuesday-night prayer meeting in which a group of eight women arranged their chairs into a circle for a prayer session, Sister Anita Edmondson (a Jamaican woman in her sixties) offered a last-minute prayer request: that women pray for the upcoming presidential election because "the country was in need of change": a veiled reference in support of Democratic contender Barack Obama. In her turn, Sister Ethel Roxbury (also a Jamaican sexagenarian woman), a long-time friend and prayer partner of Edmondson, politely countered that as Christians they should pray and support leaders who emphasize "godly values," a coded statement that signaled her backing of Republican nominee John McCain.

The exchange between Sister Edmondson and Sister Roxbury reveals the diversity of black evangelical political leanings and the inadequacies of unilaterally equating black evangelicals with the Christian Right voting bloc.[13] Black evangelicals cannot be neatly mapped onto the political axis of the Right, nor can black Christians in the US be located on the Left, or depicted as prioritizing a single set of "racial" or "religious" sentiments or positions in the election process. The coexistence of black evangelical identities with Republican political orientations and the desire of some black evangelicals to identify with a more universalized Christian identity rather than a black Christian religious community may not seem consonant with political sensibilities popularly associated with African American Protestant traditions that are authored around an intentional and self-identified blackness.

Afro-Caribbean evangelicals also hold political solidarities conditioned by transnational, postcolonial, and material locations that cannot be neatly inserted into the amorphous political slot of "African American" or the conservative or liberal poles of US political partnership or Christian civil religions. Yet the black Christian communities forged by black immigrant populations and communities outside of the Afro-Protestant mainline are nonetheless often folded into the monolithic construct of the "Black Church" rather than being engaged as juxtaposed, co-occurring, or even very different from more-mainstream formations.

This tendency to assimilate black Christian traditions within the racial, institutional, and civic construct of the "Black Church" also proves problematic in understanding the intraracial and intra-religious distinctions made by DBC and CBC members. The black evangelicals of DBC and CBC contrast their religious project with a negative stereotype they hold about black churches as misguided by charismatic, hierarchical leadership and the absence of sound biblical teaching. Congregants locate themselves against a "Black Church" trope that they create and use to authenticate their own religious project, in particular their emphasis on Bible study and biblical literalism. Thus, the black evangelicalism practiced by DBC and CBC members is very much animated by textual concerns and not just the civic and material interests that stem from the antiblack racism that is associated with a progressive Afro-Protestant mainline.

This book questions and maps the plural expressions of African American Christianity in North America that emerge across fields of religious practice, sociopolitical aspirations, and cultural imaginations. By applying contemporary scholarship, I take seriously the ways in which religion and race interface to create modes of difference, privilege, and disenfranchisement. By applying a critical perspective on religious and racial representation, I expose how morally constituted polarities of Right and Left, liberal and conservative, civil Christianity and Christ-focused evangelicalism, political and the personal, white and black—and if we acknowledge local categories, between black Bible believers and black church followers—can obscure modes of life, religious practice, and relationalities that exist between and across US social divides.

The Craft of Black Evangelical Spiritual Kinship

Although scholars may inquire about the locations of black evangelicals within a US religious landscape, the social contexts that concern black evangelical religious practitioners are often quite different. My time spent with DBC and CBC congregants exposed me to the generative project of their collective religious participation: their production of a multi-layered sense of belonging mediated by their spiritual kinship relationships. As a researcher, I held space for their stories of relationship, and I served as a witness to the language and practices of relationship they used to make themselves into a familial community. Their socio-religious networks comprise ties that bind spirit to spirit, member to member, and kin to kin. We might imagine some of these ties that bind as being composed of cords that are smooth to the touch. They bring pleasure when touched. They are a joy to discuss. Eyes light up with pleasure when discussing their beauty. Other ties are strong and durable. They invite compliments about their strength, meditations on their durability. Other ties are long. They reach far and connect people across great distances; some are trans-local, some extend across distances that surprise and are difficult to conceive. And we can imagine that some ties are rough. They are held together by knots, tied with determined hands despite the fibers unraveling. Such ties are still holding on, still a testament to a tense and textured story. And there are yet others, ones that dissolved, that did not turn out as anticipated, that are coated in silence, sighs, or whispers.

Brother Bernard Stewart, an Afro-Trinidadian member of DBC who later became my spiritual father, presented a compelling imagery of such ties—such spiritual intersubjectivity—during an interview:

> In that church family, I consider that you have church kin. Those who are near and dear to you like Todne—church kin you know? When I say Todne, I feel a sense of closeness. It's like I can almost feel myself wrapping myself around Todne or ummm . . . church kin. Sister Hamilton is church kin. I can feel myself wrapping around Sister Hamilton. I can sit down and talk to Sister Hamilton for hours and never get bored. You get where I'm coming from? [As] church family, once you're bought by the blood of Jesus Christ and you're a Christian, you're one of His. You're a part of church family but not necessarily church kin. You get where I'm coming from. There's a closeness. . . . There's a binding, right?

In Stewart's opinion, Christians inherited "church family" after "being bought by the blood of Jesus Christ." Yet Stewart drew my attention to another dimension of relatedness that stemmed from a closeness that came from deep communion and affinity. Church kinship, by his estimation, was a binding that was also pleasurable to experience and renew, that was not derivative of membership but that ignited the joys of speaking of a "we" or an "us."

Such DBC and CBC evangelicals as Brother Bernard Stewart imagine, produce, and narrate spiritually defined relationships. By inhabiting the social field of spiritual kinship, they connect religious doctrine with lived experience, join spiritual ideals with material conditions, and participate in an Afro-diasporic religious phenomenon I define as kincraft. Such DBC and CBC members inhabit a broader tradition in which Afro-diasporic religious practitioners have conscripted kinship discourse and practices that adjoin religious and spiritual worldviews.

Church members engage in the language and work of kincraft—of making one another spiritual kin—between a rock and a hard place. As Afro-Caribbeans and African Americans, church members inhabit broader political landscapes that have depicted black family ways negatively as pathological. As evangelical Christians, DBC and CBC congregants also possess a religious subculture that prioritizes the formation of heteronormative family households as an expression of religious piety.

My discussion of black evangelical kincraft is not intended to reproduce notions of black family pathology or to mute black aspirations for heteronormative family arrangements. Instead, by denoting black evangelical spiritual kinship as kincraft, I acknowledge the craftsmanship and collective labor that undergird black evangelical sociality. In the words of poet Elizabeth Alexander, I write out of a "veneration of the sweat of the craft" (2004, 52). My work is grounded in a profound appreciation of the dynamic tapestry of relationships patterned by ideological designs and collective intentions in contexts of teaching and learning, confiding correction and giving, a warp and weft fashioned by hands, starts, repetitions, do-overs, and repairs, a tapestry that I was able to see in sections, that although already a relic (for it has now become something else), I attempt to narrate here.

THE REALITIES AND HIERARCHIES OF KINSHIP LABORS

In discussing kinship in terms of craft, I draw upon important changes in the field of kinship studies. Conventionally, anthropologists have defined kinship in terms of marriage and biological relationships of descent. Such scholars have also designated nonbiological kinship relationships, such as spiritual relationships, as "fictive" kinship (Chatters, Taylor, and Jayakody 1994; Dill 1993; Ibsen and Klobus 1972; Nelson 2013). Yet to call nonbiological reckonings of kinship "fictive" presumes the singular authenticity of biological and genealogical kinship. It assumes that family is fundamentally a construct of biogenetic descent.[14] But what crowds around the margins of the "real"? What rests in the shadow of the "fictive" and therefore remains unseen or is misrecognized?

My work builds upon reconstituted kinship studies that emerged from a critique of anthropologists' ethnocentric use of the Western genealogical categories for cross-cultural kinship studies (Schneider 1984). In particular, my work draws upon a feminist and queer anthropological approach to the study of kinship that examines local idioms, categories, and intentional practices of kinship (Carsten 2000; Franklin and McKinnon 2001; Weston 1991). Central to this feminist approach is Janet Carsten's definition of *relatedness*—the lived experience of being related as conveyed in terms of local statements and practices, particularly of sentiment, substance, and nurturance. Her definition has allowed me to take seriously church members' idioms of spiritual kinship (2000, 2, 3, 22).

I also build on cultural definitions of kinship like those that Marshall Sahlins outlines. He argues against the analytical use of "the going biologism" encoded in dominant Anglo-American reckonings of family (2013, 66). Instead, Sahlins calls for an examination of kinship that gives credence to how people construct "mutuality of being" and "participat[e] in one another's existence" (2013, 2, 18). This intersubjectivity recalls Brother Bernard Stewart's description of "church kin" as feeling oneself wrapped around another self. Sahlins's outline of kinship also calls attention to cultural modes of relating that stem from the collective participation in shared existence, whether it be the talking that Brother Stewart described as creating closeness or the prayer, mentorship, or biblical study that creates opportunities for people to invest deeply in one another's lives.

My identification of black evangelical spiritual kinship as a craft is not interested in assessing whether these relationships are "fictive" or "real." Instead, I offer *kincraft* as an aperture through which to view a spiritual relatedness that emerges locally through shared utterances and performances of relationship both inside and beyond church walls. This encourages a more open-ended conceptual journey into the interiority of black social life.

My study extends feminist scholars' observations that the family is a site from which to view the oppression of women and broader workings of power. As Sylvia Yanagisako and Carol Delaney argue, social bonds and identities that are "ascribed a nonhuman basis, whether in biology, nature, or god . . . legitimize hierarchies of difference in which power relations are embedded. In short, all naturalize power" (1995, 20). Notions of family, whether grounded in biology or spirit, can be used as discursive and ontological justification for patriarchal power. Patricia Hill Collins similarly asserts that "'family values' . . . lay the foundation for many social hierarchies. In particular, hierarchies of gender, wealth, age, and sexuality" (1998, 64). The study of the family is therefore a study of the ideological constructions not only of complementarity but also inequality.

I consciously use *kincraft* (and by extension the notion of craftsmanship) to illuminate the positioning of black Christian women within broader crosscurrents of gendered kinship labor. According to theologian Dolores S. Williams, black women have been forced to serve as substitute sexual partners to white men, as mothers to white children, as managers of white plantation households, as masculine laborers, and as protectors of black households (1993). Williams also notes that black Christian women have been exposed to popular theologies that associate surrogacy with redemption: a messiah who substitutes his death for the salvation of humanity. Christian notions of salvation have thus been associated with sanctifying and even coercing black women's reproductive and familial labor.

The relationship between salvation and black women's kinwork is not merely conceptual. As Judith Casselberry discusses in her study of African American women members of the Pentecostal Church of Our Lord Jesus Christ of the Apostolic Faith (COOLJC) denomination, "doctrinal notions of black religious female personhood" motivate their institutional, physical, and emotional labors in church auxiliary organizations that support the church's male leadership (2017, 79–80). Although women become adept at managing their multiple commitments, Casselberry notes that "these women's work as spiritual mother, natural mother, and wife demands more time than they actually have" (2017, 101). The overlap of household and church work generates a heavier work burden for women than for men. The realities of kincraft are manifested in the disproportionate and unequal labors of black evangelical women (compared to men).

There is no such thing as craft without labor. I offer my ethnographic rendition of black evangelical kincraft with the awareness that all labor is not treated equally, that craftsmanship, like public sphere labor, is often made possible via differentiated and differently valued craftswomanship and women's private sphere labors. The exegetical and textual labor that frames familial ideology holds different currency than the everyday labor of churchwomen in practices of feeding, care, mentorship, and prayer, labor that I identify as a sacrament. This book's analytical lens is situated critically amid the local hierarchies of visibility and recognition that surround the production of spiritual kinship. Although patriarchal power can condition unequal hierarchies of visibility inside and outside of the DBC and CBC communities, it does not preclude the extra-institutional workings of women's spiritual authority, critique, and ingenuity.

FROM KINLESSNESS TO KIN POSSIBILITIES:
VIEWS FROM THE AFRICAN DIASPORA

This project is an ethnographic story of the black evangelicals of CBC and DBC who constructed themselves intersubjectively as spiritual kin. It is also a study of a broader collection of stories of black people mobilizing, revising, and reinventing a discourse that they did not own in order to lay claim to themselves and one another as kin. On occasion, blacks used kincraft to profess their relationality with enslaved blacks who were, at one time, literally deemed to be the property of others and marked not only as chattel but also as kinless (Spillers 1987, 74).[15] This meant that Afro-diasporic people inhabited (and to an extent still inhabit) conditions of "genealogical unfreedom" that existed "outside the precincts of protected human kinship" (Bentley 2009, 273, 276). Black families, like black people, were not free.

Yet unfreedom should not be equated with nonexistence. In her essay "Mama's Baby, Papa's Maybe: An American Grammar Book," Hortense Spillers concludes that kinship had "no decisive social or legal efficacy" (1987, 75). Yet Spillers also depicts the social worlds that would have been inhabited by enslaved black people in the following manner: "The captive person developed, time and again, certain ethical and sentimental features that tied her and him, *across* the landscape to others, often sold from hand to hand, of the same and different blood in a common fabric of memory and inspiration" (1987, 75).

Spillers acknowledges that slavery did not preclude blacks' symbolic constructions of kinship. Instead, from her perspective, ethics, sentiment, ties across landscape, same and different blood, memory, and inspiration all constituted the etchings of black kin-making during enslavement. Blacks' nonownership of a propertied kinship discourse did not prevent them from naming and claiming their kin.

Kinship in the late British and Caribbean postcolonial world and the pre- and post–civil rights US remained and remains a racialized system. Family normality, and its attendant moral capital, belonged overwhelmingly to people of European descent. The families of people of African descent were essentialized as dysfunctional. In particular, female-headed households were deemed to be epistemic of black family pathology rather than an outgrowth of socioeconomic disenfranchisement, migration, or public policy that prioritized mother-centered families for support (Moynihan 1965).

Black churches in the Caribbean and the US also popularized heteronormative family arrangements. They provided land settlements that fostered the creation of Baptist villages and approximations of bourgeois property-holding familial units, and offered other forms of material support to families navigating the social and economic disruptions of domestic and international migration (Besson 2002; Drake and Cayton 2015 [1945]; Du Bois 1995 [1899]). They also became sites for moral adjudication and political organizing around a respectability politics: the advocacy of approximating heteronormative gender, sexual, and family arrangements as a means of combating racist assumptions about black morality and sexuality (Higginbotham 1993). The yearning for normativity conditioned by racialized notions of black pathology reproduced desire and created religious projects for blacks to be born again as bourgeois kin.

Heteronormative familial aspirations and familial reckonings of black collective identity are not universally embraced. Indeed, Paul Gilroy roundly critiques the grounding of black public sphere identities within familial metaphors and imaginaries. He insists that centering the family generates a black "biopolitics" that defines community "as a radical localism and 'a simple accumulation of symmetrical units'" (1994, 58–59). This familial localism and the reproduction of racialized scripts of gender differences as a gloss for racial authenticity "narrows the horizon of any lingering aspiration towards social change" (1994, 59, 66). Given the ways in which white heteronormativity has been constructed in relation to black sexual pathology—(think of the Moynihan Report's damaging representations of black female-headed households as the source of black family dysfunction)—Tiffany Lethabo King has even provocatively called for the abolition of "the family" as a framework for black social life (2018).

I maintain that black evangelical spiritual kinship can offer us theoretical insights into the constructed character of the seemingly natural heteropatriarchal family and the alternative ethos of familial connections forged via collective experiences with disenfranchisement, spiritual imagination, and migration. In short, kincraft holds deconstructive and constructive bases. When located within the broader history of the African Diaspora, kincraft descends from a critical consciousness about the contexts and frames of conventional Western heteronormative notions of kinship. The spiritual kinship created by black evangelicals holds a *beyond* that is dually conditioned by Christian notions of transcendence but also by diasporic conditions that have required productions of kinship in and beyond normative frames. The diasporic effect on kincraft is the creation of kinship as a frame beyond a frame. This "beyond" of Afro-diasporic religious sociality is found in Spillers's depiction of the kinship created by captives that "tied him and her *across* the landscape to others" (1987, 75). Kin ties, even when not owned by enslaved people of African descent, created lateral connections across space and persons.

My research demonstrates that beyond CBC and DBC spiritual kinship, congregants not only make relationships; they also inherit a tradition of Afro-diasporic semiotic audacity (even against the literalism and orthodoxy of heteronormativity and evangelical biblicism): an audacity of black people making ways out of no ways, of the across, of creating pathways to one another amid forced displacements, of forging hybrid discourses to name those relationships within dominant nonrecognitions of black kinship. Even as they engage in auspicious modes of conformity to the heteronormative ideals of evangelical family values, CBC and DBC members are also inheritors and practitioners of this co-occurring kincraft. Consequently, they foster broad forms of connection and reflexive awareness of the enclosures created by nuclear family, ethnicity/race, and congregational membership. In so doing they themselves relativize normative kinship arrangements.

Research Setting and Methods

I came to this research as a southern African American religious subject who has a proximity to evangelical Christian religious ways. My formative religious years were spent in an African American Presbyterian church. I attended a predominately white evangelical Baptist primary school called Knoxville Baptist Christian School from kindergarten through middle school. From ages five to thirteen, I became intimately acquainted with the worldviews and scriptural readings of a neo-evangelicalism associated with the Southern Baptist Convention. Placing me in an evangelical school was a way for my parents to opt out of a segregated school system that underfunded black schools in my neighborhood relative to predominantly white schools across town. My Christian school, which emphasized biblical teaching, was known for promoting strong literacy skills and discipline. This appealed to my parents. But their decision to enroll me in an evangelical school was mostly a pragmatic response to racial segregation; it was not informed by a desire for the inculcation of evangelical religiosity.

I lived between two religious worlds, and although I inhabited both, I was raised with the idea that the Christianity at school was somehow not quite for me. When I tried to reconcile the school and church Christianity, I received tacit messages over the years that Monday-to-Friday school evangelicalism and home church religion were separate, different, and should be kept that way.

Thus, my own religious and educational history is located on the fault lines of religion and race and of liberal and conservative Protestantism. An examination of how CBC and DBC evangelicals navigate their ethno-racial and religious identities in contexts that somehow presume their incommensurability can teach us all much about our own hidden scripts about religious identities and boundaries.

My performance of a Christian identity through my familiarity with biblical and ritual knowledge, religious hymns, and Christian discourse greatly helped me participate in DBC religious life and provided a helpful footing for important research collaborations. My religious identity added another layer to members' emic categorizations of me as a curious student: it allowed them to see me as "Sister Todne." Thus, DBC respondents entrusted their points of view to an anthropologist with a Christian background, expecting that on some level their perspectives would be understood.

Despite the important common ground that we shared, there were some salient differences that shaped my locations within the DBC and CBC communities. As an African American, I came from a different ethnic background than the churches' Afro-Caribbean membership. My gender also shaped the field of my interactions, often providing deep views into women's everyday spirituality and little to no first-hand views of male homosocial spiritual connections. I also found myself philosophically at odds with church teachings about divinely mandated heteropatriarchal sexual and gender hierarchies. Also, as a participant in the Black Church tradition and a pan-Africanist in my political orientation, I was more amenable to the study of spiritual kinship (popularly known in Black Church vernacular as "church family") and less disposed to analyze fully members' claims of universal Christian connection. This is a tendency I have worked hard to correct since conducting fieldwork and one that has raised important representational questions for me about how to write about universal religious aspirations in the wake of religious and ethno-racial differences. Despite our differences, members' entrustment to me of their life stories and their overwhelming hospitality perhaps provides another powerful illustration of the ways in which they not only believed but also sought to practice their ideals of universal and transcendent connection. As I acquainted myself with their theology, I began to see these differences not as a barrier but as an opportunity that made me a teachable subject. It was not an evangelicalism I knew, but it was an evangelicalism that they eagerly taught me.

Over the course of fieldwork I employed three primary methods of data collection: interviews, archival research, and participant observation. First, I conducted semi-structured interviews with thirty-seven evangelical respondents individually and, at times, with married couples; it depended on participants' preferences.[16] I designed the interview questions to elicit the following classes of information: general demographic information, migration information, religious experience and church participation data, perspectives on church and family relationships, and participants' self-selected testimonies about church community.

Collectively, the group of participants with whom I collaborated represented a broad variety of cultural backgrounds and religious experiences. I interviewed twenty women and seventeen men. The large majority of participants were between the ages of fifty and sixty-nine. Ten interview respondents were born in the United States. Twenty-seven research collaborators were born in the Caribbean. They came from several countries of origin, including the Bahamas,

Trinidad, and Barbados.[17] The largest Afro-Caribbean population was Jamaican. They participated in a variety of non-Brethren religious traditions prior to their membership at DBC, including Baptist, Catholic, Anglican, and Pentecostal traditions, as well as having no prior religious affiliation. Congregants also listed family connections, employment and education, and difference in environment as motivating their international and domestic migrations to the Atlanta cityscape. The participants whom I interviewed resided in suburbs throughout the Atlanta metropolitan area, with church members being loosely concentrated in the Stone Mountain, Lithonia, and Decatur communities within and around DeKalb County.

Second, I analyzed church anniversary booklets, oral history archives, and the historical perspectives offered by founding church members in their recollections of the emergence of CBC and DBC. I also read the writings of Brethren theologians recommended by church leaders to learn more about the history and central ideas of Plymouth Brethrenism. Finally, I read independent scholarship about Brethrenism and the particular Brethren church network of which DBC and CBC are a part, as well as scholarship published by other Christian and academic organizations.

Third, I used participant observation to develop a firsthand understanding of the relationships, scope, and operation of church community in the religious worlds of DBC members (and, less frequently, those of the CBC). Because my participant observation took place among a group of religious participants who were serious Christians and were for the most part devoted to their church community, I attended a lot of church events inside and beyond the chapel walls. Sunday church gatherings involved at least a five-hour commitment from the beginning of the earliest service to the end of the last one. I regularly attended four Bible studies per week at church and inside members' homes. I also traveled with members to other Brethren church events in the Atlanta metropolitan area and throughout the Southeast, and attended church-sponsored conferences, retreats, and banquets. Finally, I participated in some of the impromptu gatherings of church members that were not centered on a particular religious practice but organized for the pure enjoyment of communion. Some of the scenes of my research could be as conventional as me sitting in the sanctuary during a Sunday morning service, chatting informally with church members on a weekday evening in the parking lot amid Georgia humidity and mosquito nibbling, eating the tasty foodstuffs of church banquets, working as a Vacation Bible School instructor, offering and receiving the prayer requests and praise reports of others, and speaking about the challenges of faith over a cup of tea and biscuits in church members' homes.

I was also "adopted" by two married couples at DBC with whom I spent a great deal of time. They taught me experientially about the meanings, ideals, and performances of spiritual kinship. They generously shared their life stories and knowledge, and they made space for me to do the same. More than anything else, they modeled for me the kinds of intimacies that spiritual kinship makes possible. They were indispensable to the research process.

A small number of members expressed their community solidarities by voicing their questions, desires, and concerns about how their church would be represented in my work. During the first season of my research at DBC, Sister Yvette Goode, a young mother of two, implored, "Please don't write anything bad about my church!" In a very different yet no less adamant request, a senior brother at the church challenged me to "Write it all—the good and the bad. If we're Christians, we're supposed to be concerned with the truth." Perhaps somewhere between church members' expectations of a scathingly negative image or useful critical portrait of church life was an alternative interpretation of the project as an evangelistic tool that could potentially show readers the value of being a Christian and knowing the Lord.

In recognition of the myriad concerns of church members, whose commitment to their faith and their church have earned my deepest respect, and of my own research agenda, I have endeavored to write an ethnography that demonstrates the complexities of church members' multi-layered religious attachments as well as their sincere dedication to community. Nonetheless, the images of community you will find in the chapters that follow originate from my complex placement in the webs of socio-spiritual relationships as an observer who is some parts "stranger," "friend," and "kin." I attempted to balance the competing and unresolvable demands of distance and rapport typically associated with social scientific research as well as my personal loyalties as a situated DBC community participant (Thomas 2016).

Outline of Chapters

Part I, "Contextualizing the Social Dimensions of a Black Evangelical Religious Movement," examines the ideological, historical, and ethno-racial settings in which CBC and DBC members author and mobilize their claims of spiritual kinship. In particular, the first section conducts a genealogy of the diasporic, religious, and material conditions that precipitate DBC members' spiritual kinship ideals, and it examines the critical racial consciousness and boundary-crossing aspirations of church members' reckonings of spiritual kinship. It offers a view of the ethnographic setting and the broader diasporic, historical, and local urban context in which church members render their spiritual kinship claims and aspirations.

Chapter 1, "On 'Godly Family' and 'Family Roots': Creating Kinship Worlds," explores the evangelical and diasporic sources of Afro-Caribbean and African American evangelicals' genealogical constructions of spiritual kinship. It also examines how black evangelicals often construct their kinship networks and imaginaries through the combination of multiple kinship sensibilities.

Chapter 2, "Moving against the Grain: The Evangelism of T. Michael Flowers in the Segregated US South," traces the history of the CBC and DBC communities back to their founder, Afro-Bahamian missionary T. Michael Flowers. Motivated by a critique of white evangelical racism and black Christian textual and leadership practices, this chapter provides a history of how Flowers—in conjunction with several Afro-Caribbean and African American evangelists and white evangelical donors—established from the 1950s through the 1980s a network of "black Bible-believing churches" across the Southeast, of which CBC and DBC are a part. It also examines the reformist, universalistic, and democratic theological foundations of spiritual kinship, framed by Flowers, during the context of racial segregation that would later be inherited and re-adapted by CBC and DBC congregants in the early twenty-first century.

Chapter 3, "Black Like Me? Or Christian Like Me? Black Evangelicals, Ethnicity, and Church Family," investigates how contemporary CBC and DBC evangelicals narrate the US religious landscape and their own evangelical religious subjectivities in ethnic and racial terms. It also analyzes how black evangelical congregants mobilize spiritual kinship as a tool to construct a nonethnic familial identity and a diasporic alterity that they imagine as alternatives to the ethnic and racial estrangements they attribute to US ethno-congregationalism.

Part 2, "Scenes of Black Evangelical Spiritual Kinship in Practice," turns inward and presents ethnographic portraits of the workings of spiritual kinship among the membership of DBC.[18] It is set in the black evangelical religious worlds constructed inside congregants' churches, homes, and the spaces in between. In particular, the final chapters illuminate how black evangelical spiritual kinship is animated by the social and performative dimensions of Bible study predominantly presided over by churchmen and the production of a domesticated everyday spiritual communion commonly engineered by churchwomen. These chapters also shed light on how DBC congregants use spiritual kinship relationships to reproduce and interrogate evangelical heteropatriarchal hierarchies, boundaries, and morality.

Chapter 4, "Bible Study, Fraternalism, and the Making of Interpretive Community," studies the institutional production of textual identities. In particular, the chapter excavates the relationships between biblicism and brotherhood by examining how church "brothers" used male-led Bible studies and exegetical contexts to co-constitute a fraternal interpretative community. Chapter 4 also examines the significance of Bible study, literalism, and spiritual kinship discourses as a social technology capable of generating performative and interpretive connections that generate fraternalism and socially valued modes of institutional belonging.

Chapter 5, "Churchwomen and the Incorporation of Church and Home," examines how "sisters," "spiritual mothers," "spiritual fathers," and "prayer partners" fed, mentored, and confided in one another and created a field of close, everyday spiritual intimacies. Although the location of such relationships in domesticated spaces can be conceptualized as auxiliary to the institutional moorings of spiritual kinship brokered by church brothers, chapter 5 shows how churchwomen's quotidian spiritual labors and relationships evoked the authenticated communion of the New Testament church idealized by Brethren evangelicalism. It also illustrates how their work incorporated the DBC community by generating myriad connections between church and home spaces.

Chapter 6, "Black Evangelicals, 'the Family,' and Confessional Intimacy," examines DBC evangelical productions and ideologies of "the family." It expounds upon the antiblack material conditions and moral scripts of black family pathology that shaped the context of black evangelical family life. Significantly, chapter 6 demonstrates that although black evangelicals subscribed to heteronormative family politics, their productions of "the family" were also sustained by the extended family ethos and confessional intimacies mediated by spiritual kinship that, at times, reinforced and questioned the moral premises of "the family."

The conclusion reviews the limitations of the heteronormative family as a lens through which to study the religious, racial, and familial normativity of DBC evangelicals. As an alternative, it discusses the ways in which DBC evangelicalism unfolds in spaces between religion and family, amid the intersections (and entanglements) of genealogical and spiritual kinship, and among the moral scripts of religion, race, kinship, and the emergent conditions of lived experience. It also demonstrates why the study of black evangelical religiosity in the US like that exhibited by CBC and DBC members—and its counter-hegemonic racial and relational implications—should remain an important locus of future study.

Our exploration begins with chapter 1's investigation of the religious and diasporic sources of CBC and DBC evangelicals' reckonings of spiritual kinship and the mapping of CBC and DBC members as a black evangelical constituency within the United States' religious landscape.

Part One · Contextualizing the Social Dimensions of a Black Evangelical Religious Movement

On "Godly Family" and "Family Roots"   1
Creating Kinship Worlds

During a Thursday-evening Bible study in mid-May 2008, the congregants of Dixon Bible Chapel (DBC) in the Atlanta metropolitan area gathered in the basement fellowship hall to continue their year-long discussion of Jesus, the Great High Priest. As part of an Afro-Caribbean and African American evangelical church association founded in 1955, DBC and Corinthian Bible Chapel (CBC) congregants aspired to practice a "Bible-believing" Christianity. Thus, Bible study was a common occurrence within black evangelicals' institutional and personal religious landscapes. The Thursday-evening Bible study class at DBC consisted of a small, dedicated group of approximately ten members whose warm communion was the fruit of consistent attendance, weekly prayer check-ins, and table fellowship. In many instances the formal portion of the class took on the atmosphere of a graduate school seminar. The elder, who served as a "full-time worker" for the chapel community, offered a well-organized lecture.[1] Bible study participants interjected numerous questions and insights that were, at times, topped off with good-natured and even humorous repartee.

That May evening, attendees of the Bible study were discussing the mysterious biblical figure of Melchizedek. Over the course of our discussion the elder presented Melchizedek, who is described in Genesis 4:18–20 as the king of Salem and a priest of God, as an analogue of Jesus Christ. According to Bible study teacher Elder Samuel Andrews, congregants needed to understand three concepts to comprehend the significance of the appearance of Melchizedek: theophany, "the appearance of deity in physical form"; typology, "a type of Christ . . . that points to the person of Christ"; and finally, genealogy. Here the class discussion took an interesting turn.[2]

BROTHER SAMUEL ANDREWS: There's another thing we need to talk about is *genealogy*. How important genealogy was. And it still is. Let me tell you something. It is nice if you can sit down and trace your roots. If you can just sit down and go as far back as you can. You know? You learn so much.

SISTER MARSHA LEWIS, an Afro-Trinidadian female congregant: [laughing] You know maybe some of us wouldn't want to.

BROTHER ANDREWS: You know we actually did that. We traced Joanna's [Andrews's wife's] family all the way back to Nigeria. And we came forward to today. Yeah. They were from Nigeria.

BROTHER WINSTON JOHNSON, an Afro-Jamaican male congregant: She's a gangster. [more laughter]

BROTHER ANDREWS: You tell her. They were from Nigeria. They came across the oceans. They landed in Grenada, and then they came to Trinidad, and then they spread out. I mean you can actually see the trace of history and stuff like that.

BROTHER ROGER NELSON: You do yours?

BROTHER ANDREWS: No, my cousins in Trinidad want to do it. I don't want to fight them. Let them do it if they want to do it. But anyway.

BROTHER WILLIAM EDMONDSON, Afro-Jamaican male congregant: Question. Why is human genealogy important? I have an issue with us being focused on the human family when we're in Christ. We are all in the family of God. And if you look at Acts 17, it clearly depicts that . . . we're of one blood.³ So we get caught up in that . . . wherever part of Africa we come from.

BROTHER ANDREWS: OK. That's fine. Lucky for you, yes.

BROTHER EDMONDSON: No, not just for me. For everyone.

BROTHER ANDREWS: Well, I happen to like my parents. I happen to like my parents' parents.

BROTHER EDMONDSON: But Christ said if you don't hate your parents, if you don't hate your wife, your brother, sister, you're not a part of me. [laughter] And he was saying you have to come out of that human family into the godly family. . . .

SISTER ANDREA SAUNDERS: Can I just say something to William real quick?

BROTHER ANDREWS: Uh oh.

SISTER SAUNDERS: Real quick. For us it was rather important especially to Americans because a lot of us well . . . to African Americans because we know we're African Americans, but for my family we're Americans because we knew we came from Mississippi. But when we traced our roots all the way back, we were from the Mandingo tribe. And our family name is an Irish name. And we traced that all the way back, and we found out that, um, this person had married a woman who had just come from Africa and married her and so forth and so on. He was an Irish, a free Irish man. It was very important for us. That didn't take away who we are in Christ though.

The Bible study concluded with an important lesson about Melchizedek and the central discussion of genealogy emphasized by Brother Andrews. He leaned in and explained summarily:

The high priest was well respected and all that. To Jews, genealogy was important. With no genealogy, you cannot be a priest. You have to come from a tribe of Levi, and they can track your name and everything else. But here comes Jesus. Here comes Jesus. Jesus is not from the tribe number one, and then he doesn't have . . . he had an earthly genealogy, yes, but he was born of the Spirit. So he really doesn't match up to what the Jews expected as qualifications to be a high priest. He's the perfect person to be our high priest. Why? Because He is God in the flesh. What we read here, let's look at it—Hebrews. Feel free to comment or to stop. But I really want you to pray on this. Verse 14.

Brother Andrews, Sisters Saunders, and Brother Edmondson each understood kinship differently. Although they expressed their dissenting positions affably, their perspectives represent some of the religious and diasporic influences on church members' understandings of family. How can we understand the contrasting views of kinship represented by Bible study attendees as deriving from the narrative practices of "tracing roots" and privileging "godly family" over "human family"? And how did congregants construct their kinship worlds in relation to these grammars?

The Bible study depicts divergent perspectives on kinship: the ability to hold roots and godly family in tandem versus promoting religious notions of kinship. More frequently, church members tended to combine "secular" and religious conceptions of family. Church members' constructions of their kinship worlds were located between two auspicious religious influences: Plymouth Brethren ecclesiology and the neo-evangelical emphasis on the heteropatriarchal family. Diasporic histories and contemporary Afro-Caribbean and African American migrations also significantly shaped the genealogical desires and ancestral orientations of members.

Attention to church members' pragmatic combination of kinship concepts reveals the shortcomings of isolating biological, social, religious, and racial conceptualizations of kinship. Black evangelicals' renditions and interrelationships of kinship definitions also demonstrate the need to understand the broader social landscape of evangelicalism beyond popular notions of individual religious subjectivity or the heteronormative family to a more focused attention to emic constructions of religious sociality.

Evangelicals and the "Godly Family"

Evangelical Protestantism has many contradictory impulses. Among those inconsistencies is an outward orientation toward spreading a Christian message and a tendency to create bounded social and religious memberships that segment around ideological lines. This applies also to Plymouth Brethrenism and US neo-evangelicalism, the two primary evangelical movements that have influenced DBC and CBC religious formations. For Plymouth Brethren, constructions of Christian community were created through notions of a universal church and through intensive ideological fractures that culminated in the formation of two separate religious sects. For US evangelicalism, this tension between outward and inward orientations emerges in a neo-evangelicalism that is more engaged in worldly affairs than a preexisting Christian fundamentalism but that also champions an exclusionary, heteronormative nuclear family as a centerpiece of its civic Moral Majority movement. Within this religious mélange, in which evangelical religious boundaries are extended and entrenched, exist DBC and CBC evangelicals, who fashion their kinship worlds through narrative boundaries that separate and privilege kinship types and through narrative bridges that combine sets of relationships.

PLYMOUTH BRETHRENISM: THE FAMILY OF GOD AND CHRISTIAN SUPERSESSIONISM

Afro-Jamaican Brother Edmondson expressed his opinion that black evangelicals should focus on their position within the "family of God" rather than on "human genealogy." Edmondson's universal framing of Christianity is shaped by the religious worldview of Plymouth Brethrenism: the evangelical tradition that informed CBC and DBC community life. Plymouth Brethrenism is a British nonconformist evangelical movement established in the 1830s and named for one of its foremost meeting sites in Plymouth, in southern England. Although Brethrenism was not known for being particularly successful in its early missionary endeavors, it spread throughout Europe, New Zealand, and the Caribbean during the 1860s and 1870s, particularly through the work of the most notable founder of the movement, Irish nonconformist John Nelson Darby (Akenson 2018, 431).

Formed within a historical context that was rife with criticisms of the Anglican Church and calls for disestablishmentarianism, the Brethren were decidedly antisectarian. Plymouth Brethren sought to establish a loosely connected set of local congregations, which they called "assemblies," rather than an elaborate denominational schema. According to James Callahan, nineteenth-century Plymouth Brethren endeavored to practice a primitivistic piety (1996). This meant approximating an ecclesiology that they associated with authentic New Testament Christianity. Proto-Brethren gatherings that preceded the 1830s coalescence of the Brethren movement could be characterized as "bread-breaking house-churches": a type of meeting that seemed to be located directly at the crossroads of religion and family and that demonstrated an orientation to primitivism that contrasted with the clergy-lay distinction and the separation of church and family associated with modernization (Akenson 2018, 24; Pankhurst and Houseknecht 2000). Brethren founders emphasized small, local groups of fellowship, affirmed the priesthood of believers, abolished the clergy, established collective elder governance and male biblical exegesis, emphasized biblical teaching and evangelism, and observed Communion, or the "breaking of bread," weekly. In addition to an emphasis on local assemblies populated by individual believers, Brethren held an ecumenical belief that local Christian communities together formed a complete body of Christ on Earth (Akenson 2018, 306).

Brethren also espoused a spiritual concept of the Christian church. Variously referred to as the "bride of Christ," "body of Christ," and "testimony of Christ" (and thus conceptually connecting discourse, corporeality, and kinship relation), Plymouth Brethren believed that Christians were unified through salvation and the Holy Spirit into a universal body of Christ. According to DBC and CBC members, this universal body of Christ was governed by the head, Jesus Christ.[4] Thus, they imagined the Church of God as a transcendent unity that existed in Heaven and on Earth that would congregate believers across all space and time with the coming of Jesus Christ (Akenson 2018).

Although they understood the Church to be an earthly and spiritual phenomenon, Plymouth Brethren accentuate the transcendence of the spirit in their interpretations of genealogy. This is reflected in Brother Edmondson's assertion that the "family of God" should be promoted over the "human family" and over "what part of Africa" congregants came from. Brethren also espoused Christian supersessionism grounded in the belief that Christians were the final, more spiritual embodiment of the first covenant that God made with Abraham and his Jewish descendants. Reading scripture as saying that the New Christocentric Testament was a fuller, spiritualized incarnation of God's covenant with the Israelites in the Old Testament, Plymouth Brethren understood themselves as the true children of God and as the inheritors of the mantle of God's chosen people.

The genealogical imaginaries associated with supersessionism are not benign. As J. Kameron Carter reminds us, Western Christianity was constituted through a theology of whiteness that decontextualized Christianity and the figure of Christ from Jewish religious origins and ethno-racial genealogy (2008).[5] Deeply anti-Semitic valences marked Christian supersessionism and fueled European imaginations of a superior white Christian modernity. As Robert O. Smith explains, "Darby viewed Jews not as real persons but as literary tropes in his world of prophecy interpretation" (2013, 149). This paternalistic replacement theology has been associated with Christian Zionism (Smith 2013) and thus holds significant racial, religious, and political implications. White Christian supremacy has read itself as a culmination of divine covenantal promise—an ideological matrix that has supported settler colonial imaginaries and projects. Within the racial and colonial assemblage of supersessionism, Christian conversion can be interpreted as process that promotes the renunciation of natal genealogical networks of non-white and non-Christian religious subjects (Handman 2014; Keane 2007). Therefore, Brother Edmondson's privileging of the family of God over human and African genealogy can be read as a Brethren theological practice that is built upon a logic of genealogical dispossession. Nonetheless, as I demonstrate below, reading an emphasis of the godly family solely in terms of Brethren ecclesiology misses the ways in which church members braid together religious and diasporic kinship orientations.

Plymouth Brethren are better known for their elaboration of and adherence to an eschatology that has significantly affected the US evangelical imagination of the end-times (Akenson 2018; Smith 2013). This dispensational premillennial imaginary understands the coming of Christ to unfold through a series of elaborate events and stages of history (or dispensations), such as the earthly departure or "rapture" of dead and living Christian believers before the reign of a demonic Antichrist, a peaceful millennial reign of Christ, a final apocalyptic battle between Christ and Satan that will end in Satan's ultimate demise, and a final judgment of all humans for their life deeds by God and final departure to Heaven or Hell. The effect of Brethren eschatology, according to Joseph Webster, is an "acute sense that not only is God immanent—spatially *close at hand*—but He is also imminent, that is, temporally *soon to arrive*" (2013, 33).

If Brethren ecclesiology portrays a transcendent Christian church connected across time and space, Brethren eschatology offers a notion of a dispersed community that is reunited. The rapture of dead and living Christian believers who have existed across space and time involves their reunion in heaven. One might imagine that this promise of a gathering of the scattered, rather than of the few who are chosen, could also appeal to the black evangelicals of CBC and DBC who have navigated social separations endemic to the migration process.

OPEN VERSUS CLOSED BRETHREN

At the historical intersection of the Brethren's eschatological and ecclesiological development we find another noted feature of Plymouth Brethrenism: schism. In the 1840s, Brethren infighting occurred over the different understandings of the end-times and scriptural interpretation of John Nelson Darby and Benjamin Wills Newton (Akenson 2018). The result was an effective excommunication (meaning exclusion from taking Communion or the Eucharist) of Newton and of the people with whom he worshipped by the Brethren majority that Darby influenced. These Exclusive Brethren (or Closed Brethren), who were also referred to as Darbyites, were primarily motivated by a concern with apostasy and saw the separations as important to maintaining the moral witness of Brethren communities. The Exclusive Brethren, through a doctrine of separation, would eventually restrict lines of communal fellowship by denying nonmembers access to Communion and encouraging members to minimize their interactions with non-Brethren family and community members. By contrast, Open Brethren reserved the right as local assemblies to extend Communion to nonmember Christians, provided that members confirmed their Christian status. From the perspective of sensibilities adverse to tight interconnections of religion and family that are associated with religious fundamentalism, the world of Exclusive Brethrenism may seem like a confining and self-contained world. Yet Donald Harmon Akenson notes that the group provided "a warm and comforting set of interpersonal relations in the Brethren's private sphere," along with theological, spiritual, hermeneutic, epistemological, salvific, and communal benefits (2018, 419).

This exclusive form of Brethrenism also spread to the Caribbean (Introvigne 2018). Sylvan Catwell (1995) traces the arrival of (a presumably open) Plymouth Brethrenism in Barbados to 1862, and the transplantation there of Exclusive Brethren in 1893. Several church members I interviewed mentioned their attendance of Exclusive Brethren gospel halls in the Caribbean and their limited interactions with Exclusive Brethren in their communities. Among them was Brother Carl Bailey, who described his recollections of Closed Brethren fellowship in Jamaica:

BROTHER CARL BAILEY: Because historically the Brethren, at least in the West Indies, have been known to be antisocial in a way. From what I understand there's a Closed Brethren and there's an Exclusive Brethren. My next neighbors in Jamaica I think were Exclusive, where they don't worship with anybody else.

TT: But your gospel hall wasn't like that.

BROTHER CARL BAILEY: No. They take care of their own. And . . . the only part I couldn't understand is how could they evangelize? And then they were . . . but I knew they all took care of all their members. Their children got married, and everyone pitched in and made sure their children had a home. And most of the men had their own business. And they took care of everybody from within their own group. And you marry from within your assembly.

A mixed legacy of Closed and Open Brethren communities was transplanted in Caribbean religious contexts in North America. Prior to their settlement in the Atlanta metropolitan area, some DBC and CBC members also attended a Brethren chapel in the Bedford-Stuyvesant neighborhood in Brooklyn that was, by members' accounts, an Exclusive Brethren assembly. By contrast, DBC and CBC were Open Brethren assemblies. This meant that nonmembers were allowed to take Communion and church members were allowed to fraternize with nonmembers.

In an interview, Brother Samuel Andrews voiced his criticism of Caribbean Exclusive fellowships:

BROTHER SAMUEL ANDREWS: There's a group of Brethren churches that are all Closed Brethren churches. Then there's another group that's called Open Brethren churches. Open Brethren churches would be like ourselves, where we are free to do whatever we feel is appropriate. Closed Brethren churches you cannot . . . well, that's the thing. They are closed, so that you cannot go in there and share Communion with them. Even though you are a believer in the Lord Jesus, you cannot go in and share Communion with them or anything like that. They are very tight. You know? It's just something. They . . . one of the things they do, and I don't know if they recognize what they're doing . . . they are destroying family life because if we are brother and sister and you are Closed Brethren and I am Open Brethren, we don't share meals together and different things.

TT: So even the churches don't associate?

BROTHER SAMUEL ANDREWS: No, not at all! Families! They split families down the line!

TT: Families split up over, well, you're an Open Brethren and I'm a Closed Brethren.

BROTHER SAMUEL ANDREWS: Yes, yes! I'm saying even to enjoy a meal. [silence] It's really something.

TT: Are there members here who have come from Closed Brethren churches?

BROTHER SAMUEL ANDREWS: Well there used to be. And he had a *major* issue. He has since gone.

Family and faith are not always seamless. In addition to directly criticizing the ways in which Exclusive Brethren practices that were intended to prevent apostasy caused familial and community rupture, the allusion to a former attendee who ascribed to exclusive practices prompts us to recognize that those views were incompatible with the DBC and CBC communities. As an Open Brethren community, DBC and CBC members understood Closed Brethrenism as retrogressive and consigned them to the past. Nonetheless, church members navigated their own intra-religious social boundaries and schismatic tendencies, particularly around ethnic and moral understandings, as will be discussed in chapter 3.

These DBC and CBC congregants were not alone in their critiques of the rigid boundaries of some Exclusive Brethren coreligionists. Exclusive Brethren have also been depicted negatively in fiction, religious autobiographies, and in popular media as "cults." In particular, the sundering of familial solidarities, the conservative dress codes for women, the establishment of Brethren schools, and the limitation of Brethren youths' interactions with technology and the outside world have been noted as potentially restricting voluntary religious participation (Introvigne 2018). Afro-Guyanese and Harlem Renaissance writer Eric Walrond fictionalizes the Caribbean and Caribbean migrant Brethrenism of his youth. In his 1954 "Success Story," Walrond presents the carryover of Caribbean Brethren religiosity in a New York City migrant family on the part of a Barbadian man who works as a domestic servant but endeavors to "exercise more control over them and to bring them up not 'properly' in a worldly sense, but with a true understanding of the religion of the Plymouth Brethren" (Walrond 2011 [1954], 127). Walrond's short story presents scenes of patriarchal control implemented via the protagonist's corporal punishment of children and his verbal chastisement of his wife. Thus, Walrond critically depicts the use of the familial religion of Plymouth Brethrenism as a form of patriarchy that tried to compensate for Afro-Caribbean immigrants' downward mobility (Walrond 1998).

British memoirs such as *Father and Son: A Study of Two Temperaments* by Edmund Gosse (1990 [1905]) and *In the Days of Rain: A Daughter, a Father, a Cult* by Rebecca Stott (2017) paint a picture of the repressed life of Exclusive Brethren fellowships.[6] Yet Massimo Introvigne (2018) cautions against rendering Exclusive Brethren solely in terms of such popular journalistic and literary accounts that often misrepresent decentralized, nondenominationalized movements as cults. Yet even if we examine the earliest aims of the Brethren movement to unify Christians against the fractures of denominationalism and its subsequent observance of a doctrine of separation that would create the Exclusive Brethren, a paradox emerges. The desire to create an open-ended community of believers is seemingly negated by the creation of closed-ended communities.

This tension between universal and atomized renditions of community life is reconciled, says Introvigne, by the Brethren's insistence that during the breaking of bread they are communing with the entire body of Christian believers (2018). The DBC and CBC Brethren uphold this broad understanding of themselves as members of the universal body of Christ. These understandings of Christian community can be traced to important theological constructions of intersubjectivity and contemporary crosscurrents of Christian globalism. Nonetheless, because of the moral, institutional, and interpersonal boundaries that can segment a Christian sister from an apostate, Brethren familial constructions of Christian peoplehood should not be characterized as a capacious grammar of kinship. Indeed, a review of the places where Brethren religious forms meet kinship conventions is a study of processes of association and disenfranchisement. This is also the case with some of the restrictive currents of contemporary US neo-evangelicalism—the evangelical culture that surrounds DBC and CBC practitioners—and its use of heteronormative kinship ideology.

NEO-EVANGELICALISM, THE HETERONORMATIVE FAMILY, AND ANTIBLACKNESS

Neo-evangelicalism in the United States also has inward and outward orientations. Within the clearly demarcated parameters of US neo-evangelical culture, family ideals and discourse are important markers of evangelical religious identity and moral boundaries.

In his analysis of contemporary US evangelical subcultural identity, Christian Smith observes that the strength of evangelical group membership arises from its oppositional definitions of religious identity (1998). This group identity is constructed through evangelicals' impressions and indeed insistence that they are marginalized by US public discourse. Smith explains that evangelicals perceive "hostility from the mass media, public schools, and feminism" and believe that "every racial, ethnic, religious, political, and ideological perspective existing is given fair time and fair hearing, *except* the Christian perspective" (1998, 137, 140).

Like many of their evangelical contemporaries, DBC and CBC members couch their subcultural identity as evangelicals in terms of opposition to a "secular" US culture and a Christian mainline they consider to be morally lax (Christian Smith 1998). As one DBC church elder said during a spring worship service for Youth Sunday, "We live in a culture today where there is no such thing as absolutes. People do what feels good. It's the postmodern society. It's the church of Oprah." Church members seek to sustain a sense of their cultural separation from secular society through their moral codes. These include prohibitions regarding premarital and extramarital sex, drinking, gambling, and divorce, activities that, if committed with community knowledge, could contribute to a suspension of participation in church ministries and receipt of Communion.

If late-twentieth- and early-twenty-first-century evangelicals understand the secular cultural sphere to be hostile to their ideological orientations, this complex relationship with the public sphere descended from a previous generation's disaffections with the civic challenges wrought by the movements of the 1960s. Their response was to make the private sphere of religion and family a significant rhetorical site for their ideological engagements.

The late 1970s witnessed the coalescence of the Christian Right: a predominantly white coalition of evangelicals and fundamentalists that was guided by a neo-evangelical aspiration to increase the public involvement of born-again Christians. The framers of the evangelical Right fostered a religious and political subcultural identity that rejected the social changes advocated by the civil rights, feminist, gay, and antiwar movements of the 1960s (Schäfer 2013).[7] In particular, the US evangelicalism of the 1960s "negotiated its relationship with, among other things, desegregation, feminism, deindustrialization, and the expanding welfare state" (Schäfer 2013, 4). According to Ann Burlein, for Christians like James Dobson (the founder of Focus on the Family, a conservative evangelical policy advocacy organization), "the family" became a locus for evangelicals' sense of "embattled victimization" and their understanding of liberal gender-, sexuality-, race-, and class-based threats to the nation and their interests (2002, 25, 28).

The Christian Right adroitly channeled solidarities associated with "the family" and the vulnerabilities that attend it, reproducing "the family" in support of an evangelical program: a moral program that privatized "the family" within the racial, gendered, and sexual enclosures of a white cis-heteropatriarchy and an ascendant neoconservatism that would demoralize state support for families, such as welfare (Burlein 2002). "The family" thus became a central signifier of contemporary white evangelical racial, sexual, gender, and class anxieties; an important object of evangelical religious desire; and a rallying point for an embattled evangelical civic identity.

The family imaginary and values campaign that evangelicals espoused was not simply an innocuous site of retrenchment away from public-sphere changes. Neo-evangelical family-values discourse held and still holds antiblack implications. Neo-evangelicalism responded to the civil rights movement and white evangelical concerns about socioeconomic redistribution and interracial marriage. Moreover, the morally deserving evangelical family was constructed in juxtaposition to a raced, gendered, and classed construct of the morally undeserving, black, female-headed household.

Perhaps no other document popularized the nexus of racial and moral discourse of black family formations more than the Moynihan Report of 1965. In "The Negro Family: The Case for National Action," Senator Daniel Patrick Moynihan identified "the black family"—generalized typologically as poor, urban, female-headed households that reproduced a pathological cluster of behaviors such as drug addiction, crime, and educational failure—as both the *cause* and *cure* for black socioeconomic inequality (Geary 2015). As Daniel Geary explained, the Moynihan Report was taken up by liberals and conservatives alike: "Moynihan's thesis produced conflicting notions about how to combat racial inequality. For liberals, it suggested the need to provide jobs for black men to stabilize families. For conservatives, however, it suggested the need for racial self-help: for African American leaders to morally uplift blacks by inculcating family values" (2015, 2).

By making policy recommendations to improve the socioeconomic prospects of African Americans, and in particular black men, the Moynihan Report set the stage for a corrective heteropatriarchy that was understood as foundational to black social and economic mobility and integration into US society. And for conservatives who were invested in retracting welfare benefits, the "problem" of black family life emerged as a moral problem that needed moral solutions (Greenbaum 2015).[8] Geary notes that far from just a secular policy discourse, neo-evangelicalism and conservatism jointly produced moral discourse around "the black family" and proposed that black prospects for socioeconomic mobility and family dysfunction could be redeemed and achieved by a conformity to heteropatriarchal "family values" rather than through material redistribution and equal opportunity.[9]

White neo-evangelicals did not create "the family" as a locus for moralized discussions of racial differences. Mainstream evangelical constructions of "the family" arose from a broader set of policy and social scientific discourses of kinship. These uncritical constructions of "the family" foregrounded a problematic "trope of Patriarchal man," centered the assumption of a "life-giving heterosexuality," and considered black family systems pathological (Blackwood 2005, 14; Butler 2002, 29; Ferguson 2004). Particular to the neo-evangelical and neoconservative constructions of the heteronormative family and the antiblack implications of this kinship discourse was an emphasis on decreased government spending (or small government), individualism, and free market enterprise commonly advocated by conservatives associated with fostering the ideological (moral) and economic positioning of whites disaffected by the redistributive potential of civil rights legislation. Moreover, the silence of the Silent Majority and its employment of race-neutral language introduce a hegemonic whiteness similar to that which is characteristic of mainstream US neo-evangelicalism (Rigueur 2014). By this I mean the ways in which commonsense notions of morality, and in this case citizenship, normalize and valorize white social positioning without the need for explicit reference points. The whiteness of 1970s conservatism and neo-evangelicalism can therefore be understood as kindred racial projects that exacerbated the reproduction of white supremacy in the post–civil rights era and that implicated blackness, as well as black religiosity and families, as objects of socio-moral concern.[10]

Black evangelicals in the US are located in representational economies that have marked them as racial and religious "others" to a hegemonic white evangelicalism and a white, middle-class, cis-heteropatriarchal citizenry that religious and social scientific discourses alike have constructed as the "moral" and "normal" possessors of a God-given and functional US "family." In effect, studying black evangelicals' religious perspectives in terms of their reproduction/nonreproduction of "the family" is to study them in terms of a racialized discourse that has demoralized and pathologized African American family systems.

EVANGELICALISM AND THE INTERNATIONAL MISSION OF "THE FAMILY"

The white US evangelical emphasis on "the family" as an important signifier of evangelical identity and religious piety does not have merely domestic resonance and implications for African Americans. Because of the US influence in geopolitical networks and the international endeavors of US evangelicals, the ideological weighting of "the family" as a key sign of evangelical religious identity has been exported beyond US borders and therefore also affects black evangelicals from the Caribbean.

Part of the international extension of evangelical moral discourse around "the family" emanates from US Christian Right organizations such as the Family Research Council, Concerned Women for America, the Beverly LaHaye Institute, and the Howard Center, which have formed coalitions with Catholic, Jewish, and Mormon religious agencies to effect an international lobby to protect "the natural family": mother, father (connected via heterosexual marriage), and biological offspring (Buss and Herman 2003, 2, 5). Consolidated through gatherings like the World Council of Families II, these lobbies are pitched at international organizations such as the United Nations, and its women's rights and subsidiary population-control entities, and aim to promote pro-life, anti-contraception, and heterosexual marriage and sexuality agendas.

The broader impact of US evangelical family ideals within a global field of evangelical missions and media has also been documented in the changing gender norms and family practices of evangelical converts in Latin America and beyond.[11] The circulation of evangelical family ideals is, in part, associated with the conversion of masculinities shaped by preexisting practices of machismo—hypermasculine gender constructs and performances associated with male peer groups and spaces outside of the home—to a domesticated neo-evangelical familial patriarchy (Brusco 1995; Smilde 2007; Thornton 2016). The circulation of US Christian media in places such as Jamaica has also disseminated a gendered moral economy that focuses on women's moral transgressions. In particular, US televangelist venues create an emphasis on female sexual chastity and need for women's redemption from sexual sin (Frederick 2015).[12] These evangelical constructions of family were grafted onto preexisting colonial formations of class in the Caribbean which held that heteronormative marriage was a quintessential feature of middle-class life. Many CBC and DBC members, who are located in a transnational religious field between the Afro-anglophone Caribbean and the US South, participated in this broader landscape of global evangelical religious culture and its high esteem for heteropatriarchal families. As discussed in more detail in chapter 6, black evangelicals strongly affirmed the heteronormative family as God's design for family life. Nonetheless, they also held critical perspectives on the place of heteropatriarchy within evangelical religious culture and used the safe spaces of spiritual kinship relationships to field their questions and anxieties about heteronormative family life.

DBC AND CBC EVANGELICALS: FROM "THE FAMILY" TO FAMILY

Amid the proliferation of a neo-evangelical gospel of the nuclear family fueled by the domestic and global spread of US neo-evangelicalism—which promotes the privatization of "the family"—my own investigations of black evangelical sociality revealed that church members typically imagined Christian familial belonging in broad rather than nuclear terms that equated the social boundaries of fellowship with the household or local chapel community. There were exceptions. Brother John Forde from Barbados defined family as his wife, children, their spouses, and grandchildren. He explained that his definition of family as referring to those kin who were mainly a part of the nuclear household grew out of conditions related to his profession: "Something that helped is that I moved very frequently with the company that I worked with, so we [my family and I] never really grew deep roots in one place. . . . So we basically provided a lot of our own support." Thus, we must be careful about presuming that mobility automatically generates expansive kin imaginaries.

Yet for the most part, members did not often privatize the discourse of family by restricting it to the boundaries of the heteronormative family.[13] Instead, their kinship worlds bridged biological and religious collectives. Some black evangelicals' mappings of their kinship worlds resembled the transcendent ecclesiology associated with Plymouth Brethrenism. This meant that many members included all Christian believers in their mapping of family. When I asked one Afro-Trinidadian church brother during an interview who he considered to be a part of his church community, he replied, "If someone is a Christian, they're family. To me that's the basic requirement. That's Bible."

Some members were more descriptive in their listings of Christian familial networks. When asked who she considered to be a part of her church family, one DBC member, Sister Evelyn Chapman, a Jamaican nurse in her fifties who had migrated to the US in her teens and who lived in Stone Mountain, Georgia, at the time of my research, answered:

> Church family for me extends beyond my immediate church family because in our sister churches those people . . . it's like they are a part of our group. When I say our group, I don't mean to . . . I don't want to make it sound like it's a spiritual ghetto [laughing]. You know once you get into that. It's a close-knit family. The way we function [is] if someone is hurting in another sister church, we bring it to the attention of DBC; if someone is hurting in CBC with a physical, emotional, financial matter, we bring [it] to the attention of the church; we pray about it. So, there is like a line going all over the world basically. You even think about for me, our missionaries who come and share with us, they are our church kin also. It's not just DBC. They are our extended family, and they're people we touch and people who touch us and the ministries they're involved in. If they hurt, we hurt too.

For Sister Chapman, who had lived in Jamaica and New York before moving to Atlanta, church family was the opposite of a social enclave or "spiritual ghetto," as she jokingly termed it. For her, family was an "extended family" with a "line going all around the world." Specifically, this family consisted of an international network of chapels that were located along her migration pathway from the Caribbean, to New York, to Atlanta, a network that provided vital spiritual and financial support to its constituents. Yet it was not so expansive as not to be deeply personal. This "extended family" was a feeling, praying, ministering Christian community.

One twenty-two-year-old, Lawrence Randall, an American-born DBC member with Caribbean parents, answered in a manner akin to a catechism response when asked who he considered to be his family in Christ. He responded: "Anyone who professes to be saved is a member of the body of Christ." He went on to say that his congregation was most significant to him within that body:

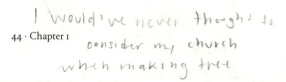

> There's just something about the local body of believers. They're my brothers and sisters in Christ. People who see you every day at church, that you worship with, that if you're in need of prayer, they're the first people who you are going to go to. If they're in need of prayer, you are gonna be some of the first people they go to. It's just closer than that broad spectrum of the body of Christ.

The transcendent family of God that connected all Christians was different to respondents than the local community that participated with them in ritual acts of worship and prayer. Conceptually, Randall valued the spiritual kinship that connects all Christians through their mutual embodiment of the Holy Spirit and their experience of born-again conversion, but also its material, lived manifestation.

In addition to the significance of face-to-face relationships, Brother Randall noted how longevity and care significantly shaped his understandings of kinship:

> There are people who have been here since I was little.... They've known me since I was a little kid. Some of them helped to raise me. There a number of people in the church I call Mom, and they all answer. They're used to this now. It's normal. What's important is that people understand that family is family. Blood family is one thing. They might get a slightly different privilege because they're blood family, but family is family. And family is to be treated as family. People that you're close to are people that you call family.

Brother Randall rendered church and family by offering his decidedly local view of kinship, a view informed by shared religious participation, spiritual reciprocity, and care. His was an ethical, performative rendering of family. Family was as family did.

Chapman and Randall mapped family differently. Sister Chapman had a broader transnational migration and religious history, and her rendition of an extended, trans-local definition of family reflects that. Brother Randall depicted a life history sited in Georgia and held a very local view of church community. Their understandings of family cannot be described solely in terms of the transcendent church imaginary or exclusive congregational communities associated with Brethrenism or the nuclear definitions of family associated with neo-evangelicalism. It is important to look at diasporic kin-tracing and kin-making practices that shape Chapman's outlines of a horizontal, cumulative understanding of family and Randall's depiction of a notion of family rendered in terms of deep and enduring reciprocal care.

"TRACING ROOTS": A STORY OF THE AFRICAN DIASPORA, RELIGION, AND GENEALOGICAL RECONNECTION

If the "godly family" could be defined by Brethren and neo-evangelical religious cultures in terms of a transcendent Christian family or more-nuclear renditions of congregational and familial life, "the roots" referred to by Brother Andrews and Sister Saunders in the Bible study, along with the lateral and care-based definitions of family evoked by Sister Chapman and Brother Randall, recall Afro-diasporic narratives of genealogy. The first roots story is one born of slavery. The second roots story is one born of post-emancipation migrations.

SHIPMATE RELATIONSHIPS: AN AFRO-DIASPORIC ORIGIN STORY

Evoked in the Bible study scene that opened this chapter, Melchizedek—a biblical figure without genealogy—is an apt analogy for the genealogical kinlessness forced upon enslaved Africans. As a result of the transatlantic slave trade, enslaved Africans transported to the New World were displaced from natal African family and ethnic lineages. In such a context of forced kinlessness, Saidiya Hartman observes that "racial solidarity was expressed in the language of kinship because it both evidenced the wound [of slavery] and attempted to heal it" (2007, 103). Afro-diasporic kinship was also shaped from the foundational experience of shipmate relationships. As defined by Alex Baroucki, shipmate networks in South America were "dyadic bonds of two persons of the same sex. Such ties originated along the lines of gender separation enforced in slave vessels. . . . Captives from West Central Africa to Brazil used the word *malungo* for shipmate networks" (2015, 61). Baroucki also observes that enslaved Africans understood the Middle Passage in cosmological terms as a movement from life to death and that making "shipmate" a synonym for "friendship" obscures how captives "came to identify themselves as brothers in suffering" through homosocial shipmate bonds (2015, 62). Shipmates shared not only suffering and other daily events but also more special ritual events. They were witnesses of one another's marriages, and in some instances they prohibited their children from marrying each other, relates Jean Besson (1995).[14] The ship is an important touchstone of Afro-diasporic kinship formation.

The shipmate relationship demonstrates the dynamism of human sociality encoded in Afro-diasporic stories. In *Saltwater Slavery: A Middle Passage from Africa to American Diaspora*, Stephanie Smallwood cautions against overstating the solidarities generated on board slave ships.[15] To be sure, one has to take into account the great ethno-linguistic variations and the challenges presented by intelligibility, illness, trauma, and violence. Yet the shipmate relationship constitutes an origin story of African diaspora kinship and of a New World blackness itself. If Melchizedek presents a biblical story of the significance of genealogy, the shipmate relationship exhibits the significance of kin-making. It is an analogy to the kinship of blackness as a collective identification born out of slavery, suffering, and disenfranchisement. This history presents compelling imagery of how shipmates were marked (consensually or not) as kin through shared experiences of forced migration and suffering. It demonstrates the significance of kinship that is constituted not by biogenetic or ethno-racial ancestry but through shared experience, remembrance, and the intentional making of kin-based community.

In that way, the DBC Bible study mirrors the ship as a context of diasporic blackness and a site of kin-making constructed through shared experiences, conversations, and debate. Such kinship is as much about making relationships as making sense of religious participants' placement in the social worlds of biblical, genealogical, and diasporic pasts and a communal present day. The kincraft alludes as much to the collective making of social relationships as it does to modes of movement and belonging that were and remain constitutive of the variety of sites collectively known as the African Diaspora.

"AND THEN THEY SPREAD OUT": KINSHIP, ADAPTATION, AND LATERAL SOCIAL NETWORKS

Congregants like Brother Andrews's wife, Joanna, and Sister Saunders used genetic testing and genealogical research to trace their "roots." Other congregants rarely mentioned Africa, slavery, and colonialism in church sermons, Bible studies, and other programs, but they did allude to Africa as a site of their own missionary activity. Church members regularly conducted missionary work in Kenya and alluded to it as a place where people "really did family." Thus, it served a metaphorical function as a site of an authenticated kinship practice that could be bettered through evangelical missionary efforts and financial assistance. The DBC and CBC church members were not necessarily turning their backs on their black cultural heritages, nor were they oblivious to the significance of blackness in the US social context. Nonetheless, they did not use the term *African* or *black* to describe their fellowship, nor did they inhabit a denominational church with an organizational history that was framed against or in response to racialized congregational lines established during slavery or Jim Crow. Slavery, then, was not part of the genealogical or institutional story told within the DBC and CBC communities as is the case for some traditional black denominations in the United States.

Yet DBC and CBC members did take part in an Africana spirituality that bridged the ontological conditions of enslavement, social death, and born-again kin worlds created by captives in the plantation context. Because diaspora was not only a historical occurrence but also a central contemporary concern, congregants also took part in a sociality that used these adaptive processes of kin-making to attend to material concerns. They and their relatives were part of African American and Afro-Caribbean migration streams between the anglophone Afro-Caribbean, North America, and Western Europe, as well as between the US South and northeastern, midwestern, and West Coast cities and rural sites (Gregory 2005; Olwig 1999a). Precipitated by economic inequalities established by the extractive relations of the plantation regime and colonialism, the structural adjustment policies that hinders the creation of self-determining national economies and economic opportunities in the Caribbean, as well as the racialization of wealth and the increased cost of living in US urban locales, black migrations are often collective family endeavors made possible through familial financial sponsorship, adoptive practices, and the collective provision of care for migrants' children (Chamberlain 2006; Jewell 2003; Stack 1974). Migrants have stretched their familial relationships into cross-regional and transnational family networks (Gmelch 1992; Goulbourne 1999; Ho 1993). Significantly, black migrant family networks are populated by church members. According to Mary Chamberlain (1999b) and Nicole Toulis (1997), family is an important language of Afro-Caribbean migrant communities and migrant religious settings. As demonstrated above, DBC congregants identify church members as part of their kinship worlds. Moreover, migrant religious settings are shaped by the mobilities of their members, creating what one fifty-one-year-old African American DBC church brother described as "a church of transients."

Yet such adaptive stretching and flexibility of social ties amid the migration process should not be too quickly idealized as harmonious. For migration is not only typically a response to economic instability, but also itself generates a number of economic instabilities, especially upon first arrival. Afro-Caribbean and African American migrations and the spatial and social distances involved can also create familial disenchantments or feelings of loss (Olwig 1999b). Moreover, when heteronormativity is commonly defined as a nuclear family household where a husband and wife and their biological children are coresident, then the cross-household or trans-local family networks that include biological and nonbiological kin relations have been either overlooked or branded by social scientists and policy makers as non-normative. Black migrant families, like African American and Afro-Caribbean families dealing with the racial and moral stigmas of heteronormativity, have had to deal with stigmas and misapprehensions of their familial networks. For instance, scholars have also tended to designate the nonbiological relationships of these lateral kinship networks as "fictive" kinship (Chatters, Taylor, and Jayakody 1994; Dill 1993; Ibsen and Klobus 1972; Nelson 2013). Yet calling them "fictive" assumes that family is fundamentally a construct of biogenetic descent. It also creates a label that delegitimizes some of the social ties that have been vital to black social life.

After anthropologists began basing cross-cultural kinship studies on the universalization of the Western genealogical grid (Schneider 1984), the study of kinship became an investigation of local idioms, categories, and practices of relatedness rather than assuming that one definition fits all situations (Carsten 2000; Franklin and McKinnon 2001). In this broader sense, kinship can perhaps best be understood as ideas by which people define "mutuality of being" and become "intrinsic to one another's existence" (Sahlins 2011, 2). Kinship can also be understood as being created through received discourse and practices that can be revised or amended when constituted against the emergent field of lived experience. The migrations and kinship tracing of DBC and CBC evangelicals reveals that fields of religion and spirituality provide grammars and rituals by which vital forms of relatedness can be created and described. The work of care, whether spiritual or material, the reciprocal exchanges of resources and time commitment that create the ties that bind DBC and CBC members together shape the ongoing process of becoming kin—what we might call kincraft—or what qualifies as such in this newer anthropological paradigm of kinship studies.

If, as Brother Andrews declared, "genealogy is important," then Sister Saunders's observation that genealogical kinship tracing is meaningful to African Americans is equally significant. If black people could excavate their ancestries without it taking "away who we are in Christ," then black and evangelical identities, Afro-diasporic and biblical genealogies, and church and family could coexist. In her terms, African Americans already know that they are Americans, but "it is important to know" where else they came from. Locating this *elsewhere* of kinship (Brown 2005) and its spiritual foundations in the current case is significant in a racial formation that is premised upon a foundational antiblackness and related ideas about black family pathology that writes black racial subjects out of a presumably normative white, heteropatriarchal citizenship.[16] Sister Saunders's discussion of the significance of genealogy for blacks in the US emerged from her critical and adaptive sensibility which knows that mainstream US ideas about black families are insufficient for how black families are conceptualized. (We might also deduce that Brother Andrews's wife

Sister Joanna, though migrating from Trinidad, was also interested in finding kinship ties that extended beyond her own Trinidadian and diasporic family network.) This search for technologies to create kinship reference points beyond the dominant frame, to find an elsewhere of kinship, can be associated with diasporic consciousness, longing, and ancestries that precede and are not restricted to church members' locations in the United States.

AFRO-DIASPORIC RELIGION AS SOCIAL SUTURE

In religious and spiritual contexts such as DBC and CBC, the New World descendants of enslaved Africans have forged ties of kinship that connect people "across the oceans." Practitioners of Afro-Atlantic traditions such as Voodou, Santería, and Candomblé invoke genealogical and spiritual descent from African nations, African-derived divinities, and ancestral progenitors through modes of embodiment (Matory 2009), the creation of transnational ritual networks and imaginaries (Matory 2005; Richman 2008), and the articulation of spiritual and material co-presences (Beliso-De Jesús 2015). Karen McCarthy Brown (2006) has noted that Afro-Creole religious systems are both relationally concerned and therapeutic in their emphasis of social ties as sites of illness, wellness, and curative rituals designed to foster social connection.[17] Moreover, these syncretic traditions aid the creation of Afro-Atlantic connections that rest upon historical, relational, and ancestral conceptions and authenticated sites of memory (Scott 2013). The ancestral, memorial, and relational functions of these traditions are mobilized to heal the alienations of enslavement and colonialism, and generate important sites of belonging amid the familial losses of slavery and the dehumanizing antiblackness encoded in Western political orders.

Yet the place of black Christian expressions within the broader field of Afro-diasporic religious traditions that use African-derived religious technologies of socio-spiritual suture is complex. African American Christian traditions are often set apart from the syncretic assemblages of African-derived New World religious practices. This is part and parcel of the differential associations of African-derived religious assemblages and Christianity within cultural and colonial orders, the former being attributed to black racial primitivism and the latter being coupled with Western colonization and the forced cultural assimilation of Western cultural mores on the part of enslaved Africans and their New World descendants. As observed by Dianne Stewart (2005), the alignment of Christianity with colonial orders was not benign. Christian colonial complexes contributed to the suppression, demonization, and criminalization of

African-derived syncretic religious systems such as Obeah in Jamaica. The distinctions between Christianity and African-derived practices were written and imprinted by those in power.[18]

The CBC and DBC members also disassociated their Christian practices from African and African-derived religious phenomena. The Afro-Caribbean and African American evangelicals of CBC and DBC do not participate in Afro-Atlantic rituals of genealogical connection.[19] Instead (at least in some instances), church members have reproduced racialized and religious hierarchies in defining their version of evangelical Christianity as distinctive and superior to other forms of Christianity, like Afro-Baptist traditions in the Caribbean and US South. Other church members, like Afro-Trinidadian Sister Constance Lorenzo, discuss their previous participation in African-derived traditions such as Spiritual Baptist practices as being rightfully replaced by a Bible-believing Christianity that possessed "more content."

Anthropologists of Christianity have theorized the relationship between Christianity and culture, noting the extent to which Christianity can generate strong forms of Christian cultural identification or processes of cultural reformation. For instance, Joel Robbins argues that Christian converts can understand born-again identity as a radical departure from their cultures of origin and hold a higher esteem of their new Christian identifications over their natal cultural subjectivities (2007). Courtney Handman proposes a different view, suggesting that Christian and non-Christian cultures and genealogies might best be studied as being dynamically engaged in "movements between critique, division, and the reconstitution of unity" (2014, 267). Both Robbins and Handman work within an anthropology of Christianity that has successfully labored to redeem Christian religious communities as an object of serious anthropology inquiry that cannot be represented simplistically via top-down colonization processes or as a repugnant cultural other to a secular liberal humanism (Harding 2001). Nonetheless, the anthropology of Christianity has been largely silent about the ways in which Christian cultural identifications interact with racial, ethnic, and diasporic subjectivities in the North American context, in particular, the religious and racial locations of black Christian religious practitioners.

Though the Christianity-culture nexus in our present case located within the cultural complex of the African Diaspora also centralizes discussions about cultural pasts, the context of the United States beckons questions about how race and diasporic locations shape the study of Christian cultures. In terms of the interactions of race and culture, Walter Benn Michaels (1992) argues that notions of culture tend to be dictated in terms of racial attribution and rights.

This framing of culture as race tends to render "assimilation into a kind of betrayal and the refusal to assimilate into a form of heroism" (Michaels 1992, 685). Though DBC and CBC evangelicals might in other cultural contexts be described as privileging their born-again identities or as engaging in Protestant social processes of cultural change and reconstitution, their position as racialized subjects in the United States would read a congregants' prioritization of a godly family over roots-based genealogy as a kind of loss: an abrogation of essentializing values associated with the workings of culture in a post-Emancipation, multicultural United States. This would render them as I proposed in the introduction as racial outliers of a sort.

Brother Edmondson's assertion that being "in Christ" and "in the family of God" should supersede "human genealogy" would thus less likely be read as an act of privileging Christian over Afro-diasporic genealogy shaped by Brethren practices of supersessionism. A race-as-culture view would read Edmondson's emphasis of the "godly family" as an attempt to assert cultural distance from non-Christian, African-derived religious cultures, or as an effort at white Western cultural assimilation. But what if the distinction between "godly" and "roots"-based definitions of kinship, as Christian versus ancestral renditions of genealogy, collapses? What if black evangelical Christian religious practitioners who insist on the prominence of the "godly family" over roots-based definitions grounded in African ancestry are engaging in more than an individual move toward Christian supersessionism or cultural assimilation?

A comparative view demonstrates that Edmondson's privileging of the "godly family" replicates genealogical practices and ethical orientations found in other Afro-diasporic religious traditions. John Pulis notes contexts in which Afro-Jamaican religious practitioners understand biblical figures to be ancestors (1999a). Given the tight associations of Brethrenism with biblical literalism and an attempt to reconstitute intimate New Testament Christian fellowship, this ancestral orientation seems fitting. Other Africana religious communities have used religion as a space to reconfigure genealogies of origin. Scholars such as Eddie Glaude (2000), Henry Goldschmidt (Goldschmidt and McAlister, 2004), and Sylvester Johnson (2010) have discussed the ways in which African American and Afro-Caribbean Christian constituents have read themselves into Judeo-Christian, Hebrew, Islamic, and utopian religious narratives of peoplehood, exile, and divine chosenness. The result of such genealogical reconstructions has been the creation of alternative histories that are not grounded in historical experiences of enslavement. In addition, by reading black people into textual and alternative histories, such ancestral reconstitutions propagated by black religious movements have often undergirded critical and even radical rebukes of imperial, democratic, and religious constructions of antiblack racism. Remember, the primitivism of Plymouth Brethrenism was located within a field of nonconformist Christianity.

At the level of ethics, an ancestral and communal orientation is key to renditions of Africana spirituality. In *The Spirituality of African Peoples,* Peter J. Paris argues that African peoples "agree that community is a sacred phenomenon created by the supreme God" and that "ancestors comprise the principal link between the ethnic community and the realm of the spirit" (1995, 51). The sacred familial imaginary and emphasis on ancestors and religious predecessors voiced even by Brother Edmondson are consonant not with an African religious essence but with an African-diasporic ethical orientation that shapes how people view self in relation to the community and the divine.

I consider Brother Edmondson's assertion of the higher importance of the "family of God" over the "human family" to arise from a diasporic genealogical imperative—a desire to trace family broadly across space and time—that is imprinted by Brethren and Afro-diasporic influences. The former is present in its transcendent ecclesiology that defines the Church as the body of Christ that connects all believers dead and alive across space and heaven. The latter is shaped by the flexibilities, adaptabilities, and imaginative capacities that have shaped Afro-diasporic kin-making in secular and sacred contexts.

According to Dianne M. Stewart Diakité and Tracey E. Hucks, an Africana religious studies hinges on not being beholden to iconoclastic distinctions between African or Western heritages. Instead, it embraces the sensibilities of broad cross sections of Africana religious traditions (2013). This approach means understanding multiple origins for black religious formations such as DBC and CBC evangelicalism. As articulated by Sister Saunders above, tracing roots of origin does not take away who one is in Christ. People construct kinship worlds based on where they are and where they tend to come from. Thus, rather than an either/or model for studying Christian and Africana religious cultures, we can consider a both/and model that acknowledges multiple origins for religious worldviews that moves beyond supersessionism and assimilation as meta-narrative frames of religious cultural identifications. In light of the ethical and capacious dimensions of black evangelicals' diasporic instantiations of kinship, I suggest that CBC and DBC members' Christian genealogical imaginaries, as well as their broader reckonings of spiritual kinship, are part of the broader terrain of an Africana religious sociality.

Moreover, as this book demonstrates in chapter 3, the history and collective experiences that constitute this evangelical association tell a diasporic story of a complex institutional and spiritual relatedness created across ethnic divides in a black Atlantic religious landscape located between the Caribbean and the US South. Thus, CBC and DBC community life is partially constituted by diasporic kinship threads that have emerged out of a recognition of histories of North American racism and Western colonialism, modes of religious and racial alterity, and shared everyday experiences and material conditions. These DBC and CBC church members were not necessarily averse to their black cultural heritages, nor were they oblivious to the significance of blackness in the US social context. Congregants like Brother Andrews's wife and Sister Saunders used genetic testing and archival genealogy as technologies to trace their "roots" and "history." Yet church members also engaged in the processes of making of kinship relationships through adaptive creations of familial ties that were spiritual (and nonbiological) and that attended to the material and political conditions shaped by racialization.

In closing, the Brethren-influenced evangelicalism practiced by CBC and DBC members and the relational ethos it distilled can be mapped onto three ways of understanding kinship: as Afro-diasporic outlines that are constructed through notions of sacred ancestry, communion, and witness shared by Afro-Caribbean and African American religious practitioners; as adaptive practices of nonbiological kinship that occur within the migrant contexts of the African Diaspora, practices that attend to the material and discursive effects of racialization on black congregants' families; and as transcendent notions of universal Christian relatedness influenced by Plymouth Brethren evangelical perspectives. For the black evangelicals who construct one another as "brothers and sisters in Christ," "spiritual parents," "spiritual children," and "prayer partners," their notions of spiritual kinship emerged from an intersection of worldviews shaped by Afro-diasporic and Brethren evangelical attunements. Yet these genealogies are not easily compartmentalized into racial or religious lineages. Instead, they are shaped by a confluence of sensibilities that derive from historical, material, symbolic, and discursive locations and imaginaries that are spiritualized by members.

As this book explores, black evangelicals take the sacred solidarities of spiritual kinship relationships and moralize them in relation to the alienations they associate with the boundaries of ethnicity, race, mainstream congregationalism, and "the respectable family" in the United States. Limiting the landscape of evangelical sociality to the construct of "the family" also misses the broader social landscape of lived religious experiences. In such a landscape, evangelicals are, as anthropologist of Chrisianity Omri Elisha observes, "expected to become closely implicated in the lives of others" (Elisha 2015, 42). Limiting that landscape obscures the ways in which contemporary Christians navigate the different values and tensions that attend individualistic as well as relational forms of personhood (Bialecki and Daswani 2015; Robbins 2015) and avoids the diasporic histories and migration experiences constitutive of church members' religious networks and reckonings of religious community.

In chapter 2 I explore the Afro-Caribbean missionary provenance of DBC and CBC. I narrate the post–World War II migration of T. Michael Flowers and his planting of "Bible-believing" churches in the US South, influenced by Plymouth Brethrenism. These stories illustrate Flowers's social location in the US South as an Afro-Bahamian evangelist located between African American churches and white evangelical institutions during the Jim Crow era. They also discuss his reformist aspirations to insert a relational vision of a universalistic Christian relatedness.

Moving against the Grain 2

The Evangelism of T. Michael Flowers in the Segregated US South

The institutional story of the Dixon Bible Chapel and Corinthian Bible Chapel communities begins with the work of the late Afro-Bahamian evangelist T. Michael Flowers.[1] Although he may not have the name recognition of some of his black evangelical contemporaries such as John Perkins or Tom Skinner, Flowers helped to establish a network of black Bible-believing chapels throughout the Southeast US in the second half of the twentieth century. He also partnered with Afro-Caribbean, African American, and white American religious participants to translate Brethren biblical sensibilities and theologies of universal Christian relationship in a region that was marked by strong racial and religious boundaries.

I learned about Flowers's life firsthand thanks to the ten months of Wednesday afternoons I spent being discipled by him, doing Bible studies on Acts, and praying in his kitchen. Each Wednesday, I drove to the suburban home of the then-octogenarian preacher in Decatur, Georgia.

We studied at a wooden table in his warm, modest kitchen. With our Bibles open, and occasionally joined by his daughter's kitten, Flowers would solicit prayer requests from me, add his own, and offer them up in prayer. He would ask for the Holy Spirit to illuminate our discussion and in his clipped and raspy brogue begin our sessions with his trademark opening: "Let's see what happens when we get in the Word, and allow the Word to get into us." Over five decades he had become renowned for his way of teaching the Bible and discipling the next generations.

In 1955 Flowers, a Plymouth-Brethren missionary, and his wife, Ella, traded the asphalt of Detroit, Michigan, for the sandy terrain of Savannah, Georgia. In a series of oral history interviews conducted by archivists for the

Wheaton College Billy Graham Center,[2] Flowers described his "Macedonian call" to the South:[3]

> I used *This Morning with God* [daily Bible devotional].... And that morning the reading was from Genesis 28, God and Jacob. And ... and ... and that morning God's word to Jacob took on new meaning. This very room seemed to be ablaze with the glory of God. There was the consciousness that God was not speaking to Jacob any longer but was speaking to [me]. "I will give you this land. I will bring you back. I will not leave you." And that morning it meant something. Today it's the driest portion of the Word of God for me but that was God's specific message to me that morning.... I was able to get here in 1955.... [My wife and] I have [been] in Georgia ever since. (Wheaton College Archives Transcript 1)

For Flowers, the glory of God transformed the Bible from a text for religious study into an oracle: a channel for divine revelation. In that moment, Flowers experienced transcendence; that day, the words of the Bible became the literal words of God addressed to him as a direct injunction. Rather than a closed book, the Bible was to him an active and open-ended text. That day, in the biblical story of Jacob leaving his father's house and receiving the promise of God's faithful presence along the course of his life journey, Flowers felt God address him. So strong was the experience of God that Flowers interpreted the narrative as an enlivened covenant that God was making with him. It was so forceful that it inspired him to move to a tumultuous and segregated US South, a South caught in the midst of large-scale racial and religious transitions.

Beyond this call event, why specifically did this Afro-Bahamian missionary decide to conduct evangelistic work in the Bible Belt with southern blacks—a population that already possessed a deep historical engagement with Protestant Christianity? Why did Flowers and his wife Ella move to the US South when African Americans and Afro-Caribbeans were migrating to northern and midwestern cities to escape racial violence and to search for better economic opportunities? What are we to make of Flowers's evangelistic project in relation to the meta-narrative of Christian missionization as a vehicle of Western imperialism?

Building on an analysis of oral history texts, church historical documents, and a collection of Flowers's reflections on his southern missionary work that I obtained through our weekly Bible study conversations, this chapter is a historical analysis of Flowers's unorthodox migration *to*, complex location *within*, and representations *of* a southern US racial and religious order. It illumines how he negotiated the missiological, ethno-racial, and imperial hierarchies between missionary and convert, between black and white evangelicals, and between emergent neo-evangelical and black Atlantic evangelical sensibilities of Christian community. I argue that Flowers's missionary work endeavored a textual reformation of a stereotyped charismatic African American Christianity and an institutional reformation of a cloistered white evangelicalism. I also reveal some of the theological discourse of Christian relatedness that has been foundational in shaping Flowers's and DBC church members' critical habitation of southern and US religious landscapes.

Yet this narration is a complicated task for three key reasons. First, one result of the anti-denominational character of Brethrenism has often been a paucity of organizational records (Akenson 2018). Second, for that reason I have had to depend on oral historical sources to reconstruct the history of Flowers's life.[4] Third and finally, the genre of missionary history is often associated with a number of shortcomings or complicating realities, including top-down and masculinist accountings of past events. Furthermore, religious studies scholars typically view with deserved skepticism missionary historiography, given the celebratory tones in which it is often recounted. Robert Priest in "Missionary Positions: Christian, Modernist, Postmodernist" notes that anthropologists have their own particular biases about missionaries. Among them is often a modernist essentialization of Christian identity and a tendency to overlook the means by which "missionary realities vis-à-vis power are more diverse and complex than modernist myths would suggest" (2001, 45). This requires an attention to microlevel stories of evangelism that is acutely sensitive to context.

Both CBC and DBC congregants celebrate Flowers as a primary founding figure of their denominations. During an interview with me, Afro-Jamaican DBC member Lemuel James discussed Flowers's legacy:

> I used to drive [Pastor Flowers] to the different churches down South. . . . It was ridiculously interesting. I loved it [though admittedly] first, I was scared. [I thought:] this old man is going to talk me to death, or he's gonna talk about stuff I don't want to talk about. I'm gonna be bored for four hours driving to Savannah. But he would pretty much share his vision driving down there. He would tell stories of the sixties and seventies and how they were treated in the South, and that was really, really interesting.

Endeavoring to reconstruct a narrative that acknowledges the various constellations of power at play in T. Michael Flowers's missionary work and attending to James's response to Flowers's self-narration calls for an ethnographic accountability on my part. Even amid my own conceptual project, I must admit that Flowers's oral history was a really interesting story.

T. Michael Flowers and Transatlantic Brethrenism

T. Michael Flowers migrated from Detroit to Savannah in 1955 to begin his missionary project of starting Bible-believing churches among blacks in the segregated US Southeast. In doing so, Flowers and his wife moved in the opposite direction of the migrations undertaken by most southern blacks and Afro-Caribbeans to midwestern and northern cities such as New York, Boston, and Chicago during the first half of the twentieth century (Drake and Cayton 2015; Johnson 2006; Watkins-Owens 1996). They also moved against the wishes of Sharon's family, whose firsthand experiences with southern segregation had earlier motivated their migration to Detroit. Nonetheless, a closer look at Flowers's religious and migration history and his location within a transnational evangelical religious network that included the Caribbean, the British Isles, and North America sheds light on his belief in and commitment to universal Christian relatedness despite the prevailing attention to social differences.

EARLY LIFE

Born in 1920, Flowers was raised in the Anglican Church in Andros, Bahamas. Nonetheless, he identifies the beginning of his Christian journey as his personal born-again conversion as a teen at a Plymouth Brethren revival there in 1937.[5] In recounting this conversion experience to me, Flowers highlighted the contested nature between evangelical and Anglican Christianity. He attested that "one day I thought I should go back and tell the priest what [had] happened to me. So I went back and I said to him, 'Father, I'm saved now. I'm a Christian.' And he turned as red as an apple and says, 'You idiot. You're what?' I says, 'Father, I'm a Christian.' And that brought our relation" [slaps hands signifying a decisive rupture] (Wheaton College Archives Transcript 1). In addition to describing the dissolution of his relationship with the priest for whom he had served as an altar boy, Flowers's observation of the white Anglican priest's insult and pejorative reaction to his conversion also exemplifies and illuminates the racist paternalism of colonial Anglicanism—the official church of the British Empire.

Flowers explained to me that when he entered young adulthood in a local community with limited job prospects, his rejection of (and by) Anglicanism limited his educational opportunities, which were traditionally mediated by

Anglican Church membership. After working as a carpenter, Flowers migrated to England and made his living doing industrial factory work from 1942 until 1946. This time, he was part of a regional movement of Caribbean migrants to England, who exchanged their labor for the war effort and potentially better economic prospects. During his time in England he was exposed to imperial racial hierarchies that segregated British metropolitan citizens and Afro-Caribbean migrants. As he remembers, "[In the Bahamas] we used to boast about being members of the far-flung British empire. . . . You know, I said, 'Boy, I thought I was British,' you know, and that's it. Then I went to England and discovered I was nothing [laughs]" (Wheaton College Archives Transcript 2). He also witnessed the ways in which intraracial hierarchies among Caribbean "colonials" created cleavages between Afro-Caribbean migrants to England and often spoke of the insults and fights that erupted between Caribbean migrants who variously identified themselves as "big island people" versus "little island people": people from islands with larger populations understood themselves as more worldly than their Caribbean counterparts from smaller communities (Wheaton College Archives Transcript 2).

Amid his tempestuous navigation of the systemic racism that was an implicit part of the British imperial regime, Flowers's religious participation with Brethren overseas afforded him an opportunity for membership in a religious community. Flowers forged connections with Scottish Brethren during his study at the Glasgow Bible Institute between 1947 and 1949.[6] Although his training at Glasgow did not culminate in a formal degree, Flowers used his time at the institute to take courses on Bible history, psychology, Greek, and Latin. His time there solidified his understanding and emphasis of biblical literalism. Living in Glasgow also showed Flowers the possibilities for interracial religious solidarity.

In sum, Flowers described the impact of his time abroad and his interactions with British evangelicals as vitally shaping his understandings of Christian kinship: "[I learned that] Biblical Christianity has no perimeters, just folks. . . . Never mind the badges. You're in Christ. And God did that and I'm glad. I am eternally glad that he took me out of the Bahamas, took me to England to give me the proper perspective of the work of the Christ of the Cross" (Wheaton College Archives Transcript 2). Flowers's stay in Glasgow also gave him the opportunity to become part of a number of interracial and transatlantic evangelical religious networks that would be central to his later southern missionary work (Wheaton College Archives Transcript 2). In addition, it was at the recommendation of one of his Glasgow colleagues that Flowers received a preaching post in Toronto, Canada.

Although Flowers navigated a number of imperial racial and regional hierarchies in the Caribbean and Great Britain, the experience of repeated migration forced Flowers to reflect, critique, and protest the tensions that resulted from myriad social differences. Flowers's migration experiences also led him to construct religious solidarities and participate in interracial and transatlantic religious communities that frustrated some of the racial and racist assumptions of British imperialism. Flowers later channeled some of his criticisms of racial and territorial hierarchies, his formative Brethren theological training, and his enlivening experiences with interracial religious collaboration into his southern missionary work.

Black Atlantic Evangelism, Respectability, and the Problem of Southern Black Religious Difference

If at least some of Flowers's experience in Great Britain illuminated the expansive and positive possibilities of Christian community, his experience in the United States was a lesson in intra-religious fragmentation. It was in Detroit, a central node of the southern diaspora (Gregory 2005), that Flowers met fellow Afro-Bahamian and brother evangelists Berlin Martin Nottage, Talbot Berton Nottage, and Whitfield Nottage. As Caribbean evangelists likewise influenced by the tenets of the Plymouth Brethren, the Nottages founded black Bible-believing churches in northern and midwestern cities in the US in the first half of the twentieth century.[7] It was in conjunction with the Nottages, who had conducted missionary work along (but not limited by) the color line, that Flowers formulated his impression of southern black religiosity and the need for a ministry in the South. As Flowers recounted, "B. M. was always saying to [me], 'Young man, there's much work to be done, and the blacks in this country are terribly neglected. They need help.' And God used that to open my eyes to get an idea of the need. But B. M. influenced me" (Wheaton College Archives Transcript 3). The Nottages and eventually Flowers came to share the conviction that although African Americans, specifically black Baptists, attended churches that were characterized by ecstatic worship and charismatic leadership, what was lacking, from their point of view, was substantive teaching of the Bible as the literal word of God and a sound understanding of born-again soteriology. This perceived state of African American religious atrophy contributed to what Flowers and the Nottages felt were contexts in which many black Christians "played church":

> Well, for the most part, it is still true that the most of our churches are given over to emotionalism without any contents. . . . And for the most

part there's very little teaching in the area of separation from wicked practices. And so for the most part there is very little change in the lives of church people.... And coming from a different country, I ... I realized that being religious was not the answer to anything, because I [too had once been] religious. (Wheaton College Archives Transcript 3)

Flowers and the Nottages framed southern black Christianity as cathartic but not textual, as performative but not salvific, as cultural but not personal. But were such criticisms valid? In her 2017 book *Doctrine and Race: African American Evangelicals and Fundamentalism between the Wars*, Mary Beth Swetnam Matthews studies the theological orientations of African American Baptists and Methodists. Matthews finds a number of similarities between the professed beliefs of African American Baptists and evangelical Christianity, including "a heavy emphasis on reading the Gospels and seeking a conversion experience that would produce life-altering behavior" and a "hewing to the traditional evangelical notions of the Virgin Birth, the inerrancy of the Bible, and the need to evangelize a fallen world" (2017, 69–70). According to Matthews, black Baptists did not subscribe to the premillennialism elaborated by fundamentalists.[8] Because dispensational premillennialism is highly associated with Brethrenism, eschatology could have been a major bone of contention between Afro-Caribbean evangelists and African American clergy.

The twentieth-century postwar period witnessed the emergence of black evangelicals who defined themselves in critical relationship to a "Black Church" Christianity that did not properly emphasize biblical teaching. Black evangelicals addressed this problem by establishing and participating in para-church Bible camps and Bible schools (Miller 2000), as well as by founding the para-church National Black Evangelical Association in 1963. Flowers and the Nottages held the same views as their black evangelical coreligionists who gave primary importance to a distinctive Bible-focused religious identity.

Nonetheless, tracing the sources of these men's constructions of intraracial and intra-religious differences illustrates how black evangelical identity—however much it was grounded in notions of collective spiritual connection—could also be negatively defined through concepts of black religious difference. Taking a broader perspective on Flowers's deprecation of southern black Christianity also reveals the structures of imperial, racial, and class-based power, as well as variegated views of black religion beyond standard denominational classifications. For this, it is useful to understand the colonial, racial, regional, and missionary discourse on Afro-Baptist and southern black religion that shaped the field of black intraracial religious interactions.

THE PROBLEM OF AFRO-BAPTIST RELIGION: INHERITED CONSTRUCTS OF DIFFERENCE, EMERGENT SIMILARITIES

Flowers's and the Nottages' views of Afro-Baptist religious practices in the US likely descended from colonial denigrations of Afro-Baptist traditions such as Native Baptist groups in Jamaica and Spiritual Baptist communities in Trinidad. Plantation and colonial orders understood Native Baptist, Spiritual Baptist, and black North American Baptist religious systems not only as inauthentic modes of Christianity but also as inferior simply because of the blackness of their practitioners and the cultural difference of their religious ways from British colonial religious practices.[9] Moreover, Afro-Baptist religion was subjected to intense scrutiny for its ability to generate self-determining black institutions that could galvanize black dissent and rebellion.

Jamaican Native Baptist and Trinidadian Spiritual Baptist communities emerged out of nineteenth-century contexts of Christian missionization, and they combined Protestant and Afro-derived religious sensibilities. As syncretized religious traditions, Jamaican Native Baptists and Trinidadian Spiritual Baptists had highly elaborate ritual landscapes and ecstatic worship practices, and emphasized local congregational leadership (Austin-Broos 1997; Desmangles, Glazier, and Murphy 2003)—norms that the colonializing missionaries then perceived as wholly other.

Although Flowers defined Afro-Baptist Christianity in an oppositional relationship to a more intellectual black Christianity that he associated with evangelicalism, there are a number of similarities between Afro-Baptist Christianity and the evangelicalism that Flowers transplanted in the US South. Like the Brethren-influenced religious network founded by Flowers, Afro-Baptist churches in the Caribbean emerged out of encounters between black North Americans and Afro-Caribbean religious practitioners. After founding the First Missionary Baptist Church in Savannah, Georgia,[10] southern black freedman George Lisle would go on to do missionary work in the Caribbean (Pulis 1999b). Assisted by fellow black American missionary Moses Baker, Lisle founded the Ethiopian Baptist Church in Kingston in 1782. As an early framer of a transnational black Christianity instituted by and among black religious agents, Lisle channeled the fervor of the First Great Awakening—a revival movement that swept across Western Europe and the British empire—into the genesis of a New World Afro-Protestant religious encounter. In doing so, Lisle helped to transform the "invisible institution" of slave religion into an institutionalized Afro-Baptist Christianity (Raboteau 1978).

In addition, Afro-Baptist communities, like Brethren, placed a high premium on the autonomy of religious practitioners and local congregational leadership (Pitts 1993). The ability of Afro-Baptist religious communities to foster self-determining black institutions also made them vectors for black dissent and rebellion to colonial and plantation orders. In Jamaica, for example, Native Baptists created institutional spaces that they used to produce sharp anticolonial protests such as the Baptist Rebellion of 1831 to 1832, led by Baptist leader "Daddy" Samuel Sharpe, who galvanized tens of thousands of slaves (Austin-Broos 1997). Although they killed only fourteen white colonists during the Rebellion, hundreds of slaves died during the incident and in its punitive aftermath. However, this sacrifice led soon thereafter to the formal abolition of slavery in 1834, which was fully enacted in 1838 after an apprenticeship period ended. In 1831 black Baptist preacher Nat Turner had likewise organized a rebellion in Southampton County, Virginia, which resulted in the deaths of fifty to sixty-five people. Notably, Baptist rebels were motivated and empowered by evangelical beliefs about the priesthood of believers and their ability to directly communicate with God (Scully 2007). Although Flowers and black evangelicals at DBC and CBC did not generate a religious culture that explicitly addressed local politics, they shared an idea of individualistic and community self-determination with black Baptists in the US and the Caribbean. Thus, Flowers's and the Nottages' constructions of Afro-Baptist religious difference replicated a number of colonial critiques of the Afro-Baptist religious culture as charismatic, disorderly, and culturally other to authenticated forms of colonial religion. Nonetheless, their constructions of Baptist religious difference also coexisted with analogical diasporic missionary histories and similar emphases of individual and local community authority. These reckonings of religious difference—though inherited and reproduced—were not absolute.

THE PROBLEM OF SOUTHERN BLACK CHRISTIANITY:
MISSIONARY VIEWS

Flowers's and the Nottages' views of southern black Christianity were also shaped by notions of cultural difference that often attend proselytizing projects. As aptly expressed by Tom Beidelman, "Missionizing makes sense only if one has a negative evolutionary view of a culture one is trying to change" (1982, 16). Flowers's perspectives on southern black religious difference was, in part, informed by the reform emphasis of Protestant evangelism and its identification of, encounter with, and transformation of a religious "other." Because missionization is often associated with Westernization and modernization, evangelism is often organized by a tacit hierarchy that privileges the missionary over the convert and post-conversion solidarities over pre-conversion identities.

The encounters between black missionaries and their black converts, though often motivated by racial solidarity, were also informed by intraracial cultural chauvinism. Waibinte Wariboko (2007) notes that Afro-Caribbean missionaries sent to Nigeria by the Anglican Church in the early twentieth century, though racialized by the white church establishment and given smaller wages and less institutional support than their white peers, often operated under similar assumptions about African cultural inferiority and the positive benefits of foreign religious interventions as their white counterparts. In *Alabama in Africa: Booker T. Washington, the German Empire, and the Globalization of the New South*, Andrew Zimmerman also observes that a number of African Americans, from Martin Delaney to Booker T. Washington to W. E. B. Du Bois, espoused the benefits of the "civilizing mission" of Christianity, education, and improved agricultural production spearheaded by African Americans and other Western powers as a pathway for African development in the early twentieth century (2012). Black missionaries and reformers during the imperial era tended to replicate the privileging of white Western cultural norms over black, non-Western ("African" or "African-descended") traditions and promoted Christian conversion and industry as a primary method for instigating blacks' trek toward modernity.

Although Flowers's evangelical missionary work took place in a late-colonial/postcolonial context among a Christianized US black population, not an African one, his missionary efforts were driven by the same missiological emphases of religious difference. In addition to reflecting the evolutionary perspective and "restlessness" of a global evangelistic Protestantism fueled by a "sense of revival, restoration and reform" (Keane 2007, 50), Flowers's constructions of southern black Christianity also took place within a preexisting landscape of missionary engagement with southern African Americans.

During the Reconstruction Era, northern missionaries and teachers employed by the Baptist Home Mission Society and the American Missionary Association applied the transformational ethos and "evangelical coloring" of missionary Protestantism in their southern educational work, which they often described in terms of "mission, missionary work and evangelism" (Butchart 2010, 87, 106). By buying into this civilizing, modernizing mission among southern blacks, these missionaries all too often cast southern black religion and lifeways as inferior to Euro-American Protestant cultural norms. The scientific racism of the era that sought remedies for a purportedly innate black racial inferiority fostered these missionaries' notions of black degeneracy (Jewell 2007). What connected Flowers to this earlier wave of missionaries conducting evangelistic work among African Americans in the US South was a worldview that generated and moralized religious differences. Flowers, the Nottages, and their missionary predecessors held a reformist view of a southern black culture that they deemed in need of change and a sense of their own capacity to institute those changes.

THE PROBLEM OF SOUTHERN BLACK CHRISTIANITY: NORTHERN VIEWS

Missionaries and northern white educators were not the only groups that problematized southern black Christianity. During the Great Migration, African Americans in urban locales outside of the South also held negative views of southern black religious ways. Those who employed respectability as a weapon in the arsenal of black protest considered charismatic folk Christianity (common among southern blacks) an affront to black racial advancement. Such advancement was a central concern for many blacks during the segregation era. As Evelyn Brooks Higginbotham notes, respectability was a tool by which blacks, a monolithic mass from the vantage point of white society, could "distinguish class and status differences among themselves" (1993, 205). Undoubtedly, Flowers and the Nottage brothers were familiar with the negative depictions of southern black religion, culture, and backwardness that other African American urban dwellers in northern cities such as Detroit advanced.

Wallace Best's historical study of southern black religious culture in early- to mid-twentieth-century Chicago investigates how black Chicagoans saw southern black migrant Christianity as a primitive religious culture. He observes that they generally considered black southern religiosity to be backward simply because it was largely rural and southern: "Indeed, the bias some showed toward black southerners indicated a stern bias against the South. Primarily because migrants were from the rural South, longtime residents felt at liberty to scrutinize every aspect of migrant speech, dress, and behavior. They insisted new migrants conform to their own values of bourgeois respectability" (2005, 37). They associated the emotional shouting, charismatic leadership, theological eclecticism, and vernacular, performative preaching with the slave past, and simply because of that negatively distinguished it from a local, urban, mainline Protestant establishment. The evolutionary urbanization paradigm popularized by the Park School of Sociology prompted black scholars such as E. Franklin Frazier (1964), St. Clair Drake, and Horace Cayton (Drake and Cayton 2015) to understand blacks' participation in ecstatic, otherworldly religious forms as hindering blacks' attention to their political marginalization. As a remedy, such scholars believed that southern blacks' urbanization would convert them into modern religious subjects who would participate in institutionalized black denominational culture and thereby close the cultural gap between them and more-seasoned black urbanites. Such seasoned urbanites in places like Chicago therefore recruited southern black migrants to established churches, driven by charitable intentions as well as "reformist and evangelical" impulses (Best 2005, 75). An intraracial mission to inculcate respectable social habits among black migrants thus ensued in migration-era metropoles.

Blacks' abilities to assimilate and exhibit Euro-American middle-class cultural norms and dispositions were considered a means of debunking naturalized racist assumptions and illustrating the ways in which biologically deterministic notions about black inferiority were socially constructed (Higginbotham 1993). Moreover, by taking on the behaviors and internalizing the values and ethos associated with Protestant modernity, blacks' ascription to and demonstration of their respectability were believed to provide a pathway for black social uplift and illustrate blacks' moral worthiness for full inclusion within the nation's body politic. Some black religious participants engaged in such measures of respectability as a tool for political advancement (Hunter 1997). Others favored religious movements that did not subscribe to the hegemonic black denominational respectability that was all too often used as an intraracial system of religious, class, and status distinctions (Curtis and Sigler 2009).

Among those new religious movements were the Moorish Science Temple Movement, the Nation of Islam, the Commandment Keepers Ethiopian Hebrew Congregation, and the Father Divine Peace Mission from the 1920s to 1940s, which Judith Weisenfeld explores in her 2017 book *New World A-Coming: Black Religion and Racial Identity during the Great Migration*. Weisenfeld suggests that these four religio-racial movements appealed to Afro-Caribbean and African American urban dwellers by offering access to alternative racial identities grounded in constructions of peoplehood that preceded the US nation or invalidated US racial categories as contrary to divine intention. The Nation of Islam, the Moorish Science Temple Movement, and Commandment Keepers foregrounded narratives of Asiatic, Moorish, and Ethiopian Hebrew descent, while Divine's Peace Mission overturned racially defined notions of identity and genealogy by promoting the idea of embodied racelessness. The religious genealogies that these movements advanced offered a sense of collective salvation (notably beyond dominant Christian notions of soteriology) and were privileged over racial categorizations of "Negro" identity and, in some instances, US citizenship itself. The movements' community contexts provided distinctive spaces for worship and even residence in the case of the Peace Mission, which was important for migrants. Some of the movements also emphasized "the heterosexual family as important for their projects of racial salvation," illustrating that their location outside of an Afro-Protestant denominational mainline did not preclude their participation in heteronormative familial aspirations (Weisenfeld 2017, 172).[11]

Black academics, Christians, and journalists pejoratively labeled these migration-era religio-racial movements as cults. And, similar to the storefront Pentecostalism associated with southern migrants in Chicago, these urban black religio-racial movements established during the 1920s to 1940s were framed as antithetical to an Afro-Protestant modernity and representative of "the problematic fracturing of the black community" (Weisenfeld 2017, 278). Yet Weisenfeld shows that the existence of religious minorities whose movements offer alternative framings of identity, community, religious scripts for intentional kinship, and a means to inhabit urban space in fact proved particularly meaningful to early-twentieth-century black migrants. Flowers would have been exposed to these religious, urban, and class-based narratives of southern black religious difference, and the intraracial tensions created in black urban spaces being transformed by black migration and Afro-diasporic dialogues would have been familiar to him. Yet if Flowers had stayed in Detroit, he would have had to choose his mission field in an increasingly crowded field of established and new religious movements. Moreover, these religious movements—however different—were offering access to religious notions of selfhood, community, and family along with a critique of the black denominational mainline. The offerings of the Plymouth Brethren–influenced evangelicalism that Flowers championed and its efforts to revise a modern sectarian cultural Christianity could potentially get lost in such a crowded religious context. Instead, Flowers turned his attention to the South—to the source and bedrock of a problematized black Christianity.

A BLACK EVANGELICAL SOLUTION TO A PROBLEMATIZED SOUTHERN BLACK CHRISTIANITY

Flowers's and the Nottage brothers' solution to the problem of southern black Baptist religiosity was to found Bible-believing New Testament churches that emphasized Bible study, literalism, and smaller, intimate, democratic modes of church association. As outlined by a twenty-fifth church anniversary bulletin in 1980, "The main thrust of his ministry was . . . 'to see independent, Bible practicing, Christ exalting communities of committed Christians in the

Southeast.'" In such Bible-believing churches, Flowers endeavored to foreground biblical teaching and to decenter the charismatic pastoral authority in southern black religious culture.

Flowers began his southern religious campaign in the 1950s by working at southeastern Bible camps like Cedine Bible Camp in Spring City, Tennessee (Wheaton College Archives Transcript 3). He then moved on to start small local Bible study fellowships that grew into local Bible churches. In 1957 Flowers established Beaufort Bible Chapel in Beaufort, South Carolina, called the "Mother Church" by DBC and its broader Southeastern evangelical community (church anniversary bulletin, 1980). As cohorts of experienced leaders arose at each chapel, Flowers placed leadership in the hands of local church elders and moved on to plant new assemblies. For instance, after helping to found a chapel in Beaufort, T. C. Taylor, Rubert Godrick from Jamaica, Leonard Mallory from the Bahamas, and Paul Beverly ministered at Beaufort as Flowers went on to "plant" more Bible chapels in North Augusta, South Carolina; Atlanta, Georgia; and Savannah, Georgia (church anniversary bulletin, 1980).

Over time, Flowers established more Bible churches, as well as the Southern Gospel Mission Association (SGMA) (1965), to oversee church constituencies in the region, and the United Bible Conference (1969), a family Bible conference designed to gather conferees "to re-examine spiritual values dispassionately and passionately reaffirm them" (church anniversary bulletin, 1980). As Afro-Caribbean migrants transformed Atlanta into a popular hub of the Caribbean diaspora in the 1980s, Flowers, together with Afro-Caribbean evangelicals from the anglophone Caribbean by way of northeastern cities and southern black leaders, expanded the scope of the SGMA church network as far as Anniston, Alabama; Conyers, Georgia; St. Helena, South Carolina; and Valdosta, Georgia. Ultimately, Flowers's missionary project coalesced into a black Atlantic church network, connecting southeastern black Brethren churches and Caribbean Brethren churches as well as other North American Afro-Caribbean Brethren church assemblies.

Black Atlantic Evangelicalism and the Problem of Southern Religious Apartheid

In addition to his critique of southern black biblical and institutional practices and his efforts to inject a more grounded biblical Christianity among black southerners, Flowers took issue with the racial cleavages enforced by white southerners during the Jim Crow era. Although some of his missionary work was funded by southern white evangelical businessmen, Flowers was critical of white evangelicals' institutionalization and maintenance of the color line. Flowers sought to heal the racial breach of southern religious culture and the increasing social difference by promoting people's awareness of universal spiritual kinship. His efforts to do so reveal his own complex positioning within the racial lines of southern religious landscapes and between a "white evangelicalism" and a "Black Church" Christianity.

Yet such work was not easy because the differences between people were deeply entrenched and often quite real. It was something his sister-in-law had warned him about. Flowers recalls her saying:

> "They're going to have [to] hang you on a special tree in the South because [laughs]... because of your funny talking self." [laughs] But, I was too crazy to understand what they were saying. You see, I have no concept of what segregation was all about because in the Bahamas it was slightly different.... And in England we have not experienced the same kind of thing. And in Canada, in that part of Canada people open up their hands and their hearts to us. (Wheaton College Archives Transcript 3)

Although his recollection of his sister-in-law's warning depicts the South as a dangerous and racially charged region that would be difficult for him as a black immigrant man to navigate, interestingly his position as a black foreigner allowed him to occupy an intermediate position between white and black Christians. According to missionary historian Waibinte Wariboko (2007), the conceptualization of the missionary as a "stranger" not only marks her as a cultural outsider but ultimately speaks to her intermediate social position between colonial elites and the indigenous majority. Similarly, Flowers's position as a stranger positioned him between southern whites and blacks. This in-between place made it possible for white evangelical businessmen to contribute to financing his evangelistic mission among southern blacks.

On the other hand, his social location as a black man of Caribbean descent amid the hardened racial regime of the segregation era gave him a proximity to the African American experience and antiblack racism. He remembers, "I went to the colored fountain and drank. I didn't bother. I didn't deal with it." Flowers depicts his observance of Jim Crow codes and his non-participation in mainstream civil rights initiatives that sought to redress the public sphere indignities of segregation.

Although Flowers's religious and racial positioning situated him between white evangelicals and southern blacks, he was more than an intermediary between white and black Christian constituents. He also acted as a moral outsider who critiqued southern ethno-racial congregationalism (Harvey 2005).

Flowers consistently took issue with the explicit use of race as a basis for religious association. In his discussion of his position on race in a Wheaton interview, Flowers insisted:

> [Some people say] let's . . . let's talk about the black situation, the black situation. Well, you see we talk about black . . . black . . . black . . . black as if there is virtue in it. My contention is if God made me black that's His problem. I don't have to solve that. If God made you white and you're not satisfied, that's your problem. I don't have to solve that either. . . . You come to the cross, you identify with the cross, you must die. Die to your whiteness, to your blackness, to your Presbyterianism, Brethrenism. You must die to all that. (Wheaton College Archives Transcript 3)

Although Flowers was more than aware of the materiality of race in the segregated racial climate of the South, he insisted on the primacy of spiritual identity for Christians. From his perspective, race was a God-ordained form of difference that was inappropriately conceived as an alibi for distinction and disenfranchisement. Christian religious identity was supposed to subsume differences like race.

THEOLOGICAL KINSHIP VERSUS THEOLOGICAL RACISM

That before God such racial differences did not matter, that all were creations of God, and therefore that all persons were brothers and sisters in Christ were beliefs that Flowers carried with him over the decades and emphasized in our Wednesday-evening Bible study discussions at his kitchen table. Flowers called on Christians to recognize their relatedness as humans and spiritual kin rather than to foreground their differences.

Emphasizing the common kinship of all people may seem a relatively innocuous dimension of Christian theology, but the deep history of theological racism in the United States made Flowers's framings of Christian interracialism ideologically significant. Different constructions of biblical genealogy were tethered to different racial projects in the US. Terence Keel (2018) reminds us that nineteenth-century polygenists such as Samuel George Morton and Josiah Nott believed that different racial groups had different origins rather than a common one. Building on the creation narrative in Genesis yet also trying to establish a rationale for a scientific racism that distanced itself from sacred historical accounts of human beginnings, polygenists sought to confine blacks to a separate and inferior human ancestry and to provide a "scientific" basis for black racial inferiority as well as pro-slavery and pro-segregationist programs (Keel 2018).

Around the time that black religio-racial movements began to emerge in northern and midwestern cities, Christian organizations began to use the language of brotherhood to promote interracial Christian fraternalism. According to Ted Ownby, the Commission on Interracial Cooperation, founded in the wake of the 1919 race riot in Atlanta, and the Fellowship of Southern Churchmen, founded in 1934, "repeatedly discussed brotherhood under the fatherhood of God as an alternative to ideas about patriarchy or any hierarchies" (2018, 65). In this way, southern Christians endeavored to establish common interracial ground, protest the relegation of blacks into marginalized social institutions, and change southern society. Yet Ownby (2018) notes that by the time of the civil rights era, the concept of interracial brotherhood evoked resistance and concern. Pro-segregationists believed that horizontal, interracial notions of Christian brotherhood in the wake of desegregation efforts would dangerously erode patriarchal familial influence and encourage interracial sex among youth. They also mistrusted framings of interracial communion because of long-standing views of black family pathology and blacks' consequent need for white paternalism. Black Christians' framings of Christian interracial kinship were therefore particularly scrutinized at the time of Flowers's southward migration.

Nonetheless, unlike in the highly variegated urban landscape of Detroit, which had experienced the rise of new movements and significant intraracial and interreligious cleavages and where Flowers's contributions might have been more easily absorbed, the emerging discourse of Christian interracial kinship in the South presented Flowers with a mission field ripe for his ideas. Flowers was able to insert into this southern society a Brethren-influenced antidenominational and universalistic ecclesiology. He presented church as a transcendent entity that could and should connect people in space and time through deep communal, familial fellowship (as discussed in chapter 1). Generating a modality of what Mayra Rivera (2007, 129) defines as "relational transcendence"—an understanding of transcendence in which "the interhuman, the cosmic, and the social" converge—Flowers's evangelicalism sought to contravene the Christian sectarianism of race in the US South.

A study of the theologies of Christian relatedness espoused by Flowers in his oral history interviews and over the course of our Bible studies reveals his emphasis on ideas about God and humanity that endeavored to assimilate ethnic, racial, religious, and class hierarchies into universalistic tropic representations of the human. Two of the most common of the tropes that Flowers as well as DBC and CBC members articulated critiqued racist distinctions between persons. These tropes reflect Christian perspectives on the relationship of the human to the divine as well as the relational imaginaries that shaped some of their broadest, extra-institutional constructions of spiritual kinship.

HUMANITY AS CREATION

Over the course of our weekly Bible studies, Flowers repeatedly and emphatically declared, "We're all God's creation!" This was also a recurring theme in the broader landscape of CBC and DBC exegesis. One elder stated this during a Sunday morning sermon as "We're God's workmanship." Another said, "Because you were born, God had to form you." Thus, the members of this black evangelical church network subjugated ethno-racial, class, and cultural distinctions to an all-encompassing human genealogy that insisted that there is no such thing as a self-made human. We are God's creation.

Black evangelicals' creation-focused anthropology was not merely descriptive. It was also rehabilitating. It responded to the assaults to self-esteem conditioned by antiblack racism. As Flowers explained to me once during an in-home Bible study, "Black and white children are made in the same way." Or again, "Everyone under heaven is a descendant of Adam. On what grounds then do people make inferiority claims?" As strong believers in biblical inerrancy, Flowers and his fellow Afro-Caribbean and African American evangelicals often buttressed their depiction of humanity as creation by referencing the genealogical lineage of Adam and Eve outlined in Genesis.

Their evangelical emphasis of the Bible as an authoritative, literal locus of divine truth also helped black evangelicals to discredit racial hierarchies and question the textual groundings of their white coreligionists. According to Vincent Wimbush in *White Men's Magic: Scripturalization as Slavery*, white imperialist self-constructions of Euro-Christian supremacy were, in part, shaped by a "discursive logic built upon literacy" (2012, 50) constructed in opposition to a non-European heathenish "other." Therefore, black Christian critiques of Euro-Christian textual orientations, like Flowers's recollection of the scriptural basis of universal kinship, challenged the hegemonic representational power of Euro-Christian scripturalization and its derivative racio-religious hierarchies.

Yet even as such notions of human kinship conveyed in black evangelical renditions of humanity as creation flattened the inequalities of Christian representational economies, they also finally acknowledged a black humanity long denied by imperial Euro-Christian anthropologies that located people of African descent as less than human. As discussed in chapter 1, DBC and CBC evangelicals, like other Afro-diasporic religious practitioners, understand their religious identity in terms of religious origins that they place in complex relationship to narratives of African descent (e.g., supersession versus juxtaposition).

However, this black evangelical creation-focused anthropology is also concerned with the conditions of lived experience. By locating black people in God's creation, black evangelicals also instilled a humanizing intersubjective integrity that enfranchised black people. It was a "theology of somebodyness," now widely associated with Martin Luther King Jr. and other black theologies (Hills and Curry 2015, 456). Rosetta Ross affirms this view in her observation that "informally, black theology names black people's belief in divine benevolence and intervention as support to their well-being" (2012, 252). Flowers likewise conveyed this anthropological redemption of black self-esteem through humorous comments during our Bible studies, comments like, "If it is the handiwork of God, then child, there's excellence in it!" They were a good reminder.

HUMANITY AS SINFUL MAN

But Flowers knew there was more to humans than excellence. Along with DBC and CBC members, he often spoke of humanity as having a shared status as fallen beings too: an inherited condition resulting from original sin. As Flowers explained to me during a Bible study, "Men won't accept the fact that they're related. . . . I thank God for the Brethren, but there's no perfect person." Racial alienation was a central focus of this critical black evangelical anthropology. Over the course of our weekly Bible studies, Flowers often repeated the statement, "God made man. Man! Not a white man, not a black man, not a red man, but man." In framing humanity as a genus rather than as a set of inalienable subgroups, Flowers underscored the biblical genealogical account of humanity's creation contained in Genesis 1:27 and noted the absence of racial designations in this origin narrative.[12]

Another great equalizer among humanity is our shared status. As one church elder stated, "Man is a sinner under the wrath of God." Thus, a black evangelical framing of humanity as man is a framing of humanity in terms of a negative discourse, a conceptualization of a humanity located on the underside of the *imago dei*. A black evangelical conceptualization of humanity in terms of sinfulness could potentially be read as reproducing a set of binaries between belief and practice, spirit and body, moral whiteness and immoral blackness that reify white supremacist moral structures (Pinn 2010a).[13] Additionally, the black evangelical understanding of humanity as fallen man reifies an androcentric religious discourse.

Nonetheless, the black evangelical trope of humanity as sinful man can also be seen as destabilizing white US exceptionalism. Even with mainstream evangelicals' promotion of a traditional moral orthodoxy (Smith 1998), evangelical

Christians commit a sin of racial disownership from the vantage point of many black evangelicals (Emerson and Smith 2000). In *Reconciliation Blues: A Black Evangelical's Inside View of White Christianity*, Edward Gilbreath (2006) illustrates that this critique of racism as sin was an important stream of black evangelical and racial reconciliation thought.[14] Gilbreath's narrative outlines a theology in which participation in and even complicity with racial alienation are outlined as a fundamental sin. More vitally, Gilbreath's account also shows how black evangelical insistence on a transracial fraternalism was pitched in a tone that could irritate the white mainstream evangelical worldview. Thus, the black evangelical theological outlines of a humanity (and an evangelicalism) as sinful in its ethno-racial alienations is prophetic in its social critique even if it does reproduce some of the Christian binaries (e.g., good and evil, salvation and sin) that have been conscripted into reifying antiblackness.

The theological anthropology of this network of Afro-Caribbean and African American evangelicals recognizes a God-ordained human genealogy and a spiritualized Christian relatedness. Taken together, black Brethren evangelical theologies outline a leveled humanism that criticizes ethno-racial and class hierarchies, which the Brethren understood as estranging humanity and Christians. The egalitarian universalism of black Brethren theological and anthropological thought creates its own hierarchies including the reinforcement of patriarchal gender norms. Their views of humanity rest upon a hegemonic masculine subjectivity (man as universalized subject) and cosmology (woman as descended from male progenitor Adam, and humanity as emanating from a paternal creator God). Nonetheless, the tropes and ideas constituting these strands of black evangelical theology flatten distinctions and bridge the spaces between racialized subjects.

CHRISTIAN INTERRACIALISM

Flowers's conceptualization of shared Christian humanity and interconnection was not novel. His and DBC and CBC members' relational theology, along with that of black evangelical racial reconciliation movement founders, resounded with the theological visions of leaders such as Martin Luther King Jr. For, according to Charles Marsh, King's concept of the "beloved community" depends on the premise that the "brotherhood and sisterhood of humankind radiates out from the fellowship of the faithful" (Marsh 2005, 66). Like Flowers, King's concept of the "beloved community" employed a genealogical concept of humanity and rested on the conviction that the relationships between Christians are of vital significance. Nonetheless, whereas King used his radical concept of community as beloved community to instigate change in the society writ large, it was in the limited sphere of southern Christian fellowship that Flowers promoted the radical egalitarianism of Afro-Atlantic evangelical Protestantism (Sensbach 2005) and a Caribbean Christian metalanguage of inclusiveness (Guadeloupe 2009, 75).

Despite their different religious backgrounds (Baptist versus Brethren) and relationships to the South (native versus immigrant), during our weekly Bible studies together Flowers expressed a profound respect for Martin Luther King Jr. and his sacrificial work. Flowers recognized their joint contention with the same violent, polarized landscape as preachers and mediators. During one of our weekly Bible studies in 2008, Flowers described his admiration for and identification with King:

> There's something about Martin Luther King that I don't say much about. I wanna say it to you. I'm talking to you personally. When I heard of Martin Luther King, I thought he was just an ordinary Baptist man. But when I came south and learned some more things about him . . . I am of the opinion that God raised him up to do what he did. Because no one else would be able to do it. Martin Luther King could've been preaching or teaching at some elite colleges. Instead, he was getting kicked in his backside.

Flowers's expression of his respect for King, a practitioner of the Afro-Baptist religion that seemingly motivated Flowers's southern missionary work, may appear ironic. King certainly fits the profile of an Afro-Baptist charismatic leadership that Flowers and the Nottage brothers associated with a southern black Christianity they typologized and problematized. Nonetheless, King's vocational humility informed Flowers's narration of a spiritual affinity with King. Flowers's view of King and southern African American Christians illustrates that black intraracial Christian exchanges, like black religious solidarities, were fraught and constantly under construction in context and afterthought.

Despite his admiration for King, Flowers was largely critical of black Christians' location and support of the "Black Church." Although southern blacks and a large host of Afro-diasporic communities located in the US and beyond "turned segregation into congregation" (Guridy 2010, 11), Flowers did not believe black churches to be authentic forms of Christian fellowship. The Bible chapels that Flowers founded were predominantly black. But he regarded the predominantly monoracial environments of these fellowships as an outgrowth of southern racial structures and religious conventions, not a reflection of his preference for monoracial religious membership. Regardless of whether racial religious membership was the product of top-down social forces that generated racial exclusions, grassroots efforts to combat the lived indignities of racism, or a desire to respond to racist social forces by creating spaces of refuge, Flowers still eschewed race as a basis for socioreligious affiliation. Although an overwhelming majority of the religious constituents in the DBC and CBC communities were people of African descent, the racial dynamics of the evangelical constituency that Flowers helped to build were not the product of his intentions to recruit a black population but of a religious landscape shaped by ethno-racial congregationalism.

If Flowers could not dismantle the tradition of ethno-racial congregationalism or stop the increasingly popular mobilization of southern Christian civil religiosity, he could at least change the exclusionary practices of his white evangelical peers and create specialized spaces for interracial encounters. Despite the vocal criticism of some white evangelicals, Flowers played an advisory role in the integration of Columbia Bible College (Wheaton College Archives). In doing so, he helped to foster blacks' access to the biblical knowledge and training that he considered essential to authentic Christian practice.

In 1967 Flowers also organized an interracial religious revival in Savannah, Georgia, with Tom Skinner, an African American progenitor of the racial reconciliation movement among US evangelicals. By his own account, the open-air revival provided a context in which blacks and whites sat and worshipped together (Wheaton College Archives Transcript 3). Far from being an ephemeral event, this revival helped him understand the creation of such interracial spaces inside and outside of southern religious institutions as having the potential to transform the racialized terrain of the US South. By creating alternative interracial fellowship in times of segregation, and by encountering one another on level religious terrain, he believed that blacks and whites could enact the integrating revivalistic potential of spiritual kinship and authentic Christian community. They could die to their whiteness and their blackness and convert mainstream practices of politicized racial religious membership into a dynamic transcendent spiritual form of association.

Flowers observed that the Savannah revival attracted a smaller number of African American attendees. He believed that the work he did with Skinner upset a number of black ministers who were unhappy with the emphasis of Jesus over race. Yet the modest number of black attendees and the reservations of local black clergy about this interracial event were likely less a reflection of the disenchantment with Flowers's particular understanding of spiritual relatedness and more a concern with the potential fallout that could result from blacks' organization of and participation in an interracial context. Moreover, blacks' motivations for attending such an interracial revival would surely be few given the safe, self-determining spaces of black churches and many whites' grudging compliance, tacit critiques, and outright resistance to institutional desegregation in the sectors of education, residence, and employment.

FAITH BEYOND AMERICA: AFRO-DIASPORIC BRETHRENISM AND MID-CENTURY CIVIL RELIGION

Flowers was also disaffected with white and black Christians' use of churches and religion as sites for political mobilization. He did not advocate for the nonviolent political protest shaped by King and a small group of Afro-Protestant mainline religious leaders during the civil rights movement to remedy institutional racism. Nor did Flowers fully support the political aspirations of black evangelicals of his generation who framed the racial reconciliation movement as a project geared toward affecting social change through material redistribution. In his discussion of the late–civil rights and post–civil rights political landscape that evangelicals inhabited, Flowers noted the work of racial reconciliation activist John Perkins:

> Perkins started the crusade for reconciliation. I think John has the right concept of what reconciliation should be. The difference between [me] and most of the rest of the competent [black evangelical leaders] is that [I] believe there can be no substitute for the church. And so my thing is the church. . . . I'm not against [politics,] but I think if we are going to have strong communities we need the church. (Wheaton College Archives Transcript 6)

Calling for building an interracial Christian community based on "relocation, redistribution, and reconciliation," Perkins founded the Voice of Calvary, a para-church organization that oversaw a conglomerate of Christian media and social service programs open to local community members. Although Flowers agreed with the discourses and objectives of the racial reconciliation movement designed and popularized by black evangelicals, he did not believe that religious institutions alone could heal the alienations that resulted from southern racism. The recognition of a divinely ordained universal Christian church and kinship uniting believers was required.

Flowers criticized how mainstream neo-evangelicals increasingly began to interact with civic politics in the post–civil rights era. He saw the contemporary mobilization of religious constituencies around political concerns as a distraction from the evangelical mission of converting others and building Christ-based relationships. He explained his views during an interview with the Wheaton College archivists:

> And right now I'm daily asking God to help me to get the saints to see the things around them are going to go up tomorrow. They're transient, they're ephemeral.... And we must see beyond America. Right today unfortunately... right today there is an expression, "We're going to save America." I'm afraid of that expression. I believe we're here to save Americans, not to save America.... I'm not so sure I'm buying into many of the Evangelicals' [pauses] teachings today.... I'm not concerned with somebody being a Republican or a Democrat. I see them as men.... And I... I think we need to be careful lest we put God on the side and say, "Let me save America." (Wheaton College Archives Transcript 3)

Flowers understood the emergence of civil religious forms that involved a diverse constituency of black Christians on the Left and a predominantly white evangelical social movement on the Right as merely creating other forms of difference that, like race, would only lead to estrangement among Christians. Flowers's critique of black Christians' mobilization of religion to address institutional racism and his privileging of evangelism and spiritual solutions to the race problem could be said to mirror the quintessential political conservatism associated with the Christian Right.[15] Flowers's resistance came from his belief in a community ideal—the transcendent spiritual collective of the universal Church—as the fundamental solution to solving racial alienation. He believed that more than any other type of religious practice or mode of connection, the universal Church possessed the greatest potential to reveal the spiritual truth of mankind's interracial relatedness.

The story of DBC and CBC and its beginning with Flowers's missionary call to the US South confounds the meta-narrative of Christian missions as purveyors of imperialism. This is, in part, attributable to the directionality of Flowers's missionary work—from global South to global North—against the grain of a conventional framework of Christian missions in which missionaries moved from Western metropoles to non-Western satellites.

In addition to the positioning of Flowers's work as mode of reverse missionization, the location of Flowers's evangelistic project in a social context characterized by great political transition also troubles its reading in terms of a colonial missions frame. In the middle of the twentieth century, the Caribbean was located between a dying British colonialism and emerging US cultural and economic hegemony in the region (Davies and Jardine 2003). The US South was in the throes of a civil rights movement that sought to generate a more equitable and racially integrated society. Flowers's positioning between two political matrices and a time period in which colonialism itself was undergoing structural changes also troubles common imperial and missiological meta-narratives.

According to Sylvester A. Johnson in *African American Religions, 1500–2000: Colonialism, Democracy, and Freedom*, there is a "complicated relationship" between the African American religious movements and colonial contexts (2015, 173). African American Christianity was imprinted with Christian supremacy and "colonial civilizationist ideology," and was born out of the interaction between projects of "racial self-determination, African redemption, Black settler colonialism, White apartheid, Christianity's civilizing mission, and the labor imperatives of Western colonialism" (Johnson 2015, 251, 172). Extending beyond the black settler colonialism of black missionary and colonialist projects in the nineteenth century, the imperialist forces shaping African American Christianity continued in the Cold War era in the connection between Anglo-Christian nationalism and neo-evangelical fundamentalism (Johnson 2015). This neo-evangelicalism coexisted with the social gospel and the racial and antiwar activism of the civil rights movement.

To be sure, some of Flowers's perceptions of southern black religion and missionary aspirations reflect a colonial worldview. His spatial imaginary of the US South, influenced by the biblical story of Jacob's inheritance of the covenant, has visual echoes of colonial Christian expansionism. His concern with the emotionalism of black religiosity reiterated notions of decorum and orderliness associated with respectable black religion and reflected the civilizing emphasis of colonial religious projects. Nonetheless, Flowers was a nonconformist. He critiqued the rigid conformity and racial hierarchy of the Anglican religiosity that mediated colonial respectability in the anglophone Caribbean. Flowers did not ascribe to Afro-Protestant denominational modernity as the sole authentic form of black Christian expression.

Flowers's criticism of the exclusionary character of white evangelicals' religious institutions and their tacit complicity with southern segregation is also a sign of his unusual location in the socioreligious order of the segregated South. Flowers knew that southern Christians' political formation included rigid constructions of difference and inequality. Flowers was unwilling to support a vision of America propagated by a neo-evangelical civil religion.

Flowers was not alone in his ambivalence about the US democratic project. In her study of how twentieth-century Afro-Caribbean male intellectuals such as Marcus Garvey, Claude McKay, and C. L. R. James conceptualized black sovereignty, Michelle Ann Stephens describes their understanding of the limits of racial integration: "In the Negro struggle for freedom, race consciousness is both the result of integration, which comes with racial hierarchies since integration itself does not necessarily imply integration as *equals*, and a response to integration, which then offers visions of a different global future" (2005, 227). For Afro-Caribbeans in the mid-century US, even an integrated nationalism did not offer blacks the opportunity for equitable inclusion or fraternity with fellow citizens. The only thing that did was their ability to imagine and enact their visions of alternative social and political collectives. In Flowers's case, this meant using the alternative grammars provided by notions of spiritual relationality and a nonconformist evangelicalism that imagined the family of God as those who recognized their common humanity.

For T. Michael Flowers, Brethren-influenced Christianity helped him to imagine and produce a broad and critical form of alterity, one that countered imperial and national understandings of racial difference. Flowers sought to reform the biblical and institutional practices of an objectified southern black Christianity by founding black Brethren churches. As a moral outsider, Flowers also sought to reform the segregated religious landscape authored by white supremacist structures and white evangelical practice by translating Plymouth Brethren ideas of familial communion and theological concepts of spiritual relatedness to white Christians and southern Christians more broadly. At times, this meant generating interracial revival spaces. In other instances, this meant working to integrate Bible colleges. Yet for him, racial integration was desirable but not the final destination for Christian community.

Flowers continued to work with the churches he established until the 1990s. At the time of my research, he was still an active church participant at DBC and occasionally preached. His sermons showed the moral inquietude of an evangelistic reformer and shared his view that Christian identities, community boundaries, and the spaces around which they are configured should always be moving beyond the familiar and toward a more universal Christian family.

Chapter 3 is set in 2008 in the DBC and CBC communities. It discusses the ways in which contemporary Afro-Caribbean and African American evangelicals understand their position within the ethnic and racial boundaries of US congregationalism. Whereas Flowers understood spiritual kinship as a universal familial mode of Christian community, present-day black evangelicals understand spiritual kinship differently: as a framework to generate nonethnic modes of fellowship and collective identity grounded in shared diasporic material conditions.

Black Like Me? Or Christian Like Me? 3
Black Evangelicals, Ethnicity, and Church Family

Over fifty years separated the context of T. Michael and Ella Flowers's arrival and the congregational environments I encountered in 2008. Rather than creating an initial foothold in a segregated religious landscape, the task of early-twenty-first-century black evangelical Brethren was sustaining their religious fellowship in a highly saturated religious milieu. Instead of asserting their presence theologically in a racially exclusive neo-evangelicalism, the Afro-Caribbean and African American evangelical constituents who I came to know were engaged in the complex processes of defining a shared ethos for community life.

Black evangelicals consider shared spiritual kinship—their relatedness to one another as "brothers and sisters in Christ," "spiritual parents and spiritual children," and "prayer partners" generated by evangelical ecclesiology, theology, and local discourse and rituals of relationship—rather than ethnicity and race, to be the most authentic basis for their group identity. Although Afro-Caribbean and African American evangelicals of the CBC and DBC were located in almost exclusively black religious congregations and sited in an urban landscape associated with African American history, culture, and social mobility, they did not identify their constituencies in racial or ethnic terms. In some instances, church members even critiqued the mention of ethnicity as the basis for religious fellowship.

It was in 2008 that I first noted a local rebuke of the ethnic frame—the idea that ethnic boundaries define the limits of Christian religious fellowship. It happened in a conversation with T. Michael Flowers. After he briefly reviewed the mandated Institutional Review Board form, which originally identified my research project as examining the familial community of Afro-Caribbean churches in the Atlanta metropolitan area, Flowers responded: "Well, you see, I would love to help you with your project here. But as I was looking over this consent form, I saw some things that I can't really support. There is no such thing as a 'West Indian' church as your paper reads. There is only one 'church.' And I can't really do an interview on something that does not fall in line with my beliefs."

Flowers resisted an ethnic classification of CBC and DBC that ran counter to the churches' primary identification as part of the universal body of Christ, which should not be explicitly defined in ethnic or racial terms. Although some members discussed their firsthand experiences with racial exclusion, church members commonly expressed their beliefs that race and ethnicity should not delimit Christian religious fellowship. Nonetheless, a small minority of church members insisted that ethnic differences between Afro-Caribbeans and African Americans did directly affect the congregational boundaries between the DBC and CBC communities.

In this chapter I assert that an inquiry into church members' religious affiliations must resist the uncritical application of ethno-religious and racio-religious lenses that try to define black evangelical communities straightforwardly as the product of ethnic and racial formations. In addition to showing the contextual influences of ethnicity and race on DBC and CBC congregants' chapel lives, my findings reveal that church members' experience with migration and diaspora should be included when considering their constructions of collective religious identities. In discussing church members' creation of a familial alterity—their familial definition of community—I uncover a local emic frame for community production. This familial alterity illustrates their complex positioning of themselves between universalistic religious aspirations and the particularities of their social locations conditioned by race, ethnicity, and diaspora.

The Social Context of DBC and CBC Productions of Church Family

According to a church anniversary booklet, the Corinthian Bible Chapel community began with a Bible study in the home of a church sister named Mrs. Walton in 1963. When the community outgrew the home space, it held services in a local YMCA instead. John Moore, "a competent worker from Detroit," came to help with the establishment of the new ministry and died in 1978. T. Michael Flowers commuted from Savannah two Sundays a month to assist: "In June, 1979, the believers purchased [their] present building at 183 Moreland SE, and it was dedicated to the glory of God in September, 1979;

thus the third New Testament assembly through Bro[ther] Flowers' efforts was established. 'To God be the glory great things He hath done.'" According to church members, CBC soon became a hub for black Brethren in the area as well as a meeting place for various campus ministries. Several Brethren I interviewed with ties to the CBC community recounted how the late John Moore encouraged them, despite their cynicism about religion and their inexperience. They described how their involvement in the church community during their early-adult years revolutionized their religious identities and informed their lifelong commitment to evangelism and service. In 1991 another Bible cell group "sprang out" of Community Chapel and began to meet in Decatur, Georgia. As it grew in size, it gathered at a local YMCA and eventually moved to a more standard congregational edifice in Lithonia, Georgia. It is now the community known as Dixon Bible Chapel.

In an interview I conducted during my preliminary research in 2006, Ann Marume—an Afro-Jamaican social worker who migrated to Atlanta in the 1980s—described DBC as a "Caribbean church" with a reputation for "taking good care" of new migrants to the area. The CBC members noted that local residents perceive their church as a typical "black church" because of its majority African American population. Nonetheless, despite neighbors perceiving them as ethnic communities, CBC and DBC evangelicals commonly defined their congregations in familial and religious terms. For church members, family was an ideological injunction and an ethos for community practice. Thus, these CBC and DBC members described their chapels as "church famil[ies]," by which they meant social collectives that attend to the spiritual and material needs of their members. During a weekend Family Life Conference at DBC, African American Elder Earl Washington led a group conversation about the social dynamics of being a part of a church family:

> We mentioned that we would try to look at what definition of family we are using. For the sake of time I'll give another Webster definition[:] "people with a common ancestry." Another [definition is] "a group of people in the same household," and this caught my attention, [a household] generally with "one head." And the other one talked about "people who are bound by the same belief or conviction," and I think that fits us as a church family. But the idea of a people who have a common ancestry being family and those who are bound by a common belief or set of beliefs [struck me]. And it's interesting [that] it's not always automatic that people who have a common ancestry are in harmony together.

Washington's depictions of church family as a construct of religious belonging reflected important institutional scripts of this community's sense of membership. Brother Washington discussed the multiple ways in which family could be defined. In particular, he encouraged participants to contemplate how shared belief could create a more binding and effective form of kinship than genealogical or cultural ties. In doing so, he displaced heteronormative definitions of kinship and instead called attention to how belief could generate intentional, enduring relationships.

In another interview setting, as a response to my question, an Afro-Jamaican church elder, Samuel Barrett, sang me an excerpt from "The Family of God":

> You will notice we say "brother and sister" 'round here,
> It's because we're a family and these are so near;
> When one has a heartache, we all share the tears,
> And rejoice in each victory in this family so dear.
> I'm so glad I'm a part of the family of God,
> I've been washed in the fountain, cleansed by his blood!
> Joint heirs with Jesus as we travel this sod,
> For I'm a part of the family,
> The family of God.
>
> (Gaither and Gaither 2005)

By responding to the question with a hymn, Barrett's response was explicitly theological. The lyrics reiterated the Brethren eschatological belief in a transcendent universal relatedness (e.g., "family of God") connecting Christian believers. Moreover, his hymn response also referenced the common language of siblinghood that has such currency in CBC and DBC settings. It evoked sentiments of relatedness (heartache, tears, rejoice, dear) that have been associated with Afro-diasporic Christian traditions and Afro-Caribbean praise songs of family (Chamberlain 2000; Sutton 2004).

Church members also depict their communities as providing a deep sense of familial belonging and care. Sister Beulah Solomon described the close-knit familial character of the early DBC community: "We basically did everything together. If someone had a party down the road, everybody was there. If there was a graduation, everybody was there since my family wasn't here. Then the church became my family. I like the small church. The kinship and the fellowship were good. A sense of caring too. That is a little bit lost because we've got[ten] a bit bigger. But it's still pretty much there." Church families provide a deep sense of presence and a communion that carries over from the church into everyday contexts such as celebrations of family milestones and even more-mundane gatherings. Sister Solomon stated that "the church became my family." To her, consistently showing up for one another made her and her fellow congregants kin.

Sister Etta Johnson described her personal experiences with the interethnic fellowship of southeastern Brethren chapels using kinship idioms. She declared that many of the adult members at DBC whom she had known as children still called her "Mama," and she referred to her longtime spiritual mentor as her "spiritual father." In such ways her narrative illustrates the many layers of belonging that accumulate over time. Members' use of kinship idioms reflects those longevities.

In addition to defining their familial communities in theological and experiential terms, this language and understanding of being family also operate as a grammar of inter-chapel relatedness. Both congregations affirm their special relationship as local "sister churches" with interconnected histories that they can trace to the evangelism of founder T. Michael Flowers. That interconnection is more than semantics. Brethren church members visit and preach at one another's services, anniversaries, and other special events, and they lend support to each church's ministries and programs. For instance, I witnessed DBC members attend the CBC church anniversary ceremony en masse one afternoon and the DBC choir perform during the joint service. The CBC and DBC members also mentioned that they had composed a "statement of unity" publicly displayed at both chapel communities that references their specific history together at CBC prior to the subsequent founding of DBC. Through such ideological, practical, and institutional means, the DBC and CBC congregational landscape is saturated with expressions of family.

"They Don't Travel Very Far": Black Evangelical Experiences of Racial, Spatial, and Religious Exclusions

Although CBC and DBC members create personal, congregational, and intercongregational relationships through language and practices of kinship, they do so in an urban landscape that bears the imprint of social exclusions of race, religion, and space.

In the United States, in the Atlanta metropolitan area, and in the domestic neo-evangelical landscape, narratives of racial progress coexist with practices of racial entrenchment. A view that race has declined in significance prevails in these narratives. Craig R. Prentiss defined the term *race* as "a social grouping or form of peoplehood that is marked by traits that are perceived to be biologically inherited" (2003, 7). Although the concept is associated with the injurious past of scientific racism, scholars now generally understand race to be a social construction rather than an innate biological inheritance. Moreover, the dominant portrayal of US multiculturalism in the post–civil rights era is of peaceable coexistence of racial groups and their cultural practices. The election and presidencies of Barack Obama as the first black president of the United States in 2008 onward—the time during which the bulk of my ethnographic research was completed—also heralded the emergence of what some have called a post-racial era. One controversial mark of this post-racial era is many people's unwillingness to talk or even to consider race and racism as central determinants of inequality in the US public sphere (Bonilla-Silva 2006; Delgado 2012). Yet talked about or not, for those marginalized by contemporary racial formations, the social force of race emerges in the very real experience of the social exclusions prompted by such antiblack racism.

ATLANTA: A CITY OF PROMISE OR PROMOTION?

Locally, the Atlanta metropolitan landscape that DBC and CBC members inhabit possesses its own split reputation as a site for black social, economic, and cultural progress and as a locale fundamentally imprinted by processes of black marginalization. In the early twentieth century, Atlanta—the "poster city" of a New South promoted by post-Reconstruction boosterism—witnessed the emergence of a local black middle class situated between a black business district named Sweet Auburn and a local set of black colleges and universities called the Atlanta University Center.[1] It was out of this institutional context that luminaries such as W. E. B. Du Bois and Martin Luther King Jr. theorized and mobilized the concept of the "Black Church" as a potential vector for black civic advancement.

In the post–civil rights era, Atlanta underwent a series of important economic changes that contributed to its rising profile as a major southern city.[2] Black mayoral leadership in Atlanta that sought to distance the city from the insularity and endemic racism associated with the South as a region (Dameron and Murphy 1997) encouraged this new stage of southern urbanization with a branding campaign that dubbed Atlanta "an international city" and a "city too busy to hate." According to Clarence Stone (1989), since the 1970s the informal alliance between the city's black mayoral elites and white economic elites has been extremely effective in courting investment capital for large-scale development projects and attending to the economic interests of the black middle class. Atlanta's successful bid to host the 1996 Olympics became an important touchstone of success for the city's interracial urban development model.

Yet the rising international profile of Atlanta came at a cost. The Atlanta inhabited by CBC and DBC residents has also been structured by overlapping processes of segregation and suburbanization that attended urban development. Together, these racial and spatial dynamics created a "separate city": an urban locale in which southern urban black populations are concentrated in inner-city cores while more-affluent populations have moved outward to suburban enclaves, in so doing creating the city's notorious urban sprawl (Silver and Moeser 1995).[3] This pattern mimicked the raced and classed spatial dynamics of white flight that emerged in the city during desegregation (Kruse 2005).

Thus, Afro-Caribbean migrants and African Americans alike weathered social opportunities and boundaries of race and class. A look at local demography illustrates the workings of Atlanta as a black urban landscape.[4] According to the 2000 US Census Fact Finder, 50.1 percent of Atlanta city's population identified as black or African American. Moreover, the local politics supported by black mayoral leadership has ultimately proven to be advantageous for white and black professionals but has had little impact on improving the life chances of the city's black majority.

This is hardly new. According to Maurice J. Hobson, "A divide between the black elite and the black poor had always riven Atlanta's social fabric" (2017, 1). Hence, attention to the ways in which local networks disenfranchise new migrants from elitist circles while city figureheads have marketed Atlanta as a mecca for the black middle class is likewise necessary (Murphy, Blanchard, and Hill 2001).[5] As John Jackson Jr. observed, black urban landscapes are constituted by the joint processes of "migration and mystification" (2001, 28). So while celebratory narratives of Atlanta as an urban landscape associated with black cultural innovation, potential, and modernity attracted Afro-Caribbean and African American migrants to the metropolitan area, the myth of the black Mecca Atlanta obfuscated the realities of racial dispossession and exclusion that continue to permeate urban interactions there.

WALLED WORSHIP: RACIAL BOUNDARIES IN THE ATLANTA RELIGIOUS LANDSCAPE

Although the overall Atlanta religious landscape is predominantly Christian, CBC and DBC members have bumped up against the racio-religious boundaries that are a reality in the city's dense, urban Christian religious geography.[6] During interviews, CBC and DBC members narrated their experiences of local white evangelicals excluding them racially and religiously. Brother Edwin Goodison, a young adult Afro-Jamaican DBC member, described his first visit to the Atlanta sister congregation that sponsored the Jamaican Baptist church in which he had grown up:

> It was kinda something like out of a movie where you walk into a bar and everything stops and the one black guy walks into the white bar.... It was all white. And I was the only black guy. The guy was preaching, and he stopped. And somebody got up and asked me if I was looking for somebody. [pause] Yeah. And I was like, "Yeah. I'm with that guy." And he turned around and said, "Yeah. He's with me." And they proceeded. And when they were through, I was like yeah, I don't belong here.

Another middle-aged Afro-Jamaican couple described attending a prominent Atlanta Southern Baptist megachurch, which repeatedly referred them to the international worship service held on Sunday afternoons in Spanish for Latinx immigrants.

More than merely a product of white Southern Baptists' racial antipathies, such ethno-racial exclusions in Atlanta also extend to the ranks of Brethren evangelicals. When describing his interactions with white Brethren in the Atlanta metropolitan area who often did not attend the black Brethren functions to which they were invited, a senior Trinidadian church member explained: "Most of them are basically older Caucasian people who . . . just don't travel very far. I don't think they dislike us. They just don't travel very far." Though cast differently, CBC and DBC members commonly discussed their interactions with local white evangelical congregants in terms of racial exclusion.

The experiences of DBC and CBC evangelicals reflect a set of racial ambivalences common throughout the nation. Contemporary evangelicals in the United States reify and disturb ethno-racial identities and institutions in different ways. White and black evangelicals have most visibly addressed racism together through the racial reconciliation movement. Michael Emerson and Jason Shelton observe that "black and white Protestants profoundly differ in their definitions and understandings of racial reconciliation" (2012, 183). White evangelicals often conceptualize racial inequality as an interpersonal problem or as a matter of salvation, and they employ discourses of pluralism that can obscure the power dynamics between dominant and marginalized groups (Emerson and Smith 2000; Smith 2006).[7] However, black evangelicals tend to frame racial hierarchy as a structural problem that cannot be adequately addressed without redistributive policies (Emerson and Smith 2000; Shelton and Emerson 2012).

James Bielo (2011) and Omri Elisha (2011) depict the challenges that white evangelicals encounter, particularly those evangelicals who are more committed to instantiating interracial religious communion and multiracial social transformation outside of their congregations. Bielo (2011) examines urban faith ministries founded by white emerging evangelicals who, disenchanted with the racial and class isolations of suburban megachurches, endeavor to create racially inclusive Christian worship and everyday communion. Bielo carefully documents white evangelicals' growing mindfulness of systemic inequalities and the potential implications of such mindfulness for urban missional work. Nevertheless, one of Bielo's interlocutors—the co-pastor of an interracial (white and African American) urban ministry—outlines the limitations of interracial evangelical religious partnerships. Bielo writes that "Kevin, in Middletown, for example, is certain that while he may be able to model racial reconciliation, a widespread social shift is never fully realizable this side of heaven" (2011, 153).

Omri Elisha documents the social position and experiences of "socially engaged evangelicals": a small group of white evangelicals who invest themselves in creating benevolent community engagements across suburban and inner-city lines in Knoxville, Tennessee (2008, 9). Despite their well-intentioned efforts, such evangelicals often find themselves located between progressive concerns with social justice and conservative emphases on personal responsibility (Elisha 2008). All too often, socially engaged evangelicals are involved in translational work between these two modes of community engagement: engagement oriented toward social change and redistribution, and engagement that foregrounds values and individualism and that tends to justify contemporary socioeconomic inequalities. The reality they encounter is that often "progressive ideas are subverted, coopted, or repressed in congregational settings where hegemonic norms seldom give up their ground" (Elisha 2008, 112). The limitations of white evangelical efforts to establish deep and long-lasting modes of connection with black neighbors and coreligionists reveal the durability of race as a social structure and the limitations of interpersonal, anti-structural efforts to support programmatic interracial connections among evangelicals.

The experiences recounted by DBC and CBC evangelicals echo these findings and suggest that religious belonging is extended impartially to minoritized religious subjects in predominantly white evangelical communities. The denial of black evangelicals' full inclusion in predominantly white religious evangelical congregations and an unwillingness to fellowship with black evangelicals in their places of worship also show that racial and religious segregation deposited by the spatial practices of the region and the Atlanta cityscape is a contemporary and not just a historical phenomenon.

The racial marginalization of black evangelicals—both in spatial terms that make interracial fellowship the work of a concerned or interested few and in ideological terms that try to explain racial inequality in terms of individual moral failings—is somewhat ironic. Black evangelicals are constructed negatively by other black Christians because of their assumed proximity to the conservative politics associated with white mainstream evangelicalism (McGlathery and Griffin 2003). An example of this is the confession of Sister Maya Johnson, an African American member at DBC, that her Baptist relatives think her religious community is a "cult," a term that often negatively evokes rigid, exclusionary boundaries that work to the detriment of community members. Yet the exclusionary concept of cult in this case depicts black evangelicals' sense of ideological distinction that sets them apart from their black kindred, Baptist and otherwise.

Although black evangelicals narrate their racial and religious identities in terms of ongoing dynamic negotiations rather than rigid polar tensions (McGlathery and Griffin 2003), the construction of black evangelicals as racial outliers is telling. It demonstrates the ways in which participation in certain institutionalized Christian religious forms is rendered in terms of racial belonging. The converse is also true. Membership in Christian religious forms that are not associated with more historically black institutions threaten a religio-racial illegibility. Thus, not only among scholars but also among black Christians in the US, African American Christianity is read through a prism of institutional legibility. This leaves certain traditions, such as the black evangelicals of DBC and CBC, doubly minoritized in racial and institutional terms. Black Christians' constructions of black evangelicals also illustrate how evangelical identity in the US is presumed to conduct the cultural assimilation of black religious participants. The association of black evangelicals with racial nonbelonging or whiteness illustrates the ways in which evangelical Christian identity continues to be racialized in the United States.

Black Evangelicals and the Ethnic Frame

In addition to the racial enclosures of Atlanta's urban and religious landscape, DBC and CBC evangelicals have also negotiated ethnic distinctions within their ranks. Occasionally, this was done through the sharing of personal observations about how ethnic differences affected congregational boundaries and interpersonal relationships. More frequently, DBC and CBC members appeared to address ethnic differences through silence and by foregrounding familial religious identity.

ETHNICITY, RELIGION, AND ETHNOSCAPE

Black evangelical congregants create community between ethnic and familial renditions of community in a domestic and local context shaped by ethnic identity processes. Although scholars predicted that ethnic communities would abandon their religious and ethnic solidarities, any straightforward trek to an integrated modern nation-state mediated by shared white, middle-class, Anglo-Saxon Protestant cultural values never occurred (McKinnon and Cannell 2013; Omi and Winant 1994). Instead, nonwhite and religious "others" have continued to hold on to ethnic and religious identities as frameworks for community formation and have mobilized these solidarities into the public sphere. Part of the reason for these ethnic retentions undoubtedly derives from the vital support that ethnic communities give and receive. Within the US landscape, ethnic congregations associated with immigrants have served as mediating civic and social support organizations for marginalized communities navigating various processes of cultural and political protest and assimilation (Ebaugh and Curry 2000). Black churches founded by African American congregants since the eighteenth century have continued to be spaces for the expression of black religious perspectives, the provision of vital information, reciprocal support systems, fraternal connections, and alternative forms of social capital for blacks in the United States (Higginbotham 1993; Lincoln and Mamiya 1990; Raboteau 1978).

Yet, like race, ethnicity mediates the discourses and practices of hierarchy and exclusion. Although ethnicity is often conceived as the more palatable doppelgänger of race, cultural agents use ethnicity "to categorize themselves and others for the purposes of interaction" (Barth 1998, 13–14). Sociologist Vilna Bashi Treitler (2013) even asserts that ethnic thinking and ethnic projects reproduce white supremacist racial structures in the United States.[8] Akin to ethnicity and race, ethnicity and religion are co-constituted through boundary-making practices, overlapping mythologies, and shared sociohistorical contexts (Prentiss 2003, 8). Like ethnic identity groups, congregations are often "particularistic, highlighting the things that set them apart rather than looking for underlying universalisms" (Ammerman 1997, 352).

Thus, CBC and DBC members inhabit social landscapes that are punctuated by ethnic identity distinctions and are imprinted by African American cultural influence. People tend to understand the "black Church" as a monolith and as a quintessentially African American social institution. The globalization of Western-centric popular culture and Christian media further consolidates African American cultural hegemony (Burdick 2013; Frederick 2015; Gilroy 1995).

Afro-Caribbean religious influence is often overshadowed by the heavy representation of African American religious ways.

The Atlanta metropolitan area, although it continues to be transformed by domestic and international migration, is also an ethnoscape heavily associated with African American history and culture (Appadurai 1996; Bayor 1996). At the time of my ethnographic research in 2008, the metropolitan area was home to a growing number of Afro-Caribbean cultural organizations, hometown and alumni associations, businesses, sporting leagues, and religious institutions, including several mainline denominations attended by Caribbean majorities. Thus, Atlanta has become a site of black ethno-racial negotiations in which Afro-Caribbean and other international migrants have had to navigate the typically exclusive social networks of US-born African Americans and white elites (Hill and Beaver 1998).

ON "BORN BRETHREN" AND "BAPTIST BLOOD":
THE DISENCHANTMENTS OF ETHNIC RELIGIOUS DISTINCTIONS

These racial and religious exclusions of the Atlanta religious landscape as well as local black ethnic identity negotiations have shaped the social boundaries and hierarchies of CBC and DBC congregational life. During interviews, church members conceded that national origins and ethnic identities shaped church members' interpersonal relationships inside and outside of church contexts. Some congregants' closest church associations were with church members who hailed from the same Caribbean nations. Some church members had known one another since their childhood days in the Caribbean or had had extensive interactions with church members' extended families in the Caribbean and Caribbean diaspora. Although the familiarity of deep histories of attachment may seem somewhat innocuous, in several instances church members referred negatively to this pattern of ethno-national association as "cliquish" and "clannish" behavior.

The most distinct ethnic identity boundaries existed between African American and Afro-Caribbean congregants. A small number of church participants told me that ethnic discord between African Americans and Afro-Caribbeans was what motivated the foundation of DBC in October of 1991. By the late 1980s, when Afro-Caribbean migration to the Atlanta metropolitan area increased, the constituency of CBC was almost half African American and half Afro-Caribbean. When the DeKalb County cell group (which was reported to be exclusively Afro-Caribbean) decided to become a separate chapel assembly, some CBC members interpreted the group's move toward independent status as a move to create an Afro-Caribbean church. In fact, several CBC members dubbed the detachment of the cell group as the "great hive-off." The DBC then became and now remains a predominantly Afro-Caribbean chapel community, while CBC was transformed into a majority African American community. The aforementioned CBC members insisted that the beginnings of the DBC community were not rooted in a concern about spatial proximity but was a response to ethnic tensions within CBC, the community from which the founding DBC cell group originated. On this topic, African American church elder Brother James Wilkerson noted forthrightly:

> The [West Indians] came, and they meet this rag-tag group of African Americans: first-generation Brethren—Baptists, Methodists, relatively young. They don't know about this Brethren thing. I mean they've been exposed, and they were told that they were Brethren, but their daddies and mommas weren't Brethren. They still have some of this Baptist blood running through them. So they come in and do the same thing the British did. The British come and conquer you and say you gotta learn the British way. Same thing went on at Corinthian. "No, Brethren, we do it this way." "Excuse me. What are you talking about? I'm just as Brethren as you." "No, we do it this way." So things start changing. And you have this cultural tension and conflict that was existing. And most of the time, the church tears apart. And most of the time it's those from the Caribbean coming and taking over. Same things as the British. So a lot of people were looking and just knew we were gonna explode. We didn't explode. And you wanna know one reason why we didn't explode? DBC started. That was the release valve. Yes, that was a church plant. I'm gonna put the best face on it. It was a church plant, and behind that is something that is not so clean and not so pretty.

Wilkerson's statement illustrates that ethnicity is an integral part of understanding the social dynamics and "cultural tension" of CBC and DBC congregational life. By his estimation, "the church plant" or the founding of the predominately Afro-Caribbean DBC community, generated an institutional division that prevented what could have been a more permanent end to black evangelical religious fellowship. Wilkerson's coinage of the terms "born Brethren" (a category that refers to Afro-Caribbeans who were raised in the Brethren traditions) and "Baptist blood" (African Americans raised in the Afro-Baptist tradition who converted to the Brethren tradition) suggests a convergence of ethnic descent and religious heritage. Local categories of ethno-religious identity appear to naturalize religious identities and hierarchies and, in doing so, suggest a reckoning of Christian identity as an inherited familial identity.

This runs contrary to conventional understandings of Christian conversion as a disruption of Christians' embeddedness in natal social and familial networks and as an instigation of a convert's prioritization of a born-again Christian individualism (Bialecki, Haynes, and Robbins, 2008).

Although Wilkerson's perspective foregrounds the impact of ethnic difference on the interactions of black evangelicals, his perspective on ethnic divisions as significantly shaping church life is not one voiced by most research respondents. The majority of the congregants did not directly discuss ethnic differences within or across the DBC and CBC communities. During a visit I made to the CBC community, Sister Lou Ellen Framingham, an Afro-Jamaican congregant who remained a member of the CBC community after DBC was founded, chimed in about the ethnic dimension of the CBC and DBC split. Yet during a taped interview, Sister Framingham did not mention the church DBC and CBC tensions at all. Instead, she asserted that she remained very dear friends with many former CBC members who went to DBC and that they spoke often.

Another member, an Afro-Trinidadian church sister, conceded that "there were a lot of cliques in the church" and discussed the virtues of silence as a response to congregational conflict:

> Like if there's some disruption that's going on in the church, I would not share that with my brother and sister because they're not saved. I wouldn't share that with my other sister because she's not a part of our fellowship.... To me, it should stay within the church family because we are a family. And I think sometimes in church we forget that. We are really [quick] to remember when it comes to our own blood family, but when it comes to the church family, we tend to be a little more loose.

Those who understand church in this way find it appropriate not to tell people beyond the church community about church conflict. Unlike congregants who used interviews to discuss some of the paradoxes of heterosexuality, other congregants understood church and family business to be the affair of family and church members only and thus protected by institutional silence.

The silencing of ethnic differences was a mark of DBC community life. The muting of dissent draws attention to the taboo character of church community conflict and the overriding ethos of church unity. The silencing of ethnic discord, at least for the ethnographic record, also illustrates the ways in which the thinning of certain sets of discourses (e.g., ethnic conflict) allows for the thickening of other modes of language. If language and narrative are significant to the formation of black evangelicals' renditions of church family, silence should be understood to be generative as well.

BLACK ETHNIC IDENTITY POLITICS: DIFFERENT GRAMMARS OF BLACKNESS

Despite the ethno-religious distinctions that Afro-Caribbean and African American evangelicals generate, scholars elsewhere have suggested that there is little difference in the intensity and types of religious practices observed by these populations. According to Chatters and colleagues, "The collectivistic and communal orientations, participatory worship styles and immediate and personal connections with a divine power are common to both African American and Black Caribbean traditions and constitute distinctive forms of devotional practice that are characteristic of peoples of African descent" (2009, 1151).

An explanation for the persistence of the ethno-religious distinctions forged by black Christians can be found by turning our attention to the identity boundaries drawn within the specific field of black ethnic-identity politics in the United States. Black ethnic interactions have been popularly cast in terms of frictions fueled by economic competition between African Americans and black immigrant groups such as Afro-Caribbean people. In particular, black ethnic tensions are reified through particular discourses about both black immigrant success and stalled African American socioeconomic mobility (Logan and Deane 2003; Pierre 2004; Vickerman 1999). Those tensions have been defined by cultural, economic, and political distinctions produced by desegregation, the liberalization of immigration policy as a result of civil rights legislation, the subsequent increase in black immigration to the US, and the conservative backlash against the legislative gains of the civil rights movement that benefited African Americans and black immigrants, backlash in which mainstream neo-evangelicals took part (Matory 2015).[9]

Social scientists have also noted the ways in which cultural and moral apparatuses construct black ethnic boundaries. Percy Hintzen and Jean Muteba Rahier argue that black ethnic frictions are conditioned by different reckonings of blackness: a structural politics of blackness often advocated by African Americans that foregrounds blackness primarily as a basis for exploitation and political mobilization, and a deconstructive political approach to blackness often advocated by black immigrants which illustrates multiple forms of blackness that are not always structurally defined (2003). In *Stigma and Culture: Last-Place Anxiety in Black America*, anthropologist J. Lorand Matory proposes that black ethnic differences actually stem from shared processes of ethnic distinction and ethnogenesis by which Afro-Caribbean and other black ethnic communities in the US assert cultural distance from African Americans, who are symbolically constructed as "homogeneous, unchanging, bereft of the characteristics and behaviors that define the normal citizen, and, according to the national mythology, uniquely embodying the characteristics and behaviors inappropriate to the normal citizen" (2015, 2). Thus, black ethnic distinctions emanate from groups' efforts to navigate the symbolic and material deprivations that attend occupying a racial bottom slot associated with an essentialized and demoralized African American blackness.

We might also envisage the ethnic lines between the Afro-Caribbean and African American evangelicals of CBC and DBC to be drawn more sharply as a result of the increasing polarization of wealth that occurred with the height of the economic recession, which bookended the year of our ethnographic engagements. Given the common occurrence of ethno-congregationalism as a model for Christian community in the US, and given religion as a mechanism for conceptualizing black ethnic difference and protesting racialization, the moralization of black ethnic difference and the ethnicization of Afro-diasporic religious experience might also be expected.

In the anglophone Caribbean societies where Afro-Caribbean CBC and DBC members originate, ethnicity and race—which are also entangled with classical hierarchical distinctions of class and color—together produce social stratification. In fact, anglophone Caribbean societies experiencing the transition from colonialism to postcolonial independence were understood to be indelibly shaped by hierarchical differences. As Deborah Thomas observes, mid-twentieth-century anthropology of the Caribbean hinged upon a foundational view of cultural difference and ethno-racial hierarchy: "The idea that West Indian societies exhibited an incompatible sociocultural pluralism was counterpoised with notions of creolized stratification" (2013, 522). Ethno-racial, cultural, class, and color distinctions were thought to create a crucible of difference that threatened the very prospect and possibility of Caribbean societal cohesion. Percy Hintzen similarly notes that national discourses of racial purity and hybridity in the Caribbean created contradictory modes of "structural integration and symbolic exclusion" and led to an "increasing crescendo of conflict and contestation" around ethnic and racial lines, as well as class and color lines (2001, 489). Thus, in addition to the ethnic fault lines that delineate Afro-Caribbean and African American cultural boundaries in the US, according to their national origins Afro-Caribbean evangelicals bring a variety of social grammars of difference and potentially interpolate a number of ethnic distinctions and hierarchies in their interactions with their African American coreligionists.

Ethnic Protest, Altered Solidarities, and the Cross-Cutting Potential of Familial Community

Yet a strict and narrow reading of black ethnic interactions in terms of entrenched differences and material competition misses the variety of ways in which black constituencies also relate through and around ethnic differences. Scholars conducting interethnic and comparative studies of ethnic identity formation note contextual shifts and ambivalences in ethnic identifications. For example, in *Black Mosaic: The Politics of Black Pan-Ethnic Diversity,* Candis Watts Smith argues that black ethnic-identity distinctions are contextual rather than absolute and that black Americans and black immigrants tend to consider each other as partners in a shared struggle against racial injustice (2014, 6), even though they are aware of their differences. Smith suggests that blackness in the United States might be better conceptualized as a pan-ethnic identity rather than always being fragmented by ethnic divisions. In *The Protestant Ethnic and the Spirit of Capitalism,* cultural studies scholar Rey Chow asserts that ethnicity is dually conceptualized as a universal condition that is the result of human cultural history and as a particular condition that results from local resistance to the capitalist assignment of particular ethnic groups to the bottom of labor hierarchies. This ambivalence between universal and particular understandings of ethnicity creates an ongoing cycle that reproduces and perpetuates difference, violence, and resistance. Chow engages Max Weber's argument that Protestant idealizations of hard work and struggle are part of the capitalist ideological apparatus and observes that ethnic protests (or certain people's resistance to the material inequalities that attend ethnicization in capitalist contexts) are endemic to global capitalism. Chow explains: "In this context, *to be ethnic is to protest*—but perhaps less for actual emancipation of any kind than for the benefits of worldwide visibility, currency, and circulation" (2002, 48). Thus, ethnic protests tend to reify rather than subvert capitalist and ethnic inequalities.[10]

Caribbean cultural agents also construct solidarities that transect ethno-racial divides. According to J. Brent Crosson, alongside the ethno-racial hierarchies of Caribbean multicultural nationalism are "altered solidarities": "relations-through-difference," which Afro-Trinidadians and Indo-Trinidadians co-construct through counter-notions of trust and intimacy that confound popular ethno-racial divides (2014, 21). Crosson observes that such counter-narratives of relationship illustrate that "relationality is, in many contexts, articulated through alterity, pointing toward the 'partial connections' and contingent coalitions that exceed notions of solidarity premised solely on shared identities, biological mixture, or part-whole relations" (2014, 24). These altered solidarities can exist at the level of neighborhood relationships in which shared experiences create an alternative reference point for solidarity rather than received categories of social difference. Crosson's emphasis on how long-standing relationships of trust and intimacy can move beyond or transcend conventional identity boundaries also helps us better understand African American DBC member Sister Etta Johnson's kinship claims that her relationship to her Afro-Caribbean spiritual father and the younger congregants (both African American and Afro-Caribbean) who recognized her as their spiritual mother were forged through their shared interactions over the years. Her description of her spiritual mothering and her reception of spiritual fatherhood across ethnic lines and the spiritual kinship that mediate both constitute an altered solidarity—or, as I claim below, a familial alterity.

Afro-Caribbean and African American evangelicals meet in a landscape that is rife with ethnic distinctions, and CBC and DBC members' kinship claims are intersected by a number of ethno-national distinctions. Even so, Afro-Caribbean and African American religious interactions cannot be adequately understood through a fixed ethnic or ethno-congregational frame. The ethnographic examination of CBC and DBC evangelical constructions of spiritual kinship gives us a different view of black ethnic interactions. It illustrates the contexts in which black evangelicals emphasize familial religious sociality over ethno-racial identities as the basis for religious belonging and as signifiers for collective identity. This closer view of black evangelical productions of familial community also illustrates the significance of religion as an arena in which intervening identities are produced between ethnic constituencies. Such a production of familial community also shows how a spiritualized (rather than a material biogenetic or ethno-national) reckoning of identity can inhabit the conceptual space between universal and particular reckonings of identity, and can do so dynamically. Such community is encoded in spiritual kinship and has social force.

"COLONIALISM IS JUST A COUSIN OF RACISM":
AFRO-CARIBBEAN AND AFRICAN AMERICAN EVANGELICALS AND AFRO-DIASPORIC SOLIDARITY

Interactions between CBC and DBC communities are deeply shaped not only by their members' racial and ethnic identities but also by shared experiences of mobility and understandings of religious alterity that resist the ethnic compartmentalization of black evangelical religious fellowship.

Although Brother James Wilkerson described the *ethnic* tensions that shaped congregational dynamics between the mostly African American CBC and the mostly Afro-Caribbean DBC, in his opinion the history of plantation slavery and imperialism that both communities shared connected them more deeply than any of those tensions could divide them. In short, their relatedness ran deep. Specifically, Wilkerson testified that "colonialism is just a cousin of racism." Although they exist in a social milieu in which ethnic and religious differences can create material and moral inequalities, Wilkerson recognizes that Afro-Caribbeans (and African Americans by extension) are not solely responsible for creating this context. He points out that there is a difference between reinscribing a pseudo-colonial religious dynamic that condones external religious authority rather than establishing its foundational structures. The same thing also applies to the politics of ethnic identity difference that is currently infiltrating religious practice. Wilkerson's acknowledgment of the broader social forces at play in these interethnic religious relationships has the same effect as silencing ethnic tensions: the avoidance of depicting local Brethren church as failed social institutions. Although Wilkerson is more than willing to analyze the social cleavages that have divided black Brethren in the Atlanta area, he does not read these tensions as being the fault of intraracial difference or Brethren exclusions alone. The ethnic differences, class inequality, and diverse religious histories that exacerbated the perceived differences between the CBC and DBC communities did not erase Afro-Caribbeans' and African Americans' shared experiences of political marginalization: the related social structures of empire and the nation-state affected both Afro-Caribbeans and African Americans. They disenfranchised both peoples and fostered "cultural conflict" that could have led to a communal "explosion." Yet instead of laying the fault for ethnic hierarchies and dissent at the feet of Afro-Caribbeans, Wilkerson emphasizes the kinship of Afro-Caribbeans and African Americans: they are religious *and* political brethren; they share a material proximity conditioned by their experiences with trans-Atlantic racisms and imperialisms. For Wilkerson, spiritual kinship recognizes the shared Christian dispositions *and* historical oppressions that CBC and DBC members experienced as communities located in the African Diaspora.

M. Jacqui Alexander reiterates this political relatedness between Afro-Caribbeans and African Americans in her book *Pedagogies of Crossing: Meditations on Feminism, Sexual Politics, Memory, and the Sacred*: "Neither of us as African Americans nor Caribbean people created those earlier conditions of colonialism and Atlantic slavery. Yet we continue to live through them in a state of selective forgetting, setting up an artificial antipathy between them in their earlier incarnation, behaving now as if they have ceased to be first cousins" (2005, 273). Like Alexander, Wilkerson uses this relatedness to challenge and flatten Afro-Caribbean Brethren's tacit claims of distinctiveness and superiority.

In another instance, an Afro-Trinidadian elder preached a short guest sermon for a Caribbean cultural celebration hosted by an Atlanta metropolitan Pentecostal megachurch. In it, he expressed the need for black people from the Caribbean and the United States to recognize their shared struggles as people of African descent. Although not many CBC or DBC members were in attendance—a fact that illustrates their enactment of congregational and religious boundaries—the elder's participation in the service conveyed a religious as well as an Afro-diasporic ecumenism.

African American Christian traditions have been associated with fostering an exilic consciousness, using the narrative frame of chosenness to validate the peripheralization of people of African descent. As Sylvester Johnson notes, the Israelitic myth and the connected community self-identifications as the people of God have constituted a "grand narrative for articulating religious, racial, or even national identities" (2004, 1). This has been true especially in the United States and for African Americans who have used the notions of chosenness in Exodus to outline a righteous exilic consciousness—a sense of anguished yet righteous alienation from a native land—and to decry the hypocrisies of racist democracy (Glaude 2003).

Alongside the uses of African American Christianity to foster a critical sense of moral outsiderness, the broader field of black Atlantic religions, including a number of Afro-diasporic Christianities and African-derived religious traditions, has been associated with suturing the wounds of spatial and cultural displacement experienced by enslaved Africans and their New World descendants, as discussed in chapter 1. Thus, Afro-diasporic Christian traditions and other religious forms attend to the social and specifically ethnonational ruptures initiated by the enslavement, racialization, and colonization of Afro-descended peoples.

Into these ruptures stepped Afro-diasporic churches. They managed to create spaces of communion for Afro-Caribbean and African American migrants navigating the socioeconomic transformations of industrialization, emancipation, and postcolonialism. This deep religious history of places of sanctuary amid racialization and mobility contributed to the social scientific construction of the "Black Church" (Evans 2008). And this ongoing Afro-diasporic vernacular engagement with a sanctuary Christianity likely shaped local Atlanta residents' reading of CBC and DBC as ethnic churches. Nonetheless, changes in patterns of migration and reckonings of blackness also raise questions about alternative understandings of black religious solidarities, understandings that do not simply reproduce more-conventional ethnic scripts of collective identity.

A TALE OF TWO ALTERITIES: BLACK SPIRITUAL KINSHIP AND OTHERNESS AS COLLECTIVE IDENTITY

Located amid a domestic US and a southern urban landscape that is shaped by spatial, ethnic, and class mobilities and estrangements, the Afro-Caribbean and African American congregants I interviewed shared an interesting commonality: the experience of serial migration—the movement between two or more locales other than the place of origin. More than 60 percent of the black US-born congregants I interviewed were serial migrants and had lived in at least two locales in the United States prior to relocating to Atlanta. And almost 90 percent of the Caribbean-born members that I interviewed had lived in another locale prior to their move to Atlanta, with 20 percent having lived in two or more locales prior to relocating to this southern city. Among the top cities of residence were the northern cities of New York, Philadelphia, Chicago, and Montreal, and the southern city of Houston. Migration research has explored how serial migration can disrupt mainstream categorical identities and instigate the formation of novel solidarities (Ossman 2004). Thus, CBC and DBC members' lived experiences of serial migration held the potential to loosen church members' relationship to their ethnic identities. Simon Coleman recognizes that diasporic identities—and specifically the mobility associated with them—can mitigate other identities, such as ethnicity and nationality.[11]

Along similar lines, social scientists Nina Glick Schiller, Ayse Caglar, and Thaddeus Gulbrandsen show how migrants in born-again religious communities in Manchester, New Hampshire, and Halle, Germany, produce "nonethnic forms of incorporation" through the creation of local religious solidarities produced through neoliberal political engagements and intercultural networks in the public sphere that are not ethnically marked (2006, 612). It therefore stands to reason that contemporary forms of mobility do not always generate the ethnic communities that are traditionally associated with migrant communities, and an ethnic analytical lens may not be sufficient to capture the productions of locality made by today's born-again Christians. For CBC and DBC evangelicals who are doubly diasporized, investing time and energy in creating thick, multi-layered modes of familial religious belonging as reference points for identity can, in some contexts, supersede their reproduction of more culturally scripted ethno-national solidarities. As observed by Kamari Clarke, "In these [black Atlantic] circuits new political economies are leading to new social configurations that are contributing to the development of new and innovative forms of practices.... These innovations are becoming even more significant with the shifts in the movement of black Atlantic populations and the state and non-state mechanisms that conjoin to provide the conditions of innovative self-making" (2013, 470).

Afro-Caribbean and African American evangelicals at CBC and DBC create a shared sense of otherness through a communal grammar of familial religious association. Thomas Csordas theorizes that the radical otherness of alterity constitutes the "phenomenological kernel of religion" itself (2004, 164). For this radical otherness is "an elementary constituent of subjectivity and intersubjectivity, and . . . a structure of being-in-the-world. Not only can it be elaborated into the monstrous as well as the divine, but it can be transformed into identity, intimacy, or familiarity" (2004, 164). The familial alterity that Afro-Caribbean and African American evangelicals create makes religious relationships central to a person's identity. Unlike the blackness written onto racialized bodies, and somewhat like the idealized renditions of born-again conversion, black evangelicals' understandings of their familial community as an othered community is an "otherness" that can be chosen. The social identities that precede conversion should not be assumed to take precedence over the social collectives that emanate from a person's decision to become a born-again Christian.

Csordas (2007) also specifies that alterity should not be understood as strictly local or only religious; it can also have ethno-racial, political, and global valences. For although white mainstream evangelicals in the US have an exilic consciousness (Elisha 2008) and perceive themselves as an embattled moral minority (Smith 1998), black evangelicals have a sense of otherness that is still informed by religious and ethno-racial notions of otherness (namely of exile and diaspora). Their position as minoritized religious subjects within a predominantly white US evangelicalism and as racialized subjects within the US social landscape frames their alterity as both a product of their spiritual imagination and of their material conditions. Black evangelicals occupy the narrative space between the countercultural imaginary of evangelicalism and Afro-diasporic blackness. One church member shared his reflections on evangelicals' cultural positioning during a worship service: "In the media they caricature evangelicals as right-wing conservatives." During an oral history interview, T. Michael Flowers noted that as black people and "as oppressed people, we are able to identify with Jesus." If otherness is imagined as an avenue to moral righteousness, then CBC and DBC members occupy a dual outsider position informed by diasporic and religious imaginaries.

Just as familial alterity is used as a signifier of collective identity, it is also used as a marker of difference. In other words, spiritual kinship (as articulated through Christian theologies and the vernacular idiom of "church family") creates a framework for community identification as well as social boundaries. As noted by Janet Carsten in *Cultures of Relatedness* (2000), kinship is not only used to convey people's understandings of their similarities with one another; it is also used to narrate their perceived differences from other social collectives. Much as ethnicity/race mediates modes of hierarchy and exclusion, familial religious identities can trace lines of belonging that bound social collectives. Peggy Becker similarly observes that family congregations can also be insular (1999). She concludes that family congregations create close forms of social belonging through the usage of familial idioms; the celebration of members' life events; engagement in quotidian acts of care, support, and communion; and the silencing of conflict. Nonetheless, Becker acknowledges that the interior orientation of familial congregations can also alienate nonmember residents in their surrounding communities.

Afro-Caribbean and African American evangelicals' understandings and practices of spiritual kinship constitute a familial way of conducting religious fellowship. Nonetheless, like ethnicity, their familial religious identity is generated through shared mythologies of origin, language, and ritual that underline common worldviews and shared experiences of local community. Spiritual kinship generates a moral divide between community insiders and outsiders around perceived differences in the right (familial) and the wrong (ethno-racial) ways of configuring Christian fellowship. Thus, although CBC and DBC members may aspire to traverse ethnic differences, their constructions of familial community reinscribe a socio-moral boundary that generates modes of religious difference in a manner akin to ethno-racial distinctions.

Similarly, some CBC and DBC members acknowledge that their churches could improve the ways they interface with their local communities. As Brother Alex Williams stated during a Sunday worship service, "We must be careful [about] creating a drawbridge Christianity and language that keeps people out." Another church brother expressed the same sentiments during Sunday worship: "We are not meeting people where they are. Sometimes we have to give up our hymns. If we're willing to give up what we want, we could reach more people." Church members also remarked that church members' reticence to engage local residents increases outsiders' perception that the church is unconcerned with attracting or interacting with new members. Such concerns of CBC and DBC members about their interactions with local community members suggest that their "church family" can generate a community of care for members only. Thus, evangelicals' ethnic protests appear to advocate that they replace ethno-religious membership with a nonethnic form of everyday familial membership that bridges social divides of interest (interpersonal/interethnic) and that remains silent on social boundaries that are not deemed vital to the production of "authentic" familial community (church community/local community).

Afro-Caribbean and African American evangelicals' constructions of familial congregational communities through idioms and rituals of relatedness show us the carefully crafted relationships of trust and the shared sense of alterity that together create solidarities that transcend ethnic boundaries. In addition to being an outgrowth of evangelical theological universalism, their own experiences of racial exclusion and processes of ethnic differentiation, protest, and ambivalence shape CBC and DBC members' negative view of ethno-religious boundaries.

Yet this evangelical association's critique of US ethno-congregationalism also sheds light on some of the limitations of ethnicity as a straightforward explanatory model for Afro-Caribbean immigrant and African American community life. The indiscriminate application of the ethnic community model can obscure the strong universalist identifications and aspirations of Afro-Caribbean and African American evangelicals and hide the interior technologies by which contemporary Christians produce interethnic familial affinities. With its capacity to mediate affinities that are interpersonal, institutional, transnational, and even global in scope, spiritual kinship is a significant framework for collective identity for Christians in a globalizing context (Frishkopf 2003). Specifically, the local community of CBC and DBC evangelicals demonstrates that spiritual kinship can actually generate shifts in congregants' articulation of public-sphere identities such as ethnicity and can anchor their emergent religious aspirations, group identities, and enactments of sociality. Spiritual kinship also facilitates the formation of boundary-crossing transethnic religious identities that are positively defined through shared institutional, quotidian, and diasporic histories.

As a whole, part 2 of the book examines how spiritual kinship mediates the institutional, quotidian, and familial experiences of DBC congregants. Chapter 4 investigates how spiritual kinship is constituted—albeit in gendered terms—through collective rituals of Bible study, exegesis, and interpretation. Because textual interpretive practices are brokered by patriarchal and biblical practices of male leadership, performances of biblicism and fraternalism are closely linked. The chapter also illustrates how spiritual kinship emerges not only as an outgrowth of the embodiment of spirit but also through shared discursive and performative conventions.

Part Two · Scenes of Black Evangelical Spiritual Kinship in Practice

Bible Study, Fraternalism, and the Making of Interpretive Community

4

Prominently displayed at the top of the DBC website is a declaration that reads "We hold the Bible to be the absolute, sole, and final authority in all matters relating to doctrine, practice, faith, life, and prophecy." As a text, the Bible underlines the foundation of DBC belief and holds a central place in church programming and ritual. Over the course of my time with the DBC community in 2008, I observed the many ways in which the Bible was not only an important influence on members' religious thought and practice but also a fundamental mediator of DBC relationships. Indeed, the Bible and Bible-centered practices constituted central ways in which DBC members constructed community belonging and narrated their religious identifications as "Bible believers."

As an integrated participant in DBC activities, I attended a minimum of four Bible studies per week during my fieldwork in the Atlanta area. My Bible study attendance convinced me of the community's esteem for biblical knowledge, but a single encounter illustrates the close connection between DBC members' emphasis on biblicism and community membership. During my last week at DBC in December 2008, Sister Evelyn Trent confessed to me and a small group of DBC members that she had been somewhat suspicious of my arrival at the church in early 2008. "However, I saw that your Bible had markings in it, and I heard you speak at Bible study. And I thought, OK, this girl knows the Word. So, then, I knew you were OK. Then I knew you were one of us." Sister Trent's candid comment suggests that aside from official church membership, biblical knowledge was an alternative and meaningful litmus test of community inclusion. To be Christians and related by a mutual embodiment of the Holy Spirit was an invisible state that could be spiritually felt. Biblical knowledge and an engagement with the Bible as a text was a highly valued and material marker of Christian religious belonging. The visual dimensions of a person's biblical groundings (e.g., reciting scriptures and marking up one's Bible) were a mode of authentication different from the formal recognition of church membership. As a result, biblical knowledge and participation in Bible-centered activities became central to members' social capital and community locations.

This chapter uncovers the contents and contexts of DBC Bible study and kinship. In particular, I argue that shared textual beliefs and practices constitute the core of DBC community formation and that the gendered dimensions of biblical teaching and exhortation create a particularly close intersection between DBC brotherhood and biblicism, and among fraternalism, literalism, and institutional authority. Although spiritual kinship—as a nonbiological mode of relatedness—is often characterized as "fictive," and although the immaterial qualities of spirit can make authenticating relatedness challenging, attention to Bible study can be productive in illustrating the discursive and performative dimensions of spiritual kinship and its grounding within institutional religious life. Moreover, a closer look at the ritual contexts of Bible study and male biblical exhortation reveals the practices by which church members make themselves into an interpretive community.

The Makings of a Translocal Brethren: An Outline of DBC Fraternalism

The black evangelicals with whom I collaborated idealized brotherhood. Influenced by Plymouth Brethren beliefs, church members understood brotherhood to be an important basis of a familial New Testament community form that encouraged collective governance and a more egalitarian approach to interpretation. Brotherhood and Bible study were also central to the establishment and organizational structures of the Afro-diasporic evangelical movement of which DBC and CBC are a part. Nonetheless, these ideological, interpretive, and institutional constructions of brotherhood coexisted with a number of exclusions.

THE INSTITUTIONALIZATION OF BIBLICISM AND BROTHERHOOD

This Brethren group's strong emphasis on biblical and fraternal elements can be traced back to T. Michael Flowers's earlier missionary endeavors in the 1950s US South. As outlined in greater detail in chapter 2, Flowers developed an evangelistic agenda to establish "Bible-believing" New Testament churches throughout the Southeast among African American Baptists, who at the time he believed to be practicing an unbiblical, charismatic Christianity. This was done through twin emphases on individual priesthood and tutelage.

Brethren consider all Christians to be "priests" capable of accessing and sharing biblical knowledge.[1] Small congregations allow members to focus on intensive Bible study. Bible teaching and learning then serve as central processes of community reciprocity and accountability. Moreover, an emphasis on the need for the collective pursuit of biblical knowledge was understood to mitigate the traditional categorical elevation of clergy over laity, which Protestants have long used to limit the textual engagements of rank-and-file members. Instead, male members were enjoined to share the exegetical labors of preaching to their peers. Churches had a collective male-elder governance system. Therefore, their efforts to generate a more democratic form of Christian communion rested upon the exclusion of women from mixed-sex teaching and preaching. For Flowers, the point was to approximate a biblical model of Christian fellowship that centered a Bible-focused practice as part of creating and cultivating an intentionally familial and nonsectarian community.

If Flowers's religious mission was motivated by a concern to extend a biblical Christianity throughout the Southeast, his work was executed through the formation of a fraternal religious network informed by processes of tutelage and local autonomy. Flowers was mentored by the Nottage brothers—Afro-Bahamian Brethren evangelists who founded Bible chapels in midwestern and East Coast cities—who assisted him in his own missionary work. As he undertook his main project of "planting" and maintaining southern Bible chapels, Flowers replicated his own personal experiences of mentorship with the Nottage brothers and extended the Brethren tradition of fraternal discipling (or mentorship). In addition to founding local Bible chapels in the US South, Flowers initiated a secondary religious project to develop the leadership capacities and religious connections between church brothers. Recounting Flowers's legacy among Brethren churchmen during an interview, DBC Elder Jacob Davidson confirmed that Flowers prayed "that God would raise up godly, gifted, gracious, and generous men for the church [and] for Jesus Christ." Transforming his prayers into a men's ministry, Flowers conducted one-on-one Bible studies that cultivated elders out of dedicated churchmen in his Georgia and South Carolina churches, even going so far as to conduct Bible studies on a Marine base in South Carolina. As he supplemented the biblical knowledge of emerging church leaders, Flowers mentored them on how to conduct effective church ministries. The elders and the evangelists who succeeded Flowers also established collaborative relationships among themselves through interpersonal communication, informal meetings, invitations to speak at church events, and extended discussions at the annual regional church conference.

Black evangelical churchmen used brotherhood as a relational framework for socializing men into the demands of biblical teaching and as a way to aid connections between Brethren Bible chapels.[2] For Flowers and a second generation of Brethren evangelists, brotherhood provided not only a connection but also a prized rendition of New Testament ecclesiology, an infrastructure for local church governance. It fostered the growth of a regional church association and provided a language for trans-local religious affiliation.

THE CONTENTS OF BROTHERHOOD: LOCAL MEANINGS

In addition to serving as an organizational framework, this brotherhood is also formational, thanks to the spiritual discourse and sustained interpersonal interactions that it fosters. Influenced by Plymouth Brethren teachings, Flowers and DBC members locally define brotherhood as a spiritual relationship (Callahan 1996). Brethren believe converted Christians to be "in-dwelled" by the Holy Spirit and to be members of the "family of God." It follows then that Christians are "brothers and sisters in Christ" because they embody the same spirit. It is because of their belief in Christians' spiritual likeness that DBC members insist that their brotherhood is egalitarian and that they ritualize this through fraternal idioms. During the course of formal church programs and everyday conversations, church members typically address one another as "brother" and "sister." Indeed, those terms prioritize spiritual connections over social distinctions.

Church members' discourse also indicates that "brother" is a label that members mobilize to outweigh other forms of social prestige. One particular example illustrates church members' insistence on the value of sibling discourses as a meaningful form of address, inclusion, and identity. During a Sunday-afternoon commemoration service celebrating the opening of the DBC senior center, Sister Mildred Douglass asked for *"Brother Pastor Doctor Andrews"* to lead the congregation in a word of prayer (emphasis added). Sister Douglass's systematic arrangement of Andrews's titles privileges his identity as a brother, rather than his other honorifics, as the reason for his inclusion and ability to address the church community.

Even as brotherhood, along with its attending ethics of egalitarianism, is manifested discursively in the kinship idioms of church members, it also emerges and is constituted by the interpersonal interactions between church brothers outside of the community. Church brothers provide personalized spiritual correction and encouragement on Sundays and during the week. Older men mentor young men on how to become better husbands and fathers, sharing intimate details about previous shortcomings and offering important life lessons. The everyday social interactions of DBC men closely resemble the accountability groups and "circular brotherhood" associated with the Promise Keepers Movement—a multicultural evangelical para-church movement designed to bolster male church participation (Bartkowski 2004, 103). The DBC brotherhood provides contexts of homosociality, in which life experiences as well as the components of masculinity are contemplated and negotiated. This proves particularly important because of the ways in which black masculinities have been constructed in the US and the Caribbean. According to Riché Richardson (2007), images of black men in the US South have often oscillated on a continuum of extremes from that of the trope of the emasculated southern black man as an Uncle Tom (and thus passive to white patriarchal oppression) to the hyper-masculine black man as a rapist and thug popularized in the post-Emancipation era (through such films as *The Birth of a Nation*). Similarly, popular cultural and scholarly representations of Caribbean men have disseminated an image of Afro-Caribbean masculinities as constituted through acts that demonstrate wit, economic achievement (via legal or illegal means), and sexual prowess (Chevannes 2001; Wilson 1969). It has also been postulated that because of the forms of manhood they propagate, African American and Afro-Caribbean men tend to be located on the margins of the biological families they help to create (Clarke 1966; Moynihan 1965; Simey 1946).[3] This pathologization of black masculinities provides a structural context for black religious organizations to show practical concern with black men's familial attachments (Lincoln and Mamiya 1990; Rouse 2004).

In "It's a Family Affair: Black Culture and the Trope of Kinship," Paul Gilroy (1993) critiques such uses of familism as an idiom of community. Explaining the increased use of kinship tropes among black Atlantic communities as the derivative of an "Americocentric obsession with family," Gilroy attributes black kin identifications to the reduction of black political and social life into "a crisis of black masculinity" (2004, 91–92). To be sure, Gilroy rightly points out the patriarchal biases instantiated by DBC kinship discourses and understanding of family, and his critiques echo a broader and understandable disaffection with familial rhetoric embedded within socioreligious movements after the emergence of the neo-evangelical Moral Majority.

Nonetheless, my ethnographic exploration compels a consideration of why Afro-diasporic people remain invested in fraternalism as a model of community and institution building. The patriarchal emphasis of Afro-diasporic family projects, however problematic in their gendered, sexual, class, and generational exclusions, is retained as an outcome of social forces that reward certain gender formations and thereby affect the material conditions of black people. Moreover, the conceptual project of masculinity that is discussed and reformed by DBC brothers may not be accurately framed as solely derivative of the US's ideological "obsession with the family," but it might be better understood as being infused by a number of religious and ethical sensibilities, some of which emerge from Afro-diasporic worldviews and community locations.

Finally, fraternalism is produced through material reciprocity. As leaders of the church community, DBC brothers organize church-wide "love offerings" that provide financial assistance to needy members and their families. Sister Lisa Douglass, for instance, received church aid in the fall of 2008 after undergoing a series of surgical procedures and losing her job. Individual members also offer personalized assistance to one another without the intervention of the church. Brother David Halliwell gave a car to Brother Joseph Richardson and his family upon their arrival in Atlanta. This support challenges a conventional nuclear rendering of "the family" as an economically isolated and self-sufficient unit. It also disrupts the dominant narrative of male familial leadership by which men head households through material provision associated with breadwinner-style masculinities.

Additionally, the provision of church-wide support evokes the mutual aid structured by a number of other Afro-diasporic social institutions, such as black fraternal organizations, burial associations, confraternities, and Afro-Caribbean hometown associations and *susus:* community credit associations that provide pragmatic assistance to blacks navigating the social dislocations of immigration and racialization, provide spaces where home cultures and familiar faces might be encountered, and also offer modes of collective saving that can be accessed by members for down payments on homes (Foner 2001; Skopcol, Liazos, and Ganz 2006; Von Germeten 2006). As scholars of Afro-Caribbean and African family and community networks have long noted, such social and financial reciprocity is vital to making and maintaining extended family kinship and community networks. Material reciprocity and exchange often foster cohesive and enduring kinship relationships (Mauss 1990; Parry and Bloch 1989). The provision of help moves brotherhood and sisterhood beyond the realm of the discursive and provides tangible signs of their mutual relatedness. Rather than simply an ideal, in such situations spiritual kinship becomes an ethics of reciprocity that is materialized through financial assistance.

Yet to outline church members' solidarity as the product of their desire for support obscures the important religious meanings and intent behind such acts of support. In part, DBC members give because their shared imagining and emphasis of New Testament collectivism motivate it.[4] As they help one another meet their most immediate needs, DBC members practice the sociality of a

New Testament model of Christian community. The solidarity, social process, and ends of brotherhood cannot be easily divorced from the textual tropes, religious meanings, and material exchanges through which it is imagined and enacted. Spiritual kinship emerges as a social phenomenon that is produced through symbolic and material mediums.

Brotherhood and Its Discontent(s): The Challenges of Brotherhood

Even with members' emphasis on egalitarianism, internal hierarchies in the DBC created contested divisions. Although DBC members criticized the institution of the pastorate, they had an officiating pastor in 2008. Rather than this being a stable designation, the acting pastor, Elder Samuel Andrews, was variously referred to as "a brother," "a pastor," "an elder," and "a full-time worker." Church members' opinions about the existence of a pastor also differed. Some saw it as a necessary concession to a US religious landscape in which pastors were important public representatives of the community as a whole. Others saw no problem with Andrews's occupation of the role as pastor because of his commitment to the church community. Those who did take issue with the church's employment of a pastor framed it as a transgression of the Brethren principles of fraternal egalitarianism.[5] Brother Moses Hamilton, a senior Afro-Jamaican churchman, explained this point of view:

> We believe in the plurality of leadership. That's why the church is elder-governed, not pastor-governed . . . and we believe that's biblical. . . . I like the fact that many gifts are being used. It's not a one-man ministry. Umm . . . the church emphasizes the priesthood of every believer. That there's no laity, you know, division. Everybody has a right to approach God. That's why in our worship services any brother can . . . umm . . . stand up and lead the congregation because he's a priest before God. . . . [The transition] was a little rocky in the beginning, but it's worked out. And it changed . . . because there needed to be an understanding of roles to be filled. . . . Older saints assemblies never had pastors. They only had elders. . . . So for many of the older saints who have been in the assemblies for a long time, to get another pastor was a new thing for them. And they had to have a period of adjustment and the pastor had to wait for a period of acceptance.

In his interview, Hamilton located elder governance within a traditional style of Plymouth Brethrenism. His description of the leadership of Brethren elders focused on interconnection, collectivism, and democracy (albeit a male version) consistent with local emphases on church familism. The discussion of elder leadership also conveys a critique of clerical hierarchy and distinction, common to US congregationalism, held by many DBC members. Brother Hamilton acknowledged that the selection and employment of a pastor at Dixon Bible Chapel is necessary because "the culture calls for that today" and because "when somebody calls the church, they need to find somebody there." Yet his discussion of the advent of a pastoral presence conveys ambivalence. This reveals a central tension between two local community orientations. The first is an *authentic interiority* in which the valuation of traditional Brethren ecclesiological conventions and horizontal associations is emphasized. Moreover, this interiority esteems an inward-looking institutional model in which the chapel is thought to cater to the needs of its members. The second community orientation is a *pragmatic exteriority* in which the church is identified as an open-ended institution that should be concerned with making a set of modifications that would situate the religious fellowship within the local religious landscape. Brother Andrews outlined an intentional process of institutional change that was designed to court an "African American public": "We paid a company to actually come and tell us some things, a Christian company. What they were saying was that our worship service needed changing, which is something I knew all along anyway. But they wanted to hear it from somebody else, so that's fine. . . . So basically we changed our worship service. So what you're seeing today is not where we started."

The pragmatic exteriority led to changes like the establishment of greeters and the official welcome of visitors. Nonetheless, while outward-facing changes were instituted, Brother Andrews's narrative illustrates that the changes were fraught. Thus, there were challenges involved in navigating the space between religious ideals and practices, as well as a horizontal fraternal versus a more vertical clerical form. Translating Brethren fraternalism and its anticlerical religious tradition to a broader urban landscape in which a pastoral model of congregational life was more often the norm was a complex process. Moreover, the change from a model of exclusive elder leadership to one that coincided with clerical presence was not a one-way process. At the end of my ethnographic fieldwork in December 2008, Brother Anderson stepped down as the pastor of Dixon Bible Chapel. This multidirectional change in institutional form is not properly captured by the notion of cultural change frequently associated with immigrant cultural assimilation and urbanization.

In addition to members' varied perspectives on the pragmatic and ideological implications of a pastor's presence at DBC, another categorical distinction existed between churchmen, who are known as brothers, and the chapel's small group of male elders, who directly oversee assembly affairs. Although in our interviews and conversations church members did not question the appropriateness of elder governance, some brothers took issue with what they saw as the frequent appointment of middle-class men as church leaders over their working-class brothers. Also, several brothers mentioned a perceived bias in favor of Afro-Caribbean churchmen raised in the Brethren tradition who were elected as church elders over African American members. Churchmen therefore protested the racial, class, ethnic, and national cleavages that affect the ties of their religious brotherhood.

Other modes of hierarchy shape the social dynamics of the DBC assembly, including those of gender. A question posed by Sister Claire Washington (a middle-aged African American CBC member) to an informal gathering of churchwomen is also relevant here: "What about the Sistren?" In short, how do we understand churchwomen's placement in this Brethren constituency? From the vantage point of church doctrines and biblical interpretations, DBC churchwomen emerge as auxiliary religious subjects. Although women are vital participants in church life, gendered ideologies of male headship and female submission limit churchwomen's religious roles. Founded upon the Pauline injunction that "women should remain silent in the churches . . . for it is disgraceful for a woman to speak in the church," Brethren traditions prohibit women from leading, teaching, or preaching before mixed-sex adult classes.[6]

Collectively, DBC churchwomen constitute half of the DBC population and are vital institutional agents who broker important contexts for church sociality. Church sisters, prayer partners, and spiritual mothers exchange personal narratives of religious experience with one another. They also make use of everyday contexts to gather and bridge the spatial divide between church and home and the institutional distinction between church and family, which I explore in more detail in chapter 5. Through their use of testimonies and ethnographic interviews as sites for reflective dialogue, some DBC churchwomen also critique DBC ideologies that call for men's exclusive leadership of church-wide Bible study. Therefore, within the broader field of DBC community life, church "sistren" emerge as far more than muted religious participants. However, DBC women are discouraged from engaging in biblical teaching and exegesis in public mixed-sex adult gatherings.[7] This institutionalization of exclusionary textual practices reinscribes the central relationship between brotherhood and biblical exegesis.

Some members also assert that the assignment of church leadership to middle-aged and senior brothers marginalizes youth perspectives. According to a young adult male member, the climate of traditionalism at DBC creates a context in which critical youth perspectives are perceived as a threat to church order and are either ignored or only partially addressed: "If [as a young person] you start doing things differently or looking at things in another light, [you're] put ... off to the side. For me and a couple of friends of mine the more we started studying and digging in the Scriptures we kinda pulled away from how my family and my group traditionally worshipped. And that was unacceptable [to the older members of the church]." Other young adults concurred. They asserted that their own engagement and interpretation of the Bible motivated them to change the manner in which they understood their religious participation. Yet older members discouraged their new way of worship and their efforts to generate independent youth-led spaces of biblical interpretation. Thus, young adults' discontentment with the structures of brotherhood reveals yet another of its limitations as a model of church-wide unity.

For DBC Brethren, brotherhood represents a shared language of male social connection, shared interpretive labor, and leadership. Even so, the centrality of brotherhood as a social structure underwriting church life does not prohibit churchmen's, churchwomen's, and young adults' present-day criticisms of how brotherhood is and should be implemented in community life. On the one hand, churchmen note the distinctions and competing allegiances that undermine fraternal solidarity. One the other hand, churchwomen and youths are the ones who chiefly have to negotiate the patriarchal social order engendered by institutionalized fraternalism. Ultimately, DBC members contend with the intra-community distinctions that have and continue to affect a host of Afro-diasporic social collectives, including the patriarchy associated with the black church (Gilkes 2001; Pinn 2010a) and the growing class divides and the changing ethnoscapes of urban spaces instigated by black migration (Harold 2007; Jackson 2001; McCoy 2000; Vickerman 1999).

FRATERNALISM AND EGALITARIANISM

Despite the gap between the ideals and manifestations of fraternal egalitarianism, DBC brothers' criticisms of this fractured standard illustrate the significance and valuation of democracy as a principle of fraternalism rather than the futility of egalitarian social projects. That social differences exist does not erase the significance of egalitarianism as a social value (Robbins 1994). Scholars of the Caribbean such as Francio Guadeloupe (2009), George Mentore (2006), and Peter J. Wilson (1973) have observed that the racist and classist hierarchies established by European colonial regimes have created Caribbean social contexts in which expressions of egalitarianism are highly valued. Rather than classifying Caribbean societies singularly as hierarchical or egalitarian societies, scholars have examined the coexistence of rigid inequitable social structures alongside fierce assertions of equality. The social classes deposited by the colonial value system of respectability institutionalized around the church and the family home are seen to coexist and at times collide with the egalitarian culture of reputation on the street (Abrahams 1983). Moreover, as Skopcol, Liazos, and Ganz observe, African Americans' formation of black fraternal organizations built upon ideas of democratic connection was informed by their experiences of their disenfranchisement from the US nation-state (2006). Therefore, the egalitarian ethos of Afro-diasporic social institutions and societies has coexisted with structuralist principles that emphasize hierarchy. Similarly, within the DBC community the presence of hierarchy does not preclude the presence of egalitarian values. This DBC emphasis on fraternal egalitarianism in the postcolonial and post–civil rights eras suggests much about what prompts people to construct and center egalitarian modes of community formation.

In some social contexts, sibling relationships are understood as egalitarian relationships, particularly in Euro-American middle-class families, as Cumming and Schneider note (1961). Various authors observe that within the families of Afro-Caribbeans and US blacks, sibling relations (as well as other connections among relatives) are highly valued relationships that also perform the primary functions associated with the Western nuclear family unit, including child rearing and the vital exchange of material goods, particularly in migrant contexts (Barrow 1998; Baumann and Sunier 1995; Chamberlain 1999a, 1999b, 2006; Clarke 1966; Goulbourne 1999; Ho 1993; Johnson 2000; Smith 1986; Stack 1996; Thompson and Bauer 2000). Of course, expressions of sibling solidarity do not preclude conflict or hierarchy. Once again, expressions of sibling egalitarianism in Afro-diasporic families are most likely concurrent with age-based and other forms of distinction. Even so, the common expressions of sibling solidarity visible in Afro-diasporic families and the centrality of sibling identifications for the Afro-diasporic church members present compelling evidence that the egalitarianism expressed at DBC is not only the product of religious ideas but also of the shared cultural logic that infuses Afro-diasporic modes of relationship making. The egalitarian sentiment that DBC members express and emphasize is therefore significant in both the sacred and secular realms.

Given the complexities involved in institutionalizing the egalitarian ideals of fraternalism, church members' interaction with biblical texts is important in promoting members' ideas of brotherhood and community. Building on Victor Turner's (1995) thesis that rituals constitute social spaces in which a community's values are expressed and validated, I analyze the biblical and otherwise sacred rituals mediated by DBC Brethren as sites where the ideals of fraternalism are exhibited and reified.

The Textual Foundations of the DBC Community and Brotherhood

Biblicism is central to black evangelical identity, and DBC members' ideologies and strategies depend on the Bible as a consistent and authoritative text. Analyzing the social process of Bible study reveals how church brothers direct the coauthorship of community consensus and connect members into an interpretive community.

DBC AND THE MEANINGS OF BIBLE STUDY

Just as Brethren church structures are built upon shared notions of brotherhood, church fellowship is built upon members' shared relationship with the Bible. For DBC members, Bible study is a central fixture of community formation and identity. The very names of Brethren chapels convey the significance of the Bible as a cornerstone of church identity. Since Flowers's founding of "Bible-believing" churches in the US South in the 1950s, black Brethren-influenced congregations that are loosely affiliated with DBC have been dubbed "Bible chapels." The central placement of "Bible" in the name of each chapel signifies the biblical emphasis that is essential to each constituency. T. Michael Flowers explained: "At the church's founding a woman said to me, 'Pastor Flowers, what are we going to call this building?' I said, 'I don't have anything to do with that so long as Bible is a part of it. Don't call it Berean Baptist, Methodist.... If this is what God sent me to do by the Word [Bible], let's call it what God says it's called.' Berean Bible Church or Berean Bible Chapel—good."

That each community's name includes the words "Bible Chapel" is a sign of the assemblies' interrelatedness, in the same way as a surname can connote kinship among blood relatives. In addition, DBC members mentioned that their emphasis on biblical teaching and Bible study established their local reputation as a community that perpetuates "sound biblical teaching." In an interview, Brother Henrick Lorne, a former Pentecostal who became a member of DBC, rendered Brethren biblical knowledge as something that distinguished them from their religious peers. "They know the scripture. They *know* the scripture.... When it comes to the scripture you can't no, no, no, no, no. They'll *tear* you up." As a result, the services of Brethren teachers have been solicited in a number of campus, youth, and Christian educational ministries throughout the Southeast. For example, T. Michael Flowers worked at Cedine Bible Ministries for a while. Members noted that during the early years of CBC's existence, the church was a clearinghouse for Intervarsity collegiate ministries. Even now, during the summer church members engage in camp ministries in the Caribbean that center Christian teaching. Bible study is a significant practice for evangelical Christians all over the world, but the Southern Gospel Mission Association (SGMA) represents the Bible and biblical study as a focal point of Brethren identity that simultaneously marks organizational connections and sets the group apart to outsiders.

Aside from the biblical nomenclature observed by DBC and its myriad "sister churches," Bible study groups are critical sites that aid DBC community formation. In his ethnography of group Bible study, James Bielo concludes that its contexts serve as spaces for evangelical cultural production (2009). The same can be said of DBC Bible studies, which socialize members into the norms, expectations, and beliefs of Brethrenism. For DBC members and their regional sister church members, Bible study is a central social process that promotes the growth of existing and new religious assemblies. Such local Bible study cell groups are effective in incorporating new church members into an existing interpretive community.

Beyond their foundational functions, home Bible studies continue to serve as important sites for social interaction. As Brother Cedric Johnson (a member of Ephesians Bible Chapel—another predominantly Afro-Caribbean Brethren chapel in the Atlanta metropolitan area) remarked, "When you come to any home Bible study . . . it's a one-on-one thing. It's more intimate. . . . You get to know people closer. Their problems, their joys, and sorrows. You have to share in those things. So it becomes a family affair." The same familial emphasis of Bible study carries over into the broader field of DBC Bible study gatherings, including church-sponsored Bible studies on Tuesday and Thursday evenings, Sunday-morning Bible studies, and member-organized cell-group Bible studies that meet on weeknights and Sunday evenings. Within these various study contexts, Bible studies emerge as energetic sites of dialogue where scriptures are debated, questions are answered, and meanings are decided. As biblical knowledge is constituted, the bonds of church fellowship are renewed. Therefore, DBC church belonging is vitally configured through the conversations and social connections that constitute Bible study.

LITERALISM AND THE PRODUCTION OF BROTHERHOOD

In self-identifying as a "Bible-believing people," most DBC members share a literalist orientation to the Bible. In particular, DBC brothers broker a biblical hermeneutic that closes the gaps between portions of biblical text (e.g., different books of the Bible, the Old and the New Testament) as well as between the biblical past and their present. Through their participation in their church's biblical practices, brothers mediate the production of biblical knowledge even as they authenticate brotherhood itself through literalist interpretation.

According to the DBC mission statement, church members believe that "the Old and New Testament are verbally inspired by God and without error in the original writings." By defining the Bible as the uncorrupted "Word of God," they also sacralize the Bible as a text by ascribing it transcendent properties. Because of its divine origins, the Bible is an inerrant reflection of God's truth. In short, rather than resulting from any particular reading of the Bible itself, its accuracy is believed to emanate from the text itself. Members frame the Bible's transcendence in terms of decontextualization or what Keane defines as "entextualization," the process by which "chunks of discourse come to be extractable from particular contexts and [are] thereby made portable" (2007, 14). DBC members also see the Bible as a text with teachings and stories that will always be relevant to the human experience. Thus, DBC members see the Bible as transcending the space between God and humans, between universal truth and variable interpretation, as well as between the past and present. In his study of US fundamentalists, Vincent Crapanzano associates such decontextualized readings with the practice of biblical literalism (2000). Specifically, he observes that biblical literalists focus on the referential rather than the pragmatic dimensions of language, meaning that literalists are most concerned with depicting the relationship between words and the things they describe, rather than understanding the contexts that endow those words with specific and shifting meanings.

Other scholarship on such communities takes issue with the ways in which their literalist ideologies commonly reinforce male religious authority and ideals of submissive womanhood (Gallagher 2003; Ingersoll 2003). Such authors have illustrated how evangelicals' interpretive practices are deeply embedded in church gender politics. The distinctive valuation of teacher versus participant and the coalescence of these roles along gender lines at DBC together demonstrate how textual practices reproduce a gendered interpretive asymmetry. At a more conceptual level, churchmen's brokerage of biblical content as the word of God automatically gives men a privileged proximity to the divine that is not completely available to women. This powerfully reinforces men's special position within the chapel community, sanctions male authority, and is an example of how DBC biblicism uniquely endorses church brotherhood.

There are likewise questions about the significance of a literalist hermeneutic in black religious contexts. In *The Bible and African Americans: A Brief History*, Vincent Wimbush summarizes what he identifies as a black fundamentalist biblical interpretation:

> The Protestant-defined Bible is considered the deracialized, depoliticized, and universal guide to truth and salvation. Radical criticism of African American religious communities and culture is expressed. Insofar as the Protestant canon is not questioned, and insofar as the foundation or presupposition for the reading of the canon is claimed to be something other than African American historical experience as remembered and understood by African Americans, it entails a severe and even disturbing rejection of African American existence. (2003, 68)

For Wimbush, the decontextualizing impetus of biblical literalism in the hands of black Christians poses two interconnected problems. First, it decentralizes African American cultural experience. Second, a black biblical literalism often leads to critiques of black Christian communities. In short, biblical literalism twice marginalizes black Christians who espouse it.[8] Nonetheless, Wimbush acknowledges that there is a need for "comprehensive investigation and psychosocial and political-ideological explanation" of black biblical literalists (2003, 70). This book attends to that deep call to context.

In my research I found that DBC Brethren observed two principles of literalist interpretation: the law of first mention and the use of biblical analogy. The law of first mention counters a common objection leveled at biblical literalists: that the Bible cannot be the infallible word of God because it is laden with contradictions. During a Thursday-night Bible study, Elder Brother Roy Fitzpatrick summarized the principle of first mention for study participants: "When something is mentioned the first time, it's important that we focus on what that means because the meaning does not change. Period. If you understand what it means the first time, we can walk through Scripture with the same thing." As a method of biblical interpretation, the law of first mention rewrites the Bible as a consistent text in which meanings are unchanging. First mention supports the Brethren conviction that accounts of New Testament churches are not archaic records and that therefore, despite the historical changes and cultural variations in how church communities have been understood, DBC Brethren still consider the brotherhood and sisterhood of early Christians to be a relevant script for how they should relate to one another in the present. The teaching, praying, communion, reciprocity, and face-to-face fellowship depicted in the New Testament Book of Acts, which exists as a canon within a canon of their biblical engagements, reveals the full potential of church life, they say, one that is recoverable if religious participants follow Scriptural imperatives.[9] As a principle informing the literalist beliefs of Brethren, first mention does not leave room for questions about variation across ancient contexts.

Rather, Brethren who observe this rule of first mention hold that what brotherhood has been and what it should be is consistently outlined in the Bible. Thus, DBC literalist beliefs transform brotherhood from an ideal to an attainable reality scripted by the Bible.

The second rule of DBC biblical interpretation connects Old and New Testament passages. As a brother explained during another Bible study, "The Old Testament is revealed in the New Testament, and the New Testament is concealed in the Old Testament." Through this rule of interpretation, the Bible became more than a collection of idiosyncratic events and characters; it is transformed into a cohesive narrative. By establishing an analogical relationship between both biblical testaments, readers are directed to see patterns across its passages. As briefly discussed in chapter 1, New Testament representations of biblical phenomena are considered fuller representations than those contained in the Old Testament. Applying this logic of New Testament revelation, the children of Israel described in the Old Testament are understood as an antecedent social collective upon which the New Testament church is modeled. However, DBC Brethren celebrate the communalism produced by New Testament Christians (a communalism with which members profoundly identify) as the fullest expression of biblical community. Thus, the inherent meanings of brotherhood alluded to throughout the Bible were most fully realized in depictions of the New Testament church.

Situated between the rule of first mention, which upheld the ongoing relevance of New Testament Christianity, and the rule of New Testament revelation, which prioritized New Testament depictions of community over other biblical models, brotherhood emerged as a privileged element of Christianity. As Bible teachers, brothers contributed to the reproduction of DBC as an interpretive community. As they shaped literalist biblical readings, they actively remade the Bible into a consistent, linear narrative. They also endeavored to keep biblical meanings constant and narrowed possible biblical interpretations. In doing so, brothers built consensus about biblical meaning. Although one can criticize the brothers' production of shared biblical meaning through literalism for its decontextualization of biblical writings, it is important to depict the ethnographic ways in which that production underwrites religious identities and fraternalism.

Aside from the intertextual and interpersonal implications of DBC members' literalist interpretations of the Bible, it is also important to think through the significance of literalist ideology for DBC members' kinship claims. Typically, scholars have characterized spiritual kinship as fictive kinship (Frishkopf 2003; Thomas, Malik, and Wellman, 2017). Nonetheless, DBC members' assertions about the truth of the Bible and its contents, including its representations of the church as a family, raise important questions about whether they see their relatedness to one another in strictly metaphorical terms. I argue that, given their textual literalism, they do not see their relationships as merely metaphorical. Because of the authoritative weight they give to the Bible as a source of God's truth, categorizing the relatedness defined in the Bible as "fictive" would directly contradict DBC members' textual approaches as well as their beliefs about sociality. Keane insightfully comments on this conceptual paradox enshrined in Protestant discursive practices in which the portability of language made possible by entextualization potentially runs against religious concerns with truth and transparent representation (2007). In his analysis of Sumbanese Calvinism, sincerity emerges as the means by which religious practitioners navigate the murky terrain among words, objects, and selves. By sincerity, Kean means that they insist on the genuineness of performative discourses and religious language.

For DBC members, literalism provides a means by which they can fix biblical meaning and ensure the authenticity of biblical content. This has social implications. Instead of seeing themselves as approximating fictive kinship, DBC members use the decontextualization of literalism to read the antiquity and spirituality of New Testament Christianity into their own fraternalism. In doing so, they enliven the Bible as a text and sacralize the bonds of their own fellowship, and their kinship is realized through a mutual discovery of the Bible's lessons about God and humanity.

THURSDAY-NIGHT BIBLE STUDY

First begun as a cell-group Bible study that was originally hosted in members' homes, the Thursday-night Bible study expanded to include a broader group of participants. Housed downstairs in the small fellowship hall that adjoins DBC's kitchen, the collegial atmosphere of the Thursday-night study attracted not only chapel members but also the spouses, siblings, and friends of chapel members, who came from a variety of non-Brethren Christian religious constituencies, including Pentecostal and Anglican fellowships.

The Thursday-evening Bible study is best characterized as an interactive seminar. The teacher served as an instructor, mapping out the lessons for each season and structuring each meeting with carefully planned discussions and PowerPoint presentations. The core group of ten regular attendees, who were middle-aged and older, established a great sense of rapport with one another. As a result, attendees were frank in their responses and disagreements, and comfortable posing questions that they would not ask in other contexts such as the

Tuesday-night Bible study. Participants engage in lively biblical debates. Even so, serious discussion was accompanied by smirks and peals of laughter after Sister Angela made one of her witty asides or Brother Graham posed one of the cheeky questions or critiques for which he was infamous. In addition to the free-flowing dialogue characteristic of the weekly meeting, the gender dynamic of Thursday-night studies varied from that of other church settings in that women were vital participants in the study context, posing tough questions, responding in kind, and making points on a par with their male counterparts.

Beyond such generalities about interactions, the following describes how the social process of Bible study unfolded in one particular case. In an April Bible study about "The Mystery of Melchizedek" (discussed in chapter 1), a brother and a sister opened the meeting in prayer. The teaching elder then initiated the study by asking for three volunteers to read Genesis 14:17–20, Psalm 110:4, and Hebrews 7:1–10. After the Scriptures were read, the elder who directed the study posed questions that fostered textual analysis, such as "What is the common element mentioned in both scriptural passages? What are the analogies connecting both texts?" Participants responded, noting all three texts' discussion of priesthood and the conceptual connections made between Christ and Melchizedek in the New Testament Scriptures. To fill in the lines of discussion, Andrews reminded members of previous lessons in which they had learned about Old and New Testament notions of priesthood. He also pointed to finer details in the selected Scripture passages, encouraging group members to notice other relevant information. He then invited more discussion by asking members, "So who is Melchizedek?"

A debate ensued. One camp of attendees argued that Melchizedek was a mysterious yet very mortal man. Another contingent held that Melchizedek was actually an Old Testament incarnation of God. Andrews posed trenchant questions that forced attendees to construct their argument and to use Scriptures to prove their claims, reminding them: "Don't just [have] an opinion. Be a Berean.[10] Look it up for yourselves!" After more than an hour of heated discussion, interspersed with jokes, muted rivalry, and even some passionate disagreement, the elder brought the discussion to a close. Although members had developed various interpretations of Melchizedek, some having even gone to great lengths prior to the evening's group meeting to conduct research, the Bible study teacher closed the study with the *right* answer: "Melchizedek is a human man with no genealogical record who serves as one of the many Old Testament antecedents of Christ. He is a man because the Bible does not state otherwise. He has no genealogical record, which is very uncommon in Old Testament narratives, because his sole purpose is to precede Christ."

Despite the open environment of the Thursday-night study group in terms of gender relationships and collegiality, the leader did not leave biblical meanings open-ended. Although all attendees took an active part in searching for and contemplating the solution to the interpretive puzzle afforded by Melchizedek (sometimes vehemently disagreeing in the process), the study ended with the revelation of the true, singular answer revealed by the pastor. Questions were answered, and alternative interpretations were dismissed. As the appointed teacher of this Bible study group, despite its conversational tone the teaching elder and his interpretation carry the weight of church authority. Thus, Thursday Bible studies concluded with a clear statement of the correct reading of the text in question. In these contexts, piety was still a process of each person's deep engagement with biblical meanings. Like most Bible studies, the Thursday-night meeting intersected the three vital elements of Brethren brotherhood: fellowship, democratic modes of Bible study, and the production of a consensus that knits people into the fabric of an interpretive reading community. Although the Thursday-night group was particularly close and inclusive, it nonetheless rearticulated the familiar pattern of authoritative male interlocution of Bible knowledge and social process found in other Bible study settings.

PRAYER-MEETING BIBLE STUDY

On Tuesday nights, DBC members gathered in the sanctuary for a weekly church-wide prayer meeting. After collecting prayer requests from attendees, an elder selected two to three brothers to pray over the concerns and good fortune that their fellow members had mentioned. The men then left the sanctuary to convene a separate prayer session downstairs while the women divided into smaller prayer groups to pray about more-intimate concerns. Bielo and Griffith remind us that as a collective act, prayer creates settings in which Christians share narratives of life experience and build intimacy (Bielo 2009; Griffith 1997). For DBC members, prayer was a common spiritual language of their community. It affirmed members' reliance on God as a father and divine provider. It also expressed empathy and concern in which praying persons stood in solidarity with those encountering difficulties or changing situations. But besides praying, meeting attendees also spent half of their time together studying the Bible. This regular occurrence of Bible study in a prayer program illustrates the centrality of the Bible in DBC community life. It also generates questions about the significance of Bible study for the creation of DBC brotherhood.

When the first half of the prayer-focused program was completed, the twenty or so regular attendees convened a Bible study session. Churchmen and churchwomen assembled in the sanctuary and arranged their chairs into a circle before beginning. Led by elders or more-senior brothers, some teachers used multiple Bible references to shed light on a biblical theme. Other brothers fostered a context that encouraged group discussion. The interactions in this Bible study within the prayer meeting were more formal than those of the Thursday-evening study. For example, members raised their hands to show they wanted to respond. Perhaps because of its location in the sacred space of the sanctuary, or the reassertion of gender lines established through the gendered prayer circles, or because of the presence of multiple elders, sisters were less vocal in this context than in the Thursday-night study setting, and the opinions and perspectives of brothers therefore predominated in this Bible study setting. With all heads bowed and eyes closed, a brother offered a brief prayer asking for God's blessing on their time spent taking "a closer look into the Word." After the group's "Amen," the teacher began by introducing the lesson's theme and by inviting another brother to read aloud a Scripture, thus transforming the passage from written text to spoken word. The teacher then proceeded with the key points of his study.

On one evening, a brother teaching the study may have enjoined members to compare Judas's and Peter's betrayals of Christ. On another Tuesday, the teacher may have crafted a lesson on how obeying biblical principles on marriage can foster improved communication between spouses. During a prayer meeting in June 2008, one elder took up the popular topic of evangelism. Using Matthew 28:16–20 to frame that evening's discussion, Brother Rookwood began the study by asking the members in his distinctive baritone voice, "What kinds of evangelism have *you* accomplished in Christ's name? How do we feel a part of the Great Commission to evangelize? Why is evangelism important?" Members contemplated the answers to such questions as they sat with their Bibles open on their laps. On the wall to the left of the study circle is one of the many banners that hangs in the sanctuary. Its declarative statement was particularly relevant to this study: "Go, or Send a Substitute."

Many of the open Bibles on members' laps were worn, had loose bindings, and included marked passages as badges of honor testifying to years of use. All the DBC members there were quite intentional about centering the Bible as the authoritative source of information on evangelism. One sister used New Testament references to outline examples of the Apostle Paul's missionary work throughout the Greco-Roman world as critical case studies for evangelism. However, other attendees employed the Bible not as a source of information but as an interpretive tool to unlock interior meanings of a particular passage.

For example, Brother Joseph read the Bible passage closely and encouraged attendees also to read the previous and succeeding verses to make sure that they understood the full meaning of the text. During another study, an elder examined the Scriptures in both a King James Version and a Greek translation, sharing the etymology of key words for attendees' benefit. By contextualizing Bible verses and locating central meanings, members were expressing their desire to discover the "real" meaning of the text rather than just answer the few questions that framed the study at the outset. Bible study discussions did not take place amid a wide field of interpretation. Rather, members (and brothers in particular) narrowed the range of interpretations on a particular topic and thereby brokered religious knowledge. Thus, the interpretation of the Bible was not the sole task of the teacher but was a shared labor undertaken by the group. It was this shared work of discussion that informed the central process of Bible study. The production of biblical meaning was like social glue that connected study participants as spiritual kin, and the gendered work of guiding interpretation connected churchmen as brothers. Brother Rookwood concluded the lesson with a simple rejoinder: evangelism "is not all about eternity" but is about ushering in God's kingdom on Earth. Different from the lengthy and decisive conclusions given by the pastor at the close of the Thursday-night Bible discussions, Rookwood could end the study succinctly because his co-elders and other brothers had already done the framing work.

In addition to generating biblical meaning, attendees also engaged the study context in other ways. Some proposed comments that connected the Bible study discussion to their own experiences. One brother endeavored to inspire study participants by describing how rewarding his missionary experiences in the Caribbean had been. A sister admonished members to think of the Great Commission (Jesus's final call to Christians to spread the gospel before his ascension, discussed in the Gospel of Matthew) in local terms by depicting how members should engage coworkers and neighbors in order to bring them to Christ. Such acts of applying biblical concepts to everyday life were concerned with creating a bridge between text and context associated with practices of entextualization. Some members were adept at introducing life narratives or everyday scenarios to help Bible stories and commands travel from the page to members' everyday realities.

According to Sister Brighton, women were particularly adept and concerned with relating the Bible to everyday life: "There are women who can speak just as well as those brothers and some even better. They've been studying the Word. They know the Word. They can deliver the Word. . . . They're able to bring things down to our [level]. We talk about current things and everyday things. Really common life issues not all up there."

Sister Brighton suggests that there are gendered languages of Bible study: men's language of biblical hermeneutics and women's grounded language of the everyday. Studies on conservative Christianity have likewise observed a dichotomy in male and female textual practices and spiritual concerns (Frederick 2003; Griffith 1997). Yet despite women's contributions to such discussions, in the context of church-wide programs it was primarily the language of interpretation voiced by DBC brothers that propelled Bible study discussions. Ironically, life experiences expressed via prayer or framed as a method of biblical application were of secondary importance even in prayer meetings. Instead, the collective and reciprocal act of biblical interpretation emerged as the main process that drove discussion and consensus as well as sociality. The "breaking of bread" emerges as a ritual site in which text and emblems that were key material markers of members' Christian religious identities were consumed. It also constituted a social event through which the democratic mores of brotherhood were ritually performed by churchmen.

Breaking Bread, Breaking Text: The Ritual Performance of DBC Brotherhood

As is often the case, Communion was associated with remembering Christ's resurrection and with ritually consuming bread and wine. As it is performed by DBC Brethren, Communion also emerged as a ritual in which the textual foundations and ideals of brotherhood in particular were performed. The DBC Brethren observed Communion every Sunday during the nine o'clock service. Although the service was interchangeably referred to as Communion and the "breaking of bread," the latter term evokes the biblical language of Acts, describing the ritual fellowship of New Testament believers.[11] In contrast to the monthly commemoration of Communion that is widespread in other Protestant communities, DBC Brethren "break bread" once a week. Consequently, many members understood the "breaking-of-bread" service to be a distinctive marker of Brethren identity. One sister explained the Brethren approach to Communion: "Brethren assemblies are very Word-centered . . . and so it was important to have the Word. And it didn't matter what Brethren church you went to you, you're gonna have the breaking-of-bread service every Sunday morning." A DBC brother confirmed her view: "The Brethren assemblies pay great attention to the Lord's Supper—the breaking of bread, which is a service in itself. For me, I find that it is the best in the world, what every Sunday the Pilgrim Holiness and Pentecostal church have as an add-on service usually the first Sunday in the month. . . . My once a week breaking of bread and meeting to commune sets me up for the next week."

The breaking-of-bread ritual was also distinctive because of the absence of musical instruments and because of the intermittent silences that punctuated the sharing of communal singing and biblical reflection. Combined, these forms of silence marked the breaking of bread as a distinctive and solemn ritual space.

An outline of a typical breaking-of-bread service follows. Every Sunday morning, members entered the modest suburban Georgia sanctuary and greeted their fellow members with silent nods and smiles. Most women were dressed in their common attire of skirts, blouses, and hats or small lace head coverings. Their male counterparts were outfitted in suits or dress slacks and shirts. Most attendees were middle-aged and senior assembly members. The service started promptly with silence. After some time had elapsed, a brother stood and recited the words from a hymn chorus. After calling out the hymn number, the attendees stood and responded by singing the appropriate song a capella. As the song filled the modest meeting room, members looked off into the distance, contemplating the meaning of the words, or tapped the pages of their hymnal, keeping time. After the final chorus, members sat down, and the previous silence resumed.

After another pause, another brother stood and made his way to the podium to share a biblical reflection. He named a passage and paused while attendees found the specified text. He then went on to describe the manner in which he had encountered the passage, whether during a family devotional time or during a cursory scan through his Bible. Creating a mini-sermonic text, the brother weaved his biblical reflections and personal experiences around a theme, this time the importance of obedience to God's commands. Next, a different brother read a biblical passage and offered a brief message on the importance of forgiveness. The members responded to his comments with nods, subdued "amens," and the service's quintessential silence. Another brother stood and offered a hymn that took up the theme initiated by the previous discussion. The following brother shared his interpretation of a Bible passage. He related his reflections to the previous texts, exegesis, or songs, in so doing contributing to the emerging theme of the morning. The cycle of song and biblical reflection separated by silent contemplation continued for about an hour.

To instigate a shift from the "breaking" of text to the breaking of bread, an elder then walked to the front of the sanctuary and stood behind the Communion table. He added his own insights to the theme crafted by his brothers' intersecting reflections on biblical texts. On some Sundays, such an elder might begin by reciting a Bible passage describing the Last Supper, in which Jesus shared bread and wine with his disciples on the eve of His crucifixion. On another occasion, he might remind those present that the bread and wine symbolized the body and blood of Jesus Christ and should be received sincerely and with clear hearts. Quoting 1 Corinthians 11:27–28, the elder warned believers that "whoever eats the bread and or drinks the cup of the Lord in an unworthy manner will be guilty of sinning against the body and the blood of the Lord. A man ought to examine himself before he eats of the bread and drinks of the cup" (NIV).

Instead of reciting from a liturgy, it was the Bible itself that provided the DBC Communion discourse. The elder then prayed over the bread and wine. After an "amen," four deacons (another class of male church-appointed leaders) moved to the front of the sanctuary. They folded back the tablecloth that covers the ritual table and took up the trays of bread and wine. They distributed the Communion elements to assembled members. As church members received, pulled, and tore a small piece of bread from the hard loaf (a type of bread popular in the Caribbean) and drank Manischewitz wine from individual plastic cups, they consumed their present-day incarnations of the unleavened bread and wine that their New Testament predecessors had consumed. As the platters of food circulated among the rows of seated people, some bowed their heads in silent praying. Others waited quietly for their portion. After all had been served, an elder concluded the breaking-of-bread ritual with church-related announcements, the greeting of visitors, and the sounds of fellowship that broke the previous silence as members greeted one another warmly and moved on to their Sunday School classes.

In participating in the Communion service, the brothers performed the egalitarian ideals of Brethren brotherhood. The breaking of bread constituted a ritual space open to only adult male perspectives. As a result, it served as a vital site at which fraternal egalitarianism was enacted and maintained. Although individual men shared individual meditations informed by personal Bible study, they also took care to relate their reflections to those previously offered by others. In doing so, they validated the exegesis of their brothers and authenticated brotherhood as a category of relatedness. Moreover, they created cohesion among ritual texts in the same way that literalist practices cohere biblical content. The breaking-of-bread service thus required brothers to share the labor of biblical exhortation. The exclusive presence of male voices and biblical perspectives made it a unique site from which to view the democratic contents of DBC brotherhood. Women's voices provided a responsive backdrop (of sorts) of singing and silence between textual reflections, but their insights did not propel the course of the service itself. During the breaking of bread, women provided the response to their brothers' calls. Although church sisters arranged the display of Communion foods on the table and could consume the ritual bread and wine, they did not distribute them to the assembled members or share their textual ruminations. Thus, women's restricted participation further illustrates the ritual's centering of brotherhood.

The breaking-of-bread service also revealed the textual foundations of DBC brotherhood. As a vernacular term used in the Caribbean, "breaking bread" here refers not simply to the literal breaking of eucharistic bread but to a dialogic speech event initiated by a small group around a particular topic or theme. The DBC brothers reenacted the "authentic" relatedness and collaboration of New Testament brotherhood through their textual communion and became the ancient brethren depicted in the biblical book of Acts. Through the breaking of bread, DBC brothers collapsed the distance and time between themselves and their biblical ancestors. At the same time, they substantiated fraternalism as a core religious value and the sacred significance of the Bible as a text through their shared ritual performance.

After these churchmen broke the "bread" of the Bible together, all attendees consumed the material bread and wine of Communion. Therefore, in addition to its particular relevance to brotherhood, Communion incorporated the DBC community as a whole. As anthropologist Gillian Feeley-Harnik (1981) concludes in her ethno-historical study of Christian Communion, ritual food sharing demarcates a community of belief and kinship. As attendees partook in Communion fellowship, they affirmed their identity as Christian believers and local assembly members by consuming the same bread and wine with their "brothers and sisters" in Christ. Although Protestant Communion is often oriented around symbolic foods that represent the blood and body of Christ, DBC members transform it into a site at which participants collectively consume the Bible as a text. The DBC Communion was thus a discursive communion between brothers that materialized as much through the fraternal sharing of the biblical text as through the church-wide sharing of bread. Similar to the social contexts of other church-wide Bible studies mentioned above, the breaking of bread served as a site for the production of church unity.

Nevertheless, as a special ritual context that compelled men to submit individual biblical insights to shared ideas and concerns, the breaking of bread uniquely integrated fraternal fellowship. Therefore, through the breaking of bread and through other church-wide Bible studies, DBC men textualized and performed brotherhood as a democratic form of association that incorporated male participants above all, but also the community at large.

Thus, there are many connections between DBC brotherhood and the Bible. For Flowers and the early members of the SGMA church network, brotherhood constituted a model for church and inter-church association as well as the formation of productive, incorporative, interpersonal relationships between church members locally and regionally. Yet, aside from its grounding of the religious order, DBC brotherhood most fully coalesced in church textual practices. Biblicism is an important avenue by which church-wide identity, consensus, and unity are produced. As illustrated in the opening vignette with Sister Trent and throughout the course of this chapter, the production of biblical knowledge is a significant gauge of community identification and belonging.

A close examination of the social interaction of church textual practices demonstrates the ways in which Bible study and Communion were sites where brothers emerged as authoritative brokers of biblical knowledge and conduits for brothers' democratic religious participation. Amid DBC members' authentication of fraternal and church relatedness through the Bible, external and internal hierarchies of race, ethnicity, gender, and class posed challenges for members' translation of biblical ideals of fraternal egalitarianism from the page into the contexts of everyday life. Yet through literalist and textual practices like the breaking of bread, DBC Brethren attempted to move beyond the boundaries established between past and present, word and thing, text and life, member and member, and brother and brother.

Finally, understanding the connections between DBC biblicism and brotherhood also generates important insights about DBC members' broader understandings of relatedness. Text emerges as a vital element of DBC spiritual kinship that materializes and authenticates their relatedness. Members' approaches to their sacred text as truthful and authoritative have implications for how their relatedness should be read and categorized. The study of DBC members' biblical literalism reveals that they inhabit a context in which their relatedness is more appropriately characterized as spiritual and textual, "sincere" if not "true," and performative rather than "fictive."

Chapter 5 turns to examine the everyday spiritual work and relatedness of DBC churchwomen. Patriarchal church leadership and evangelical valuations of biblical knowledge production generate gendered zones of spiritual kinship production that are differentially valued. Chapter 5 offers descriptions of the quotidian domestic communion authored by churchwomen, illustrates the ways in which their social labors integrate church and home and tighten belonging, and suggests that women's kinwork should be considered just as vital as men's for its generation of the face-to-face familial fellowship that Brethren evangelicals associate with New Testament Christianity.

Churchwomen and the Incorporation of Church and Home

5

More often than not, an institutional view of DBC relatedness foregrounds church brothers as the primary mediators of biblical knowledge and overseers of church affairs. However, this overlooks an important set of relationships and spiritual processes that reinforces church fellowships: those of DBC churchwomen. Moreover, exclusive attention to formal church programming also overlooks the myriad contributions that DBC women make to their community and to the production of relatedness. Although church doctrines and practices prevent churchwomen from holding official leadership positions, they offer their presence, time, and spiritual and material resources to the DBC community. They craft spiritual relationships in and across households, such as prayer partnerships and spiritual parenting ties, that infuse a sense of intimacy and familiarity into community sociality.

Although scholars of African American Christianity and evangelicalism might typically represent Afro-Caribbean and African American evangelical women in terms of their religious agency vis-à-vis their religious and familial roles (Singh 2015), my concern is with the qualities and contexts of churchwomen's everyday spiritual relationships and their impact on the community as a whole. Specifically, I contend that DBC women reproduce and tighten the preexisting bonds of the broader church community through quotidian domestic practices, such as hosting, feeding, and talking, as well as through the domestication of socioreligious practices of prayer and fellowship. By denoting this field of everyday relatedness as a sacrament, this chapter illustrates how DBC women's church and relational work generates many of the inter-institutional connections between church and family that shape Afro-diasporic evangelical religious life in substantial and characteristic ways. Rather than contemplating the breadth or circumscription of DBC women's religious agency, this chapter applies black feminist, theological, and historical conceptualization of black domesticity to their everyday spiritual work and communion—that is, to what bell hooks describes as "a sacrament of the everyday" (1990, 193). In particular, the chapter illuminates how this sacrament emerges through the ritualized use of mundane practices, materials, and spaces for the purposes of spiritual communion.

Gendered Spaces and Moralizations of Christian Womanhood

Like other evangelical groups, the gender ideologies espoused by DBC members uphold the necessity of "traditional" gendered roles of male governance and female support as well as the acceptance of derivative gendered spaces. As Low and Zúñiga define them, *gendered spaces* are "particular locales that cultures invest with gendered meanings, sites in which sex-differentiated practices occur, or settings that are used to inform identity and produce and reproduce asymmetrical gender relations of power and authority" (2003, 7). Within the religious setting of DBC, female spaces emerge as sites to which women are relegated as flawed, auxiliary, and submissive religious subjects. Whether it be women's secondary placement within a cosmological spiritual order or in the social institutions of the church and the family, DBC church teachings relegate women to spaces that are productive of social order. Nonetheless, because this section explores local moralizations of gender, space/place, and power, it also elaborates on how women conceptualize and construct their own placements within the church amid changing understandings of gender and women's changing relationship to the public sphere.

BAD FRUIT AND THE PROBLEM OF WOMEN'S PLACE

Like many other DBC beliefs, members appeal to the Bible as an authoritative source on women's social position. Perhaps the most foundational biblical narratives that inform gender relationships are those of the Fall in the Book of Genesis, in which Eve's transgressions are interpreted as being responsible for the advent of original sin. Over the course of a series of young adult Sunday Bible classes at DBC, I received the following account of Eve's temptation and the origins of female submission.

According to this account, prior to their Fall in the Garden of Eden, Adam and Eve had different roles but were arranged in a complementary rather than a hierarchical relationship. However, Eve upset this divine social system when she ate the fruit from the Tree of the Knowledge of Good and Evil, believing she "would be like God, knowing good and evil" (Genesis 3:4 NIV). Her desire to "be like God" ultimately reflected her disaffection with her assigned role as Adam's companion and her rebellion against the exclusive authority of God as Creator. In response to all that transpired, God meted out eternal damnation to Satan for deceiving Eve and punished Adam by making manual labor and death requisite for Adam and for all humanity. Eve and her female descendants were given the exclusive punishment of experiencing extreme pain in childbearing. God also instituted male leadership over Eve and her lineage with his pronouncement in Genesis 3:16 NIV: "Your desire will be for your husband, and he will rule over you." More than a narrative of the beginnings of sin, Eve's narrative disruption of a gendered cosmological order becomes an allegory for the morality of asymmetrical gender relations. In this account, male headship (or divinely mandated patriarchy) is perceived as a divine response to Eve's spiritual rebellion against an ordained set of social relations. All women (essentialized as Eve's descendants) are represented as requiring male authority and mandated to take on the appropriate posture of submission, and the problem of women's place—that is, contestations about women's placement within gendered relationships and social institutions—becomes a fundamental social concern of the Abrahamic faiths and human existence.

The biblical justification of women's subjugation as social and religious subjects extends to New Testament prescriptions for women's auxiliary placement in the Church, albeit with some modifications. The image of Eve's capitulation to Adam's authority is translated into women's deference to male religious perspectives. As a religious community that seeks to uphold New Testament church traditions, DBC Brethren practice exclusive male leadership. Most often, church members cite the injunction in the Pauline letters (letters believed—by Brethren—to have been authored by the Apostle Paul and that make up a good portion of New Testament Scriptures) against women's vocality in the church as justification for their leadership practices. A biblical passage commonly used in DBC settings to justify male church leadership is 1 Corinthians 14:34-35 NIV: "Women should remain silent in the churches. They are not allowed to speak, but must be in submission, as the law says. If they want to inquire about something, they should ask their own husbands at home; for it is disgraceful for a woman to speak in the church."

In such a text, churchwomen appear as muted, auxiliary church members. Submission or deference to male authority and religious knowledge appears as requisite for female community belonging. As discussed in chapter 4, institutionalized literalist interpretations present biblical content, such as the

Fall narrative and Pauline gender imperatives, not as the product of historical context but as a time-transcendent truth. Thus, biblical narratives about Eve as a female ancestor as well as about early churchwomen have important implications for DBC gender norms.

However, feminist theologians have criticized what they consider to be andocentric readings of the Bible and, in particular, Pauline doctrines, which foreground representations of female culpability and naturalize male authority. Dennis T. Olson, for instance, proposes an alternative reading of the Genesis Fall in which Adam is held accountable for not assisting Eve in her verbal exchange with the serpent (2006). Furthermore, Adam neglects his responsibilities as Eve's partner when he does not stand with Eve during her encounter with God and when he blames her rather than accepting his share of responsibility. In Olson's reading of the Fall, guilt is equally apportioned between Adam and Eve for disrupting the mutuality of their relationship and God's commands. New Testament theologians such as Amy Jill-Levine have long debated the erasure of women's contributions and place within early churches, noting their leadership and even their patronage of early apostolic work (2008). Such works call into question the gendered culpability and patristic focus of Brethren biblical readings and the patriarchal institutional practices they moralize.

Yet in the realm of church practice, DBC brothers are uniquely invested in their right to offer church-wide biblical exegesis while churchwomen occupy more restricted roles. Women are allowed to make church announcements and sing, but not to teach mixed-sex adult audiences; they are allowed to lead women's and youth organizations, but not church-wide ministries. The gendered conceptual apparatus established in Genesis and reiterated in the Pauline Scriptures heavily informs the social position of contemporary DBC churchwomen, who are seemingly positioned either as being rebellious daughters of Eve or silent, submissive religious participants. As might be expected, many DBC women cannot be cast as either dissident or conforming religious subjects. The following section raises important questions about women's perspectives on the existence and their habitation of gendered religious spaces.

SISTER REGINA: GENDERED CRITIQUES AND THE PRICE OF COMMUNITY

I spoke to Sister Regina Manchester only briefly at church two or three times over the course of my year at DBC. She was a petite woman with almond-colored skin and medium-length hair, and I found her to be personable during our infrequent and brief exchanges. Although I rarely spoke with her, I often heard her name mentioned during prayer meetings when the church collectively prayed for the recuperation of her husband after a severe bout with diabetes almost cost him his sight. To the great relief of all, he fully recovered over the course of several months. I was almost a week away from completing my fieldwork in December 2008 when I met Sister Manchester in her family's North Atlanta suburban home. Following my interview with her husband, Walter, Sister Manchester sat down for an interview with me. A middle-aged entrepreneur who migrated from Jamaica to the United States with her family and pursued her undergraduate and graduate degrees at northeastern universities, Sister Manchester confidently and candidly answered interview questions about her religious background, church commitments, and relationships. She used concise language, speaking with intention and making her points quickly. Throughout the course of the interview, her critical social insights were often tempered with gracious concessions and even laughter.

In many ways, Sister Manchester depicted herself as a moderate churchgoer, a regular attendee who occasionally participated in special church activities. Having grown up in a noncharismatic Church of God, which she likened to the Southern Baptist tradition, she joined DBC because of her husband's background in the Brethren tradition. In addition, she finds the "family atmosphere"—and the church's role as a religious and cultural socializing agent for her children—most appealing: "They nurture the children. That is the number one thing that I find very attractive about that church. The congregation embraces the kids, and I think they get a firm Bible-based upbringing there. . . . It [is a church that] embraces the Caribbean culture."

Although she spoke of the church primarily in positive tones, citing the oft-repeated praise of DBC's biblical emphasis, Sister Manchester's motivations for DBC membership seemed to emanate from her concerns for other family members rather than a personal preference for DBC church fellowship. I do not presume that an individualist (consumer) model of church selection should be the operative framework for understanding church membership or that Sister Manchester's family-oriented motives for participation are unique. In fact, as discussed in chapter 6, religious participation is often heavily shaped by family traditions and concerns.

Sister Manchester's lack of personal motivations for church membership partly resulted from the critical views she has of church social dynamics, in particular DBC gender politics. Sister Manchester especially took issue with the church's prohibition against women speaking or teaching in mixed-sex adult groups, women's practices of wearing small circular lace head coverings, as well as simplistic notions of female submission that do not fit women's lived realities. From her perspective, her vocal nature—set against the backdrop of mandated female silence—caused discomfort among other members. In some instances, Sister Manchester represented herself as an outsider of sorts, or at least qualified her insider status by noting she was "a little bit of the rebel" and had not "grown up Brethren." For her, another distinguishing feature was her "rational" investigative approach to religion and church practices, rather than an uncritical conformity to church protocols of behavior.

Despite the fact that Sister Manchester was at odds with some of the central, gendered aspects of church sociality and expressed some ambivalence about her church belonging, she willingly paid the price of community. She adhered to most community norms and was more than merely a Sunday-morning participant. Despite her work and family commitments, Sister Manchester mentioned her involvement with the youth ministry as well as her recent participation with the women's retreat: "Yeah, they ambushed me to [get involved]!!!! I was like, I'm gonna sit in the back, and nobody's going to notice me. I got there, and they said, 'You know you're [helping], right?' And I was like, 'What? Nobody told me!' 'Oh, sister so-and-so didn't call you?' I was like, 'No, she did not.' I said, 'OK, girl, you're gonna have to take this one.'"

As she concluded her story of her church service, Sister Manchester hinted that refusing another churchwoman's request was not an option. Whether her acquiescence resulted from her appreciation of women's gatherings (in which women did not exist as auxiliary religious subjects) or a felt sense of pressure to participate in some of the demands of community life, she agreed to take on a very public role without advance notice. At a moment when her rejection of such a responsibility would have been easier for her, Sister Manchester conceded to her church sister's request. Thus, her disapproval of church gender norms did not mean nonparticipation in church life. She even acknowledged her participation in everyday church networks when she mentioned her recent visit to a bereaved church sister as well as her participation in small informal home gatherings of church members during the week.

Throughout the interview, Sister Manchester oscillated between favorable and critical representations of the DBC community, initiating a cycle of positive responses and critical personal interjections. Taken together, Sister Manchester's depictions of her stance in and toward the DBC community uncover her complex religious placement. Her concession to the requirements of community belonging raises larger questions about churchwomen's negotiations of the patriarchal religious establishments as well as their status as religious subjects.

Sisterhood: Foregounding Experience and the Sacramentalization of Women's Work

The DBC women understood sisterhood as a category of relationship built upon their shared identity as Christian women and church members. But unlike church brotherhood, which served as an institutional title and a framework for church governance, sisterhood was not explicitly outlined in institutional doctrines or reified through Bible study or exegesis. Instead, sisterhood emerged as a form of relatedness anchored in rituals of nourishing and experience that fostered a sense of camaraderie among churchwomen. Church sisters, even when performing "traditional" women's work, produced their own valuable form of community by bringing vestiges of the home into the church and the church into the home.

THE SOCIAL PROCESS OF SISTERHOOD

During DBC women's gatherings, sisterhood is mediated by religious practices such as testimonies and prayer, in which churchwomen create and share experiential narratives. As discussed by a seasoned and active church participant, "If they were to ask who has a testimony and you were to stand up and give a testimony, then you could be female or whatever. You recall that most of the people who spoke [during the church-wide testimony service] were women." In the wake of church practices that constrain their abilities to make exegetical contributions, DBC women use testimonies as a means of sharing their personal experiences and voicing their spiritual discoveries. In the course of women's meetings, testimonies are a common occurrence. Different church sisters are invited or volunteer to share their life experiences with other churchwomen.

For instance, during an annual DBC women's retreat in 2008, Sister Briggs, a soft-spoken but faithful church attendee, began her testimony by saying that "I don't know what to say, but I will be honest and share what God has done for me and my family." She then delivered a narrative that gave numerous examples of God's provision in her life. She described the economic difficulties she and her four children had to navigate in Jamaica after her husband died unexpectedly. Whenever food supplies in the house dwindled to nothing, a neighbor would leave a parcel of groceries on her doorstep—with the exact items that she needed. After her family moved to New York City, her children were placed in good public schools in the same area in which they lived, and transportation was often provided by persons in her neighborhood. One year, a neighbor provided the exact amount of fabric she needed to sew her children's school uniforms. In another instance, neighbors donated their children's old schoolbooks so that her children had all the required course texts they needed. In the midst of her many economic difficulties, she confessed that she felt frustrated because her husband used to take care of household finances. Eventually, however, she had a conversation with God in which she said, "You are my provider now, and I'm gonna look to you to take care of all this like my husband." Sister Briggs's testimony followed a cycle of need and divine intervention, and culminated with the discovery that the loss of her husband would be tempered by a providing God. Though mentioned less often, Sister Briggs's narrative also spoke to her embeddedness in local community networks that helped her navigate economic insecurities. Rather than reciting a Bible story that would attest to the theme of God's generosity, Sister Briggs used her own life as a script to speak about the nature of God and God's provision of community. She, and other church sisters like her, use their lives as the basis from which to teach and to speak to their sisters and fellow church members. Thus, through their use of testimonies, DBC women access the form of speech and authority available to them.

Lived experience is also a site of authority, particularly for longtime church members. The perspectives of senior church sisters are often heard and heeded by all church members. In some instances, women can intentionally access the age-based authority that they feel is their due. For instance, at a women's prayer breakfast organized to welcome new members, a new church member referred to an elderly churchwoman as "Sister Warren." She was quickly corrected: "It's Aunt Warren. I approached the throne of grace and was saved before you were even born." She responded by graciously agreeing to address the older woman in the way she preferred. Shortly after the incident, the younger woman sat at our table and confessed to her neighbor that she had never used that term "Aunt" as a title for older women during her previous Brethren church experiences. Shortly after this misstep occurred, I asked Sister Harris, another churchwoman, who was seated across from me, how I should address other churchwomen. She responded that pairing the term "Sister" with a woman's last name should work, but that I should not worry: "Trust me, they will correct you if you're wrong." On another occasion, a senior Jamaican churchwoman introduced herself to me as Tía Anglin. She told me that the church addressed her as "Tía" (the Spanish term for "Aunt") because she had spent time living in Cuba and was fluent in Spanish. However, it stands to reason that the designation of "Tía" came from her status as a senior church member, and Tía Anglin confidently accepted the title as her due. Therefore, the perspectives of experienced persons are valued, legitimated, and, at times, discursively marked.

This focus on experience is also visible in church sisters' prayer practices. Quite frequently, a praying person recounts individual experiences to fellow religious participants in order to receive divine assistance. Prayers, like testimony, often consist of experiential narratives (Ochs and Capps 2001). A women's prayer service provides a clear example of how central experiential narratives are to the social process of sisterhood. On a rainy Friday evening in December 2008, I was among a small group of church sisters who gathered in the finished basement of Sister Johnson's home. Over the course of the evening, we shared prayer requests, gave personal testimonies, sang a few hymns, and prayed extensively. Sisters brought numerous issues before God and their sisters through the collective language of prayer, issues such as the failing economy, children finding their way, health problems, and friends facing difficult times. Altogether, the prayer service lasted more than five hours, until after 1:00 a.m. Even after the meeting itself ended, the women stayed to eat the refreshments provided by Sister Johnson: zucchini bread prepared by her son George, escovitch fish cooked by Sister Marshall, chips and salsa, and an assortment of other vegetable trays, desserts, and beverages. Even after the long prayer session, the church sisters appeared to revel in the fellowship with one another. New convert and member Sister Claudia Phillips described her ongoing preference for younger men while Sister Johnson gently countered that God can change our tastes. Sister Robbins sucked her teeth and, wearing her signature smirk, stopped the exchange with her characteristic wit, which as usual prompted the women's laughter. The night ended with more talk and humorous exchanges.

Establishing familiarity, confiding in one another, and sharing the labor of divine supplication are central to the social processes by which sisterhood is constituted. Much more than a spiritual discipline, prayer emerges as a portal to sisters' lives, a ritualized invitation into pressing personal problems and concerns. Although the moralized mandates of respectability typically contribute to members' suppression of personal and familial problems, sisters' prayer and testimonial practices can break such silences by creating therapeutic ritual spaces that allow women to voice their past and present insecurities and struggles (Griffith 2000).

THE SOLIDARITIES OF SISTERHOOD

Aside from outlining sisterhood as a form of relatedness produced through experiential narratives and authority, it is important to understand the type of solidarity mediated by DBC sisterhood. *Sisterhood* is typically defined as a genealogical category associated with shared parentage and childhood coresidence.

However, a variety of different collectives have employed the term to envision group relatedness. Feminists have employed sisterhood as a model of women's community. First-wave feminists have imagined sisterhood as a discourse that would garner mutual appreciation and respect between women. It was ideally constructed as inclusive and egalitarian. Even so, the construct of feminist sisterhood has been critiqued by blacks, Latinas, and feminists in the global South for making invisible the power dynamics that cut across the ranks of the international women's community. Maria C. Lugones and Pat Alake Rosezelle conclude that feminist sisterhood was and continues to be burdensome to women of color who, under the guise of egalitarianism, are enjoined to accept the inequalities perpetrated by white feminists (1995). Consequently, they propose that friendship better recognizes the plurality of women's experiences because it is not grounded in preexisting institutional components or rules. Furthermore, friendship does not assume unconditional bonding, and it is sufficiently individualized to take notice of particularities produced by ethnoracial, national, class, and sexual differences. If, like Lugones and Rosezelle (1995), we assume that friendship is a relationship most suitable for plural contexts, we are able to see how micro-interactions between DBC church sisters are built upon the ground of common experiences. Some church sisters build relationships with one another that move the church into the realm of everyday experience and that transcend ties of provenance. Those church sisters become more than religious co-participants who engage in rituals that foreground experiential texts. They use sisterhood as a spiritualized basis on which to build friendship and more intense forms of camaraderie.

Sister Washington, an African American church member, fondly describes the close bonds she has developed over the years with several Afro-Caribbean churchwomen such as Sister Sanderson. For her, it was their mutual joys and struggles of being mothers in large families with four or more children that brought them together as friends. They shared practical advice about mothering and even kept an eye on one another's children in church. At times, they provided child care for one another's children outside of church. Sister Washington's connection with Afro-Caribbean church sisters was therefore predominantly an outcome of common familial experiences. Thus, DBC church sisters considered family relationships and identifications to be common ground on which women's sociality can be built. As Hazel Carby argues in her theories of black feminism, black women's sisterhood emerges as somewhat different from mainstream feminist sisterhood (1997). Rather than conceptualize the family as a site of oppression, Carby observes that black women's mutual locations in kinship and friendship networks afford them key sources of survival and empowerment. In a similar manner, the sisterhood produced by DBC women does not necessarily critique women's family moorings. Rather, DBC sisters help one another negotiate familial obligations and dynamics. Church sisters advise one another on how to maintain their marriages and how to raise their children in the midst of the problems and questions that inevitably arise. Like their black feminist counterparts, DBC sisters organize themselves into multiethnic and multinational friendships that emanate from women-focused concerns, particularly those grounded in the family.

THE ENDS OF SISTERHOOD

As illustrated above, sisterhood provides a channel for women to enjoy fellowship and friendship through their ritualistic and everyday sharing of experiences, history, and practical information. More broadly, sisterhood also galvanizes women's labor on behalf of the church and church members. Women's contributions to church-wide events—such as anniversary celebrations, revivals, summer youth Bible camps, weddings, funerals, and holidays—are vital. Often the women contribute Afro-Caribbean and US-style food. Tucked away within the enclosed modern kitchen situated within the large meeting hall of the Family Center, church sisters can often be found preparing a variety of culturally distinct cuisines. At special church anniversary and missionary banquets that host members and invited guests, DBC churchwomen provide restaurant-quality cuisine, such as marinated fish, rice, roasted vegetables, green salads, and pies and cakes—all neatly arranged in an evening buffet. For church-wide occasions, such as the annual Christmas dinner, churchwomen prepare special Afro-Caribbean foods, such as stewed chicken, rice and peas, raw vegetable salads, and cold drinks. For more informal events, such as Vacation Bible School dinners for youths or day events requiring lunches, common fare includes hot dogs, sandwiches with luncheon meats, and chips, often accompanied by lemonade or fruit punches.

Examination of DBC sisters' practices of nourishing others illustrates not the circumscription of themselves to the domestic domain but their position as vital makers of community. According to Afro-Caribbean theologian Lorraine Dixon, Afro-Caribbean churchwomen's practices of cooking as a mode of communal care represent a specific ethos of "open pot spirituality" (2007, 76). Describing the cooking done by her mother and other churchwomen, she continues:

> Chicken with "Rice and Peas" (rice with kidney beans or gunga peas) was a sacrament in these circumstances enabling those who feasted on it a

taste of the Divine through earthly substance. Jamaicans know this dish as soul food and indeed it was, for human spirits as well as bellies were fed until they were full ("till them ready fe bus!"). . . . My mother [had] a commitment to others, generosity, and a passionate spirituality which informed her sense of right and responsibility to the community. From the table to the community, Black women like my mother have always held (and continue to do so) a central place in the support, protection, and advocacy of the Black community. (Dixon 2007, 77)

Dixon's description of the centrality of Afro-Caribbean women's work to maintain the vitality of their church communities very much resonates with the DBC sisters' offerings to the chapel assembly. Despite the fact that performing the work of cooking reinforces a gendered division of labor and an image of female domesticity, Dixon reminds us that Caribbean women's church work is informed by their own spiritual convictions that hospitality should be an indispensable feature of church life. In other words, rather than interpreting women's church work solely as a concession to patriarchal gender politics, she encourages us to examine women's motivations for nourishing others, as well as the broader impact of their church contributions. These women's offerings of food to the church also tie together church and home spaces, what Dixon calls going from the "table to the community" (2007, 77). Church sisters prepare home-style food in both church kitchens and domestic spaces, and thereby create the intimacy and familiarity of religious community.

In chapter 4 I outlined the ways in which DBC brotherhood is produced via textual rituals. Presided over by church brothers, DBC Communion becomes a literal and figurative breaking of bread. Bread and wine are blessed, distributed, and consumed by religious participants while brothers share and relate their biblical insights. Sisters provide full meals and share personal experiences with one another and the community as a whole. Familiarity, intimacy, and home infuse their religious rituals and commensality while tradition, knowledge, and ideology inform the ritual praxis of their brothers. In both instances, sisters and brothers materialize their spiritual relatedness (an immaterial relationship) as children in Christ through rituals using food as well as (female) experiential texts and (male) biblical texts. Both Communion and churchwomen's feeding allow for the corporealization of community. However, while brothers' ritual work contributes to the *institutionalization* of the DBC community, sisters' work contributes to the *incorporation* of DBC members as an everyday, familial community that shares common religious and cultural ground.

Scripture, which is understood as the divinely inspired word of God, is legitimated as the dominant way of knowing. Experience, as a mundane ground for acquiring spiritual knowledge, is valued less within the church community as a whole. The ability to learn from everyday life and to process spiritual revelations from the uncharted path of everyday life requires a skill set similar to biblical exegesis. Phenomenological research has concluded that in some Christian traditions such as Pentecostalism, it is spiritual revelation and a person's unique experience with the divine that are centered and given credence (Austin-Broos 1997; Engelke 2007). For the evangelicals at DBC, it is the materiality of text—its possession of physical qualities as well as the fixed meanings brought about by local literalist practices—that is believed to be verifiable and collectively understood and that gives it asymmetrical value. On the other hand, the transient qualities of personal experience as something that is seemingly subjective, singular, and unverifiable makes it a secondary pathway to spiritual truth.

Thus, if we apply Dixon's characterization of Afro-Caribbean churchwomen's food as a "sacrament," we are able to move beyond the analytical impasse that comes from internal and intellectual asymmetries that value the text over the experience, the religious over the mundane, and institutions over everyday sociality that would contribute to the under-theorization of DBC women's church work. Furthermore, we are able to reevaluate the problem of women's place, their habitation of female spaces, and the scope and significance of their church contributions (Dixon 2007, 77). Their work of feeding, then, becomes a central and institutionalized feature of church life. Although DBC members do not identify the everyday work of women as a sacrament, they do consider the everyday connections between religious practitioners to be vital to the Christian lifestyle. Referred to in vernacular terms as "walking together," this quotidian fellowship is idealized as the type of everyday closeness experienced by early Christians, whose sociality was not only limited to formal meetings but was also a fixture of participants' everyday lives.

It was this form of close collective piety that early Plymouth Brethren sought to re-create in their religious movement as a counterpoint to the institutional rigidity of mainline Protestantism (Callahan 1996). Despite the lack of an official church discourse to categorize this widely practiced feature of Brethrenism, the significance of everyday sociality is not diminished. If DBC sisters' domestic labors and their everyday spirituality are reconsidered to be sacraments, then regardless of church gender politics and ideological traditions, the belonging they broker is an indispensable and foundational part of church community life. As administrators of this sacrament, churchwomen are transformed from religious subjects into religious agents who preside over traditions that have fed, and continue to feed, black evangelical socioreligious worlds.

DBC Women and the Cultivation of Community

Understanding the spiritual relatedness and social contributions of DBC women requires an investigation not only of their articulation with the DBC church community but also of their lived religious experiences. In so doing, the recognition that DBC sisters bring material and symbolic elements of the home into the church is compounded by their insertion of church and Brethren religiosity into home and quotidian life. The domestic locations and spaces of DBC women and the means by which they employ those spaces on behalf of the broader church community illustrate the interstitial placement of DBC women and the everyday spiritual sociality of the DBC community.

REMEMBRANCES OF SISTER ELLA: IDEALIZATIONS AND REVELATIONS

For DBC members, Sister Ella Flowers epitomized this Christian and southern hospitality. The deceased wife of T. Michael Flowers (who preceded him in death), mother to their two children, and grandmother to their many grandchildren, "Sister Ella," as she was and is still known, lives on in the memories of the DBC community. Memorialized and idealized for her many contributions to individuals, families, and the church writ large, narratives about Sister Ella reflect not only scenes from her life but shared community values about womanhood as well.

I was first introduced to the legacy of Sister Ella in a conversation with Brother Grainger over the course of our lunch at a Piccadilly Cafeteria in DeKalb County. Grainger, a DBC member of Afro-Caribbean origins, recounts how he was in the military and stationed in Georgia during the 1960s. As a young black man transplanted to a racist South, Grainger struggled to find a place in his new social world. To him, the Flowers were instrumental in providing him with both a sense of direction and belonging: "At that time there were not a lot of West Indians in the South, and I struggled with how poorly black people were being treated." Grainger fondly recounted his weekend rides from his military base to the Flowers' Savannah home and their conversations about God, religion, and his future. He also warmly remembered Sister Ella's kind welcome of him. Despite the presence of the Flowers children and other evangelists and their family members who frequently visited their home, Grainger noted that Sister Flowers always made sure that he had a place to sleep and warm meals to eat.

Other stories of how nurturing Ella Flowers was have even been institutionalized by the church community and performed by individual church members. On the Sunday afternoon of April 27, 2008, the church gathered in the Family Life Community Center to commemorate the opening of Ella's Caring Hands Day Center, an activity center for elderly adults that commemorates Ella Flowers's legacy of care and raises awareness about the practical needs of seniors coping with Alzheimer's disease "who are unable to take care of themselves at home alone while their family members are away" (program brochure). During the opening ceremony, a cofounder of the Day Center and the former prayer partner of Sister Flowers publicly spoke of Sister Ella's community involvement as well as her contributions to her own development as a Christian. In private, Sister Brenda Halliwell connected herself to Sister Flowers's legacy through her own deeds. On Tuesday nights after the church prayer service, I witnessed Sister Halliwell clandestinely give Brother T. Michael Flowers home-cooked food to take away. As I witnessed their regular exchange of meals—plated on Styrofoam dishes, covered with aluminum foil, and transported via plastic bags—as well as the usual pleasantries, I thought of the ways in which Sister Halliwell's support of Brother Flowers recalled her relationship to Sister Ella, as well as the actual community work performed by Sister Ella during her lifetime.

Sister Wanda Hutchins, the other cofounder of Ella's Caring Hands Day Center, also fondly recounted her relationship with Sister Ella during an interview: she "was just like my mom. I felt honored that they wanted to leave her with me [to take care of her after she became sick]." Sister Hutchins provides an even more explicit picture of the care network established by her and Sister Flowers, in which each extended and received care. The motifs of Grainger's story about Ella Flowers—open doors, home-cooked food, and the frequent entertaining of visitors—are reiterated in many members' recollections of Sister Ella. Of course, the preeminence of Sister Ella in the collective memory of DBC members is partly the result of the significance of the Flowers family to the evangelical social network of which DBC and CBC are a part and the idealizations that all too often accompany memory. Nonetheless, the celebrated images of Ella Flowers's openness and domesticity point to a gendered model of community building in which churchmen provide ideological oversight (Grainger's recollections of Brother Flowers's mentorship of him in ministry work) and churchwomen make members feel at home (Grainger's recollections of Sister Flowers's hospitality). Sister Ella emerges as an archetype of

Christian womanhood that continues to be highly respected and considered worthy of emulation.

However, it was through the memories of her husband, T. Michael Flowers, that I received the most intimate and complex portraits of Sister Ella. As we sat in his home during our weekly Wednesday-afternoon Bible studies, I saw vestiges of Sister Ella's presence. Although Flowers's daughter lived with him, the house still appeared to reflect the homemaking sensibilities of Sister Flowers. Across from the kitchen table where we normally conducted our Bible studies hung a corkboard pegged with pictures of missionary families for whom she prayed regularly. A small workroom two doors down from the kitchen was oriented around a desk covered with tidily arranged papers with a covered green typewriter that had not been touched for years and a bookcase with Bible-related books. On the other side of the kitchen was a living room with velvet chairs and a couch and dark-colored carpet that appeared to come from another time. In that room a display of framed family photographs of three generations of Flowers sat on multiple end tables. Perhaps the most recent picture of the family depicted Sister Ella, an elderly, petite African American woman with tidily curled gray hair and glasses, positioned next to pictures of her family members.

Able to connect her face with her name, I listened to Pastor Flowers reminisce about his wife. Over the course of ten months, I learned from him about Sister Flowers's Georgia roots, about how they first met while he worked at Cedine Bible Camp in Tennessee, as well as about their courtship and marriage—interspersed with his evangelical work in the Caribbean, Canada, and the northern United States. He admiringly described Ella's support of his decision to undertake church work in Georgia despite the objections of a member of her family that the South was an unsafe place in which to build a home, a family, or a church. Even as he described her hospitality and kindness, Flowers described some of the lessons she had taught him. As he tried to build his new ministry in the South, financial concerns inevitably resulted. Raised with more conventional understandings of gender roles, Flowers insisted that he combine his full-time ministry work with part-time carpentry work. However, Sister Ella objected and insisted that they could live off her full-time teacher's salary while his ministry work developed. Flowers's endearing recounting of his wife's life and ministry reflected the place she held in his life and his memory. Yet his depictions of his wife also contain traces of a later, newfound, complex appreciation gained through years of contemplating her legacy following her death.

In many ways it was images of her service and her open home that were publicly celebrated while it was her subversion of her family's warnings and traditional gender notions that won Ella her husband's respect. T. Michael Flowers's remembrances appear to break Sister Flowers out of gendered strictures, even as the church community's celebration of her domestic offerings reinscribes images of female domesticity. To connect the legacy of Sister Flowers to the contemporary contributions of DBC women, I employ bell hooks's concept of "homeplace." This also helps me think through the qualities and politics of the social spaces brokered by DBC women in and beyond their homes. Through that line of thinking, Afro-Caribbean and African American women at DBC emerge as institutional agents who make connections between homes and communities and who work within and beyond traditional gender norms.

DBC Women as Community Agents: Productions of Homeplaces and Yardspaces

bell hooks offers an interior view of African American home and community life through her concept of "homeplace." According to hooks, homeplaces are the domestic households that African American women build as

> spaces of care and nurturance in the face of the harsh reality of racist oppression . . . where all black people could strive to be subjects, not objects, where we could be affirmed in our minds and hearts despite poverty, hardship, and deprivation, where we could restore to ourselves the dignity denied us on the outside in the public world. This task of making homeplace was not simply a matter of black women providing service; it was about the construction of a safe place where black people could affirm one another and by so doing heal many of the wounds inflicted by racist domination. (1990, 42)

hooks's outlook on black women's domesticity sidesteps explanations that frame black women's domestic labor as the product of naturalized gender differences. Furthermore, her emphasis on the type of social space cultivated by black women also evades mischaracterizations of black women's relationship to the household as a pathological, emasculating matriarchy. Rather than trying to restrict black domestic spaces and women's relationship to those spaces, hooks concerns herself with the internal textures of black home life. She primarily depicts black homeplaces as spaces of care and nurturance presided over by African American women, not as an outgrowth of their social location as women but out of their commitment to producing recuperative spaces for their community.

To be sure, the homeplaces of DBC women experienced their provision of material and spiritual resources to family and community members as well as how they strengthened kin relations among themselves and the broader church community. As stories of Sister Ella illustrate, DBC community members' experiences of home care were often sensory occasions seasoned by the food that the women prepared. Initially, it was a Jamaican non–church member living in the Atlanta area who explained to me this connection between home and food sharing. When I asked her how she defined *family*, Ann Marume responded that "family and home was where you can get your rice and peas; where you can visit without calling first." For Marume as well as DBC members, opening up one's home for visiting and sharing meals is an important way in which Afro-Caribbeans order belonging. It follows, then, that noting who eats and cooks with one another is a useful way of gauging which persons and spaces are engaged in creating relatedness. Women and kitchens emerged as central fixtures in the production of homeplace and community. By creating and embodying shared substances in the kitchen, Afro-Caribbean and African American churchwomen occupied important social and spatial locations for kin-making.

In her discussion of Caribbean women writers and migration, Meredith Gadsby also points to kitchens as important sites for Afro-Caribbean women's "kitchen talk," in which women foster their relationships with one another through "the ordinary speech of the kitchen space ... to talk politics, swap advice and gossip, and share hopes and dreams for the future" (2006, 143). In homeplaces and kitchen spaces, women make food—the material substance of kinship—even as they coproduce the immaterial dialogue of shared intimacy. Kitchens, then, become sites for making kinship and community, everyday talk and women's speech, and, more broadly, the construction of religious subjectivity.[1]

Connected to the domestic spatial analysis evoked by hooks's concept of homeplace and Gadsby's outlines of kitchen space are Afro-Caribbean understandings of the "yard" as a site for family and community meeting. Within Caribbean contexts, yards are the spaces between homes shared by local neighbors. They are typically fenced in and distinguished from public streets. As common spaces, yards are inter-household contexts in which family and community ties are incorporated as members gather and witness the ebb and flow of everyday life. With the familiarity fostered by the sharing of space and experiences come the collaboration and even the conflict that punctuate persons' cohabitation in shared social worlds. In yardspaces, community members convene to chat; to exchange pleasantries, gossip, and quips; to hang out; to borrow things from one another; to study the Bible; and more (Austin-Broos 1997; Chevannes 1997; Korom 2003). Yards are interstitial spaces in which communal collectivism and identifications are produced and seasoned. Essentially, they are junctures at which family, extended family, and community relations figuratively and literally meet. Not to be confused with the entertaining visits of bourgeois domesticity, the production of yardspaces is less about the performance of family status and respectable womanhood and more about the enjoyment of everyday sociality.

At first glance, the urban sprawl of the Atlanta metropolitan area makes the intimacy and spatial proximity of Caribbean yards appear a distant memory. Moreover, Atlantan suburban arrangements of domiciles as separate units surrounded by private lawns and demarcated by gated areas evoke the very opposite of the inter-household intersections that organize Caribbean yards. As a group, DBC members live in a variety of counties within and around Atlanta. Although these local residential ties are different from those found in Caribbean yards, they illustrate how local residential connections can contribute to the production of church relatedness despite the decentralized nature of Atlanta. Church cell groups and informal enclaves of members form proximal and neighborly ties with one another. Groups of church members who live in the same or neighboring housing developments in the Decatur and Stone Mountain areas, for instance, not only stop by for informal visits but also gather to socialize.

One Friday night I attended one these informal gatherings of church members hosted by the Marshalls—a middle-aged Jamaican couple who were relatively new to the DBC community. As I entered their modest, well-furnished suburban home, the smell of goat stew cooked by Sister Marshall mingled with the sound of Caribbean gospel playing in the kitchen. Occasionally, loud jokes and protests uttered by DBC men playing dominos in the basement game room made their way up the stairs. As I was explicitly invited by Brother Marshall "to keep Sister Marshall company," I made myself comfortable in the kitchen area talking with her while she finished her stew. Although she and her husband were relatively new to the faith, I learned that they frequently hosted such gatherings. Over time, I gleaned that Sister Francine Marshall and her husband, Delroy, had garnered a reputation among the church community for their hospitality and open home, and throughout my time in Georgia I experienced this hospitality many times as their "spiritual child."[2] During the course of the Marshalls' Friday-night gatherings, the recuperative offerings of *homeplace* and the familiarity of the *yard* converged. The desire for everyday connection and the enjoyment of community embeddedness were both experienced there. The Marshalls engineered a space in which church members—as part of a diasporic community (once and even twice removed from Caribbean homelands or US places of origin)—could experience home. Over the course of that night, home smells, tastes, sounds, language, and play converged. Rather than remaining a faraway location, they not only invoked home but also transformed it into a sensory experience. More than a religious affair, fellowship was an expression of common identification; more than an obligation, it was a pleasure: not just church praxis endorsed by precedent, but a shared desire for a return home experienced by a familial community. In unpacking the conceptual space of home with which DBC women such as Sister Marshall are closely associated, the material elements, the sensory and symbolic space of home, converge.

Another female church member described her regular social interactions with church members in similar terms: "We socialize, like sometimes you get together and play games, or we take trips together, like we take trips together down to Destin [Florida] once a year. Sometimes we go to get-togethers at each other's house." Her brief description of "get-togethers" and "games" evokes the levity of community life even as her mention of trips suggests that DBC members re-create the ethos, if not the spatial order, of the yard through informal and frequent domestic gatherings and trips. If the old adage often paraphrased by DBC members stands that the church is not the building but the people, perhaps a related insight should also be considered: that the yard is not just a space; it is a nexus for neighborly kinship. Moreover, members' investments in experiencing re-creations of homeplaces and the yard—despite the spatial and socioeconomic restraints that conspire to channel resources into household family units—can no doubt be traced to the diasporic experiences shaping some members' aspirations for and investments in community.

As we came to know each other better through our own kitchen table talk, Sister Marshall and I often discussed the difficulties of performing expected everyday domestic work like cooking while working. Even amid her critique of gender roles that typically attributed domestic work almost exclusively to women, she often described how much she enjoyed having large gatherings of church members over and how pleased she was that people enjoyed her cooking and the time spent in her home. Sister Marshall's domestic work on behalf of community members does not arise from her tacit acceptance of hegemonic community—her status as a church member and accompanying sense of requisite service—but from her own enjoyment of having an open home. Yet the work of Sister Francine and the late Sister Ella Flowers illustrates their unique articulations of gender ideals and domesticity and their contributions as women who built needed spaces for community gathering despite its personal costs and devaluation in the midst of sexist socioreligious structures that tend to privilege male contributions. The rituals of feeding, talking, and creating spaces for extra-institutional spiritual communion do not only have the effect of reinforcing DBC church membership. In contexts mediated by prayer partnership, churchwomen engaged in close spiritual relationships in which they fostered one another's faith.

DBC Women and Everyday Relatedness: Prayer Partnership

Differing from church sisterhood, prayer partnerships are more nuclear forms of interpersonal relationships formed by DBC women outside of church contexts. Specifically, prayer partnership is a form of relatedness intentionally formed by churchwomen in which a pair or small circle of women regularly meet to talk and pray about everyday occurrences, concerns, and crises. Like other forms of spiritual kinship formed among DBC women, prayer partners establish a unique, intimate line of spiritual relatedness born out of their common spiritual work and sharing of ritual experience. Because of their frequent meetings and location in domestic contexts, prayer partners especially reveal how "everydayness" is an important facet of spiritual relatedness. Moreover, an exploration of how prayer partners bring church relationships and practices into the home illustrates the ways in which DBC churchwomen drafted elements of church culture into the service of everyday concerns.

THE SOCIAL PROCESS OF PRAYER PARTNERSHIP

> Well, you know ... I have two people, two women in the church, Sister Wanda and Sister Gertrude, that I'm really close to. And I call them my prayer people. And we pray; we have sort of this little group. If we hear something, then I would call one, and we'd call the other one, and we'd pray, and we keep praying. They are the people that I talk to most on like a personal level. [As] prayer partners, we [interact] on a daily basis. That's a daily thing. They will call and see what's happening, or we will chat, and so, you know, I call them my lifeline. I have them and my sister-in-law. They're the three.

As Sister Lola Trent—a Trinidadian woman in her early sixties—outlines, the social process of prayer partnership involves daily (or frequent) talk and prayer. A typical meeting between prayer partners involves two or three women calling one another by phone at a regular time. In some instances, neighboring church sisters visit each other's homes regularly for face-to-face prayer. Prayer partners might begin their prayer session with greetings and light banter. Or they might begin their session with brief overtures, taking prayer requests, and sharing news of any answered prayers. As one partner speaks, the other partners listen in silence or quietly write the requests on prayer cards or other paraphernalia. Illnesses, family concerns, friendships, occupational concerns, spiritual struggles, and current church issues are some of the substance of partners' apprehensions. Prayer partners then pray for one another, recalling the requests by memory or using written materials as a script to guide their supplications. After all the partners have prayed for one another and uttered their "amens," prayer partners close the meeting with more chatting. Thus, the ritual cycle of prayer partnership begins with everyday talk, centers on the sharing of requests and prayer, and closes with more mundane talk. The everyday speech—the talking for talking's sake—establishes and maintains the affinity between partners. Good-natured fellowship cements the foundation of the relationship and allows more personal matters to be shared.

In contrast to the secular character of everyday talk, prayer is intentional speech; it is motivated and directed language guided by shared conventions such as supplication, confession, divine adoration, and thanksgiving. As previously mentioned, prayer often involves the exchange of experiential narratives—of personal problems, victories, and general happenings. Thus, for this as well as other reasons, the prayers undertaken reflect the experiences of the prayer partners. However, prayer partnership exhibits other important dimensions of prayer. More than a language of experience, prayer is a language of asking and gratitude, of empathy and support. In his ethnography of group Bible study, Bielo focuses on the social dimensions of prayer by denoting it as a language of intimacy (2009). As partners approach God in prayer, they reconcile themselves as limited, religious subjects. Through prayer, they ritualize their vulnerability and build an intensive fellowship through everyday confiding. Therefore, prayer is an inherently social act; it is open-ended discourse capable of brokering an intensive form of fellowship, and its ritualization involves straddling sacred and profane talk and realms.

Also shaping prayer partnerships are the qualities of the spaces in which women meet as well as the spaces they create. Whether their dialogues took place in the physical spaces of sisters' homes or in the spaces between phone lines, prayer partnerships were enshrined in and across domestic settings. Face-to-face interactions and phone conversations drew lines of connections between prayer partners and their households. Domestic spaces constituted important spaces of refuge for Afro-diasporic people as well as privileged sites of Brethren spirituality.

However, if the paternalistic nature of church history prevents comparison of DBC women to church founders, the in-home meetings between prayer partners can be easily considered a spiritual form of the kitchen table talk depicted by Caribbean women writers (Gadsby 2006). Because prayer partnerships were frequently incorporated across households through phone conversations, they also constituted a virtual and religious yardspace.

In their study of Jamaican cell phone usage, Horst and Miller noted that Jamaican women commonly used cell phones to communicate with close, local neighbors while they performed domestic duties (2006). For Jamaican and other Caribbean transnationals, phone communication has long integrated households across great geographic distances.

Whether prayer partnerships tie households together across nation-states or across town, they create unique ritual spaces in which multiple individual and household concerns are brought together, discussed, and prayed over daily. Prayers partners collectively deal with close issues and concerns in a manner almost akin to spiritual housekeeping—attending to trouble spots and praying consistently in a manner to preempt bad outcomes.

THE SOLIDARITIES OF PRAYER PARTNERSHIP

Just as prayer is a purposeful language, prayer partnership is an intentional form of fellowship. The term *partnership* implies a relationship based upon a shared action. In the same vein, the core of the prayer partnerships formed by DBC women is a shared interest in prayer and a belief in its efficacy. However, prayer partners recognized that amid their common interest in prayer, distinctions do exist. Sister Marshall, a newer member in the DBC community, is the prayer partner of Sister Michaels, a seasoned church member and the wife of a senior elder. Sister Marshall commented on Sister Michaels's giftedness as a Christian woman and prayer partner: "I see in Sister Michaels such a praying woman. She trusts in the Lord. Her faith . . . I just can see. Seeing spiritual things is not like seeing that microwave over there. In her I see faith, and I connect with the faith in her."

Women such as Sister Marshall are distinguished by reputations of hospitality and culinary skill, and women such as Sister Michaels are known for their spiritual talents. The common purpose engendered in prayer partnership does not erase the differences in partners' spiritual experiences. Nor does the ritual focus of prayer partnership preclude the formation of other modes of affinity. According to Sister Trent, she and her prayer partners have other commonalities:

> [Like] people . . . tend to gather, you know? Would we interact on a different level? *Yes!* Because we've become more close and discovered we

have like interests. We clown a lot. We laugh a lot, you know what I mean? So you have that. We're around the same age. The relationship I would have with them as nurses. So it depends on where we are and [what] our interests are, but really there is also that same level of caring.

More than the exchange of information and ritual duties, prayer partners also share laughs and develop friendships. Other commonalities, such as shared occupational interests, dispositions, or local residence, can also affect the formation of prayer partnerships. However, Sister Trent's description of prayer-partner sociality still privileged a shared interest in prayer as the source of these relationships. For her, the discovery of commonalities and the building of collegiality with her prayer partners came *after* their central concern with prayer.

The organization of prayer partnership resembles the orientation of brotherhood around textual rituals or sisters' emphasis of experiential rituals. However, prayer partnership is the only type of DBC kinship that is explicitly named after a religious ritual. It is smaller in scope than the relationships between church brothers and sisters. But prayer partnership does, in fact, constitute a type of spiritual kinship. For DBC women formed prayer partnerships only with other Christian women. Although in some instances DBC women created prayer partnerships with nonmember women, these ties were nonetheless inherently Christian. Because DBC teachings define all Christians as brothers and sisters related through the same internal spiritual substance, prayer partnership is inherently a spiritual relationship by local standards.

Research on religious small groups also raises interesting questions about the impacts of voluntary associations on US religious involvements. In general, small-group members provide one another with a meaningful sense of rapport, closeness, and efficacy in solving personal problems (Erzen 2006; Wuthnow 1996). Such groups are considered a therapeutic resource for members negotiating everyday concerns and life crises. Prayer partnerships exhibit many of the positive social benefits of small groups, such as everyday collegiality and support. Sister Hutchins described how her prayer partner encouraged her to pursue a difficult course of action. After she lost touch with her best friend, Sister Hutchins prayed for her friend and their reunion. She explained, "My prayer partner had been praying with me. My prayer partner and some of my Christian friends have continued to pray, and some of my friends have said 'Let it go. You seem to get hurt.'" Her case provides a glimpse into part of the ethos of prayer partnership: a commitment to prayer should come before personal feelings of frustration. Sister Hutchins's situation suggests that prayer partners should continue to pray until an issue is resolved. Therefore, a glimpse into prayer partnerships reveals that they may take up individual concerns but do not necessarily cater to personal emotions that go against the common mission of Christian morality.

The frequency of partnered prayer (almost every day) versus church gatherings (which happen three to four days a week) shows its preeminence in shaping women's religious subjectivities. However, rather than an anti-institutional or alternative form of religiosity, the prayer partnerships constituted by DBC women appear to complement partners' church commitments. Through prayer partnerships, DBC women are able to shape their broader community. As they regularly prayed for the church, church leaders, and church missionary ventures, prayer partners bring church concerns into the space of everyday life and thereby exert a form of spiritual influence over the church as a whole. They create another pathway by which churches and homes as well as institutional and everyday social worlds are connected.

THE ENDS OF PRAYER PARTNERSHIP

Prayer partnership offers a valuable form of community to DBC women interested in developing their commitment to prayer and transforming their lives, their church community, and broader social collectives. As Sister Hutchins noted, prayer partnership is an effective, meaningful relationship because prayer can change things. She confidently and repeatedly testified, "Continue to pray. Never give up, and God will come through in His own time. If you believe in who you pray to, He will." Because of their belief in the efficacy of prayer, prayer partners used a language that they understand will positively affect their social and spiritual worlds. Prayer partners cultivated a relationship that centered their shared identity as ritual agents. In contrast to the male literalist ideology, which members mobilize to stabilize biblical meaning, prayer is a transformative discourse. Whereas brothers supervise biblical explanation and concern themselves with governance and tradition, (female) prayer partners engage in an improvisational ritual language and focus on changing outcomes.

As they prayed for their church communities, prayer partners saw their work as influencing the church. Their prayer connects churches and homes, institutional religion, and extra-institutional spirituality by submitting church concerns to the ritual space and authority of everyday spirituality. In the process, prayer partners cultivate an important form of relatedness, often creating everyday kin relations in return.

Spiritual Motherhood

Although women's church fellowship is primarily ordered around the lateral relationships between "brothers and sisters in Christ" and the egalitarian ties of prayer partnership, spiritual parenting relationships are also an important part of women's religious networks. Spiritual mothers mentor the early spiritual development of new converts and of their other spiritual children. Spiritual mothers also oversee the pragmatic dimensions of their daughters' and sons' incorporation into the broader church community as well as interpersonal networks of spiritual support. Spiritual motherhood (and by extension spiritual parenting) is a line of everyday religious kinship that is almost always constituted amid members' navigations of sacred transitions (such as conversions and crises of faith) and social changes (such as migration and changes in church affiliation). Though primarily located in the domestic sphere, spiritual motherhood is vital to the reproduction and strengthening of the broader church community and is an essential example of the types of religious authority wielded by DBC churchwomen.

THE SOCIAL PROCESS OF SPIRITUAL MOTHERHOOD

Although spiritual motherhood is not an institutionalized relationship at DBC, many members mentioned to me spiritual mothers and fathers and their positive impact on their spiritual growth. During the earliest stage of my research with the DBC community in 2008, I conducted an interview with Sister Pauline Robbins. As I entered the hallway of her neat, modern home located in Lithonia, Georgia, I heard advertisements being broadcast on the Christian radio station to which her living room stereo was tuned. After we greeted each other, she ushered me to a wooden kitchen table. On the walls hung a clock painted with the Jamaican flag, the text of the Jamaican national anthem, and a regulations poster for home health-care workers. We sat next to veranda doors that let in the afternoon sunlight and a view of her fenced backyard. Seated, we spoke about everyday concerns, like the current economic downturn and the rising cost of gasoline and utilities.

After a while, we began the interview process. Sister Robbins told how she began attending a Brethren church in the Trelawney parish of Jamaica at the age of nine. Since then she has been a member of Brethren communities in Montreal, in Boston, and, since 2005, at DBC. As she recounted her church history, she described the marginalization she experienced as a single mother during her participation in the Montreal and Boston church communities, in which other members did not fully accept her into their personal social networks or fully include her in church activities because of her status as an unwed mother. However, she mentioned her affection for an elderly woman at the Boston Brethren assembly who encouraged her to remain in the church despite other members' exclusions:

> I took her for my mother. She keeps calling to find out how [my daughter] is doing, and we talk, we talk.... I mean she's from back home, from the old school back home, and most of the people in other Brethren churches, we know them.... We really talk. And she, when I tell her things, she really encouragin' me, and I really love her as a mother. Her and her husband they like opened their arms and opened their doors.... Her ways and her principles and her faith. I just ... she just remind me ... not her stature because she's just a little lady, but the things she stand for and her principles and her love for the Lord just remind me of [my mother].

Sister Robbins's narrative uncovers some important features of spiritual mothering relationships. First, the relationships between spiritual mothers and their spiritual children are built through regular communication. For Robbins, it was her spiritual mother's words of encouragement that ultimately reinforced her sense of church belonging and motivated her to remain in church despite her frustrations. When interviewed, other DBC members also acknowledged that everyday talk and confiding were at the foundation of their most valued spiritual relationships. Often these shared words take place via phone conversations or around kitchen tables over shared meals. Hospitality and the comforts of home infuse the kitchen-table dialogues and the relationships between spiritual mothers and their children.

However, spiritual mothers do not simply offer words for words' sake but also for instruction. As devoted Christians and church participants or, in Robbins's own words, as women of "principles ... and faith ... [who] love the Lord," spiritual mothers are women respected by their church communities who transmit religious knowledge to those in need. Sister Lisa Johnson, a Jamaican mother of three and new DBC member, was mentored by Sister Haliwell into the Christian faith and the DBC community through intensive Bible study and through discussions about the church's moral codes and social dynamics. Similarly, Robbins's spiritual mother offered guidance as she navigated the personal dilemma of her church membership. The process of spiritual mothering is steeped in the language of discipleship, a term used by many evangelicals to describe the socialization of new Christians into the faith through intensive biblical study. Some members' decisions to mentor and care for new and questioning members such as Sister Robbins are informed by biblical representations of new Christians as "newborn babies" in the faith who "crave spiritual milk" (1 Peter 2:2, NIV). Just as infants need sustenance, so do new "believers" require spiritual nurturance and mentoring. Despite the local use of Pauline scriptures to support male church governance, nurturance of children is typically considered women's work. The Apostle Paul's reference to "spiritual milk," though disembodied from women's reproductive capacities, invokes a female presence. Nonetheless, the work of spiritual mothers falls somewhere between rigidly defined gender roles of male instruction and female nurturance, combining both practices to affect the institutional church from a noninstitutional vantage point.

Situated in the homeplaces (and yardspaces) cultivated by the Afro-Caribbean and African churchwomen of DBC, spiritual children accept the kindnesses and advice of their spiritual mothers. The material and spiritual sustenance offered by spiritual mothers is not visible from the vantage point of Sunday churchgoing. Brothers are the public face of church evangelism and teaching. In contrast, spiritual mothers use their homes as sites to incorporate female and male church members.

THE SOLIDARITIES OF SPIRITUAL MOTHERHOOD

In addition to the discursive properties and feeding practices through which maternal spiritual ties are constituted, these two church communities model the adoptive and trans-local characteristics of spiritual parent-child ties. The bond constituted by Sister Robbins and her spiritual mother resonates with Afro-Caribbean kinship practices in which nonbiological kinship relationships are constituted to aid the settlement of Afro-Caribbean migrants (Bashi 2007; Chamberlain 2006). Spiritual mothers assist young Christians such as Sister Pauline Robbins, a Christian woman "from back home [in Jamaica]," because of their shared conviction that they should not be left to navigate spiritual and social transitions and crises alone. In particular, the adoptive tradition in which kinship is created from above (or in the case of Sister Robbins, her own creation of kinship from below ["I took her for my mother"]) is a common feature of Afro-Caribbean and African American kinship and is widely practiced by many members of the DBC constituency (Jewell 2003). Brother Earl Whittam, a young adult Jamaican member, depicted his adoptive relationship with his spiritual family at DBC:

> When I came here, my family wasn't here. It was just my brother and my dad. My relationship with my dad is kind of strained, so it's just me and my brother. We became friends with like Yvette and Evan and all

of them—their families just kinda took us in. Literally, there are people there who think we are brothers and sisters and cousins. They took me in and took care of me at a time when there was no one else around to do it. They literally took me into their home and into their families. It's hard for me not to think of them as family.

Brother Whittam's depiction of his adoption by other church members aligns with the description that Sister Robbins offered. The motifs of care and the recurring image of being taken into a home and a family (echoing the open homes associated with homeplaces and yardspaces) appear again in Whittam's description. The process by which a person becomes attached to a home and a family is through table fellowship. In the words used by a senior Trinidadian church brother, adoptees are "strays," unattached persons who become a standard household presence after they are fed by a family member. In the case of spiritual mothers, this feeding is double: people are literally fed food and figuratively fed or taught biblical and community knowledge. As an adoptive relationship, spiritual motherhood, and parenting by extension, is an incorporative relationship.

Spiritual mother-child bonds in many ways appear to transcend the limitations popularly associated with institutional church relationships. Rather than being local in scope, contingent upon church membership, and characterized by polite collegiality, spiritual motherhood has been depicted as a loving relationship that members maintain after their migration to other locales and communities. Sister Pauline Robbins notes that her relationship with her spiritual mother is trans-local in scope and that it remains important to her despite her migration from Boston to Atlanta. Therefore, spiritual parenting is not confined to a particular locality or to the boundaries of local church membership. In her discussion of the spiritual motherhood practiced by Afro-Caribbean Spiritual Baptists in Toronto, Carol Duncan writes that "the spiritual family . . . include[s] relationships that transcend conventional barriers of time and space" (2008, 198). The case of Sister Robbins confirms this view. She insisted that her relationship with her spiritual mother remains important to her, despite her current residence in Atlanta. As migrants, Robbins and her spiritual mother also forged their relationship in a diasporic context away from their home country of Jamaica. So although spiritual mothering ties originate within a local church community, grow within home settings, and reinforce church membership, the reach of spiritual mothering relationships extends beyond locality.

THE ENDS OF SPIRITUAL MOTHERHOOD

Given the role that Brethren spiritual mothers play in the social lives of their children and churches, why do their contributions remain a private fixture of community life? The most obvious answer would appear to be that spiritual mothering is an undervalued form of women's work and bounded by the domestic sphere. However, spiritual mothers are publicly recognized leaders in Afro-Baptist, Afro-Pentecostal, and Latin American Catholic churches, all of which have patriarchal Christian traditions (Brown 1995; Klaits 2010; Sault 2001). To be sure, comparing the social locations of DBC spiritual mothers against other instances of spiritual motherhood raises interesting questions about the intersections of gender and the institutionalization of evangelicalism. But the significance of spiritual motherhood to the broader DBC community must still be located. For DBC, spiritual motherhood, prayer partnership, and sisterhood are incorporative relationships that knit together the DBC community via microlevel interactions. Different from the public nature of institutional church membership, the private and mundane cast of everyday relatedness makes it an important site at which the intimacy of spiritual kinship is nursed and at which women exert spiritual authority. However, the patriarchal tenor to Brethrenism contributes to its being a less visible dimension of members' religious worlds than formal church practices.

In his landmark work on the slave religion of New World blacks, Albert Raboteau presents a complex picture of the institutional moorings of emergent Afro-diasporic Christianity:

> At first glance it seems strange to refer to the religion of the slaves as an *invisible institution*, for independent black churches with slave members did exist in the South before emancipation. [But] the religion of the slaves was both institutional and noninstitutional, visible and invisible, formally organized and spontaneously adapted. Regular Sunday worship in the local church was paralleled by illicit, or at least informal, prayer meetings on weeknights in the slave cabins. (1978, 212)

Although Raboteau's descriptions of Afro-diasporic religion speak of another time, his conclusions raise provocative questions about the institutionalization of black Atlantic Christianity. If his insights are applied to DBC community formation, there is a multi-layered belonging that combines public religiosity and private spirituality, institutionalism and incorporation, collective and personal identifications, as well as sacred and mundane practices. The invisibility of everyday spirituality allowed the survival of black religiosity in a plantation regime that outlawed black religious communalism. The political landscapes encountered by Afro-Caribbeans and African Americans have changed, yet black social institutions such as the church remain complex, resilient, and nonconforming to mainstream social patterns. This proves all the more pertinent to a religious movement imprinted by the antisectarian nonconformist religious project of Plymouth Brethrenism. In the case of the DBC community, churchwomen oversaw the invisible, everyday church: an adaptable community that tightened church bonds and attended to the personal needs of church members in this current sociopolitical era. The invisibility of spiritual mothering work from the vantage point of institutional church life, then, does not erase its impact or its meaningful grounding within Brethren church traditions that privileged everyday religious ties as evidence of authentic religious communion.

Churchwomen's work and everyday spirituality are recognizable fixtures of black religious life. Whether it be the small-group Bible studies conducted by religious participants in homes, coffee shops, or in Caribbean yards (Austin-Broos 1997; Bielo 2009), the everyday spiritual networks and lived religion of black churchwomen (Frederick 2003), or the everyday provision of care for dying church members (Klaits 2010), the sacrament of the everyday (hooks 1990)—meaning the increased infiltration of everyday spaces as sites of ongoing spiritual connectedness and the enrichment of faith—is an important aspect of contemporary Christian religioscapes. The domestic locations of spiritual relatedness and the sacrament of the everyday as a feature of Christians' lived religious experiences make apparent the limitations of strict institutional analyses of Christianity, which would likely ignore the substantive contributions of women to DBC community life as well as contemporary religious constituents' embeddedness in multiple religious and spiritual collectives. Although all too often religious scholars divorce institutionalized religious involvement from noninstitutional forms of spirituality, the everyday relatedness of DBC women encourages ongoing investigations of between-Sundays fellowship and religious practices (Frederick 2003), not as a separate or secondary dimension of Christian religiosity but as an expected and increasingly common feature of Christian social worlds.

Thus we see that DBC women participate in a dynamic field of everyday spiritual relationships and processes that provides specialized fellowship for churchwomen and for community members as a whole. As mediators of homeplaces and yardspaces, DBC churchwomen structure everyday contact, meaningful sociality, and reciprocal ritual action, and in all these ways enrich religious life. Most significantly, through the spiritual work they conduct in everyday domestic spaces as well as domestic practices, DBC sisters, prayer partners, and church mothers demonstrate that the social boundaries between church and home are not stopping points. These women resist and blur them. Similar to the ways in which some women's productions of homeplaces and yardspaces resist the visiting practices of respectability, the bounding of social collectives observed under dictates of respectability are not observed by some members. Social spaces should not be demarcated as separate from religious space but should be infused with collective religious experience because to these women, Christianity involves the movement beyond spatial and identity boundaries. The everyday relatedness of DBC women gives us a way to contemplate the materialization of spiritual kinship, the relationship between institutional and mundane religious experiences, the special interstitial spaces engineered by women between the church and the home, as well as the transcendent logic that infuses the field of spiritual relatedness interconnecting DBC members and broader religious collectives.

Chapter 6 is also located in the inter-institutional space between church and family. In particular, it presents an ethnographic analysis of how DBC congregational relationships reinforce heteropatriarchal kinship amid the challenges that besiege black family maintenance, challenges such as the material marginalizations of antiblack racism and the discourses of black family pathology and family morals propagated by neo-evangelical, neoconservative, and neoliberal orders. It also explores how spiritual kinship generates therapeutic spaces of confessional intimacy, whereby members share their challenges and criticisms of heteropatriarchal family norms.

Black Evangelicals, "the Family," and Confessional Intimacy

6

As spiritual kin, the Afro-Caribbean and African American evangelicals of CBC and DBC sanctified their relationships with a thick sociality fostered through everyday reciprocities of prayer and table fellowship. This everyday relatedness was located in a broader social field of relationships that overflowed from churches into homes, from congregations into families. After conducting an interview with Sister Wanda Hutchins, I confided how difficult it was for me to sort through the webs of relationships I encountered in the DBC community. She responded with laughter and replied, "Everybody at DBC is related. I just found out about two people being related the other day!" In the midst of our shared moment of levity, Sister Hutchins's comment illustrated that the black evangelical congregations were populated not just by individual members but by families. I relied upon people such as Sister Dolores Rodney as kinship consultants who knowledgeably uncovered the numerous ties that related a number of church members. Through the interventions of members like Sister Rodney, I was able to see how the DBC was simultaneously a church family—a context mediated by a shared sense of spiritual relatedness that generated familial grammars and practices of membership—*and* a family church, a setting in which genealogical families (and heteronormative families in particular) were welcomed and nurtured.

The DBC congregation was overwhelmingly peopled by nuclear and extended families. In one instance I learned through a series of interviews that DBC had a member family that comprised four generations of attendees! The dense sociality mediated by the inter-institutional overlap of church and family relationships provided a context of witness and support for members' genealogical relationships more broadly, and nuclear family relationships in particular. Congregants celebrated family milestones such as engagements, births, weddings, anniversaries, and graduations. Church members praised God for their ability to sustain their marriages and raise their children, and they celebrated each other for their faithfulness. They also provided moral support and supervision for families. I witnessed one such scene—of informal marriage advising—one Sunday.

It was almost 11:30 a.m., and DBC members were filing into the sanctuary for the main worship service of the day. As they found their seats, members greeted each other with warm hellos, hugs, and handshakes. Brother Bill Myers, an African American member in his sixties, greeted another brother in his thirties with a hearty handshake and, upon taking a quick glance at his hand, inquired, "Brother, why aren't you wearing your wedding ring? It's important that you remember to wear it." The overlap between church family and family church emerged in the intersection of spiritual and genealogical family discourse, in the familial attendance of DBC congregants, and in relation to the congregational reproduction of heteronormative family ideologies exemplified by the brotherly exchange depicted above.

Of course, DBC members do not live completely in a social world of their own making. Congregants live out their family relationships within a US cultural milieu that tinges African American productions of kinship with an aura of pathology. Afro-Caribbean congregants hail from postcolonial societies that are similarly shaped by Victorian norms of bourgeois citizenship that center the white heteronormative family as an icon of middle-class life. Taken together, DBC members create spiritual and genealogical relationships within an Anglo-American cultural field that racializes nuclear family kinship. My ethnographic engagements with DBC members poignantly illustrated that the moral weight of heteronormativity (and black family pathology) was particularly acute for black evangelicals who also inhabit a religious movement that moralizes the patriarchal nuclear family unit and marginalizes ethno-racial subjectivities that are stereotypically written out of a (mythological) white heteronormativity.

Perhaps the most poignant example of this moral bind emerged in an interview I conducted with Brother Earl Littlefield, a sixty-five-year-old active church member at DBC who migrated to the Atlanta metro area with his family from Trinidad in 1992. While seated at the dining room table of his comfortable suburban home in Lithonia, Littlefield transitioned into a discussion of his family life. Although at the time of our interview Littlefield was married to Wilma Johnson, an African American woman in her sixties, he spoke tearfully about how his first wife's passing from cancer sharply illuminated his remorse over his marital infidelity:

> Now the person that you see sitting here talking to you now has not always been the person that's talking to you now. You name it. I did it. Does that tell you anything? Carrying the Bible under my arm saying that I'm a Christian and doing some of the worst things you possibly could think of. I never stole. I was never a homosexual. I never smoked. I never drank, but I did the rest. And it took God dealing with me in my wife's hospital room five years ago. It took him dealing with me five years ago in a hospital room. And he wrung me dry. Took away the best thing I had in my life—my wife. Took her *away*. I asked him to. When I stood in the hospital room and saw her condition and she could not have been of any use to anybody. Where if she drank anything, it went down to her stomach and came out through a tube into another thing. And God dealt with me in that hospital room. It was a time of singing, a time of praying, a time of commitment, a time of recommitment. . . . Those are the things that have influenced my life and have brought me to this point. If today is the last day in this here Earth [crying], Lord make me an instrument. That's it.

Littlefield's reflections were ordered like a testimony. His narrative was built around moral and temporal contrasts between heterosexual monogamy and adultery, between evangelical notions of sanctified sexuality versus sexual sin.[1] Littlefield's emotionally charged account also testified to the enduring guilt that can result from a moral transgression. In between the lines of his story was the unvoiced transcript of his late wife's experiences and the affective hauntings that occur when one does not keep a vow, when someone disappoints a loved one or even oneself.

If we contextualize Littlefield's narrative within the broader context of his reflections, we also find a critique of the moral hierarchies instantiated by institutional ideologies of "the family" itself:

> The Bible says, "All have sinned and come short of the glory of God." And sin is sin in any bracket. So, if I catch you stealing, and your name is mentioned stealing, it is no different than if I were going to commit adultery. But to everybody adultery is a big sin. The church is going to read you out of fellowship because you commit adultery. And the person who stole lookin' down at me sayin', "Uh huh!" You get that kind of thing. Whereas if the man who has committed adultery. . . . If I commit

adultery and a man comes to me and puts his arms around me and says, "Brother, in the eyes of God all of us are the same, but for the grace of God I could be like you," that man is kin. Because in my mess he is willing to accept me and not put me down. . . . He is willing to put his hand around me and say, "Brother, you['ve] mess[ed] up you know. I've messed up too, and God has forgiven me too. So I don't condemn you. . . . I'm here to encourage you—encourage you in the ways of the Lord because I mess up too. It's only that your mess was made public, and nobody knew about my mess except God. But in the eyes of God all of us are even."

Littlefield depicted his navigation of the stigma he experienced after he was read out of fellowship—barred from attaining church eldership or from participating in active church ministries (e.g., singing, Bible teaching, evangelism) for a probationary period—after news of his transgression broke. In narrating the weight of that stigma, Littlefield makes two observations: First, he noted that church members interpreted adultery and acts associated with sexual sin as the gravest type of moral offense. Second, he held that authentic kinship emerges when church members embraced, put arms and hands around one another, and accepted one another despite those moral transgressions.

Littlefield's comments about the moral weight given to sexual transgressions and the interventions of spiritual kinship poignantly illuminate the paradoxical position inhabited by many Afro-Caribbean and African American evangelicals. And that location—betwixt and between a mainstream religious culture that esteems the formation of the "traditional" family and a racial milieu that reproduces discourse of black familial and, in particular, black sexual deviance—makes respectability a particular mark of piety (with religious, racial, and class implications) and a locus of angst. To be black and evangelical in the first decade of the 2000s meant to inhabit a racial and moral paradox. It meant to carry a burden of proof of one's conformity to a moral standard that was widely believed to elude people for moral rather than structural reasons. It also meant to be caught between the morality of evangelicalism and neoliberalism when both center the family as the sacred and secular building block for social order and the middle class while obscuring the racial double standards encoded in both moral orders of kinship.

This chapter explores black evangelicals' ideologies, discourse, and practices of the heteronormative family, in particular parental relationships and marriages. It also illustrates how the dense relationality mediated by the institutional and everyday workings of spiritual kinship helps to make "the family" possible. In addition to providing ideological and interpersonal support, black evangelicals use spiritual ties to create spaces for a confessional intimacy—reflexive interactions among spiritual kin—that allow them to navigate the racial and moral demands of evangelical and neoliberal family values. Specifically, confessional intimacy emerges in conversations in which church members share familial experiences and concerns, laud familial devotion and commitment, vent experiences of familial stigma and shame, and air questions and critiques of the moralization of heteronormative kinship. Thus, the study of black evangelical productions and reflections on "the family" once again illustrates black evangelicals' mobilization of spiritual kinship as a form of sociality that allows black evangelicals to meet the demands of Christian living and to interject their critical moral visions on family, community, and Christianity into the US racio-religious landscape.

Between Pathology and Idolatry: Black Evangelical Family Values in the US Religious Landscape

As discussed in chapter 1, the Black Church in the US exists at the nexus of academic discourse that emerged amid political exigencies of early twentieth-century antiblack racism and historical institutions of African American Christian expression. Although it is a powerful locus of black sociality within black theological, political, and cultural imaginaries, there is no such thing as a monolithic "Black Church." Along similar lines, there is no such thing as the "black family." Rather, there are a number of familial arrangements generated within Afro-diasporic communities. The kinship of Afro-Caribbean and African American working-class and middle-class families has been framed as a deviant social phenomenon. Black middle-class families in the US and the Caribbean have been associated with patriarchal nuclear families that detach from extended-family kinship networks to keep economic resources within the nuclear family and to transmit middle-class status and economic standing. Afro-diasporic middle-class families have also been highly associated with a class-based social orientation that includes a worldview that emphasizes respectability, Christian marriage, thrift, a future-oriented outlook, and private property ownership (Barrow 1996; Besson 2002; Douglass 1992; Frazier 1957; Lacy 2007; Patillo-McCoy 2000; Schneider and Smith, 1973; Smith 1965; Wilson 1969). Conversely, black working-class families have been framed as matrifocal (mother-centered) domestic units characterized by low rates of marriage and the emphasis of extended-family kinship relationships (Clarke 1966; Smith 1986). Such families were theorized to be pathological approximations of Western kinship norms (Frazier 1939; Simey 1946). Some researchers have discussed the means by which extended-family networks structure reciprocal financial support between relatives navigating socioeconomic instability—including between "fictive" or nonbiological kin (and we can insert spiritual kin here) (Barrow 1996; Chamberlain 2006; Ho 1992; Sobo 1993; Stack 1974). Yet matrifocal households and extended-family types, however adaptive, have been understood as counterintuitively organized for the purposes of social mobility and private property ownership (Olwig 2010; Stack 1996).[2] It is the trope of the working-class or the "dysfunctional black family"—meaning an impoverished, nonheteronormative, female-headed household—that emerges as a stand-in for black family life. It is a focus of academic, political, and religious discourse and a site of social and moral concern. This trope of "the black family"—its statistical occurrence, the reasons for its existence, and the policy and religious prescriptions for its conversion—has been used as a glyph to discuss African American and Afro-Caribbean racial pathology and unfitness for citizenship and sovereignty throughout the twentieth and twenty-first centuries in the United States (Ferguson 2004).[3]

The familial communities produced by CBC and DBC members that tend to the material needs and enable the moral reproduction of religious practitioners resemble the familial church environments that are widely associated with African American and Afro-Caribbean milieus. Such churches have been conceptualized by black churchgoers as surrogate or extended families and depicted via familial idioms that characterized such congregations as "church famil[ies]" (McAdoo 2007). Scholars have typically conceived of the closely knit congregations found in black church settings as at least partially an African cultural inheritance—in particular, a translation of a West African extended-family ethos into a religious institutional context to enact ritualized modes of solidarity and communal joy (Austin-Broos 1997; Du Bois 1995 [1899]; Sudarkasa 2007). The familial connections found in some black congregational contexts has also been explained (and at times naturalized) as an outgrowth of the kinds of ethno-religious institutionalism associated with preserving the ethnic cultures and attending to the pragmatic needs of migrant communities weathering the social dislocations of migration, as discussed in chapter 3. In their fulfillment of a set of social work roles, African American churches have also been cast as family support systems that buttress the maintenance of black heteronormative and nonheteronormative family households through the provision of material, social, and affective support (Billingsley and Morrison-Rodriguez 1998). The CBC and DBC members who are the subject of my research were located in a broader landscape of Afro-diasporic church projects that make ideological, institutional, material, narrative, and ontological interventions into black family experiences.

US CONSERVATISM(S), NEO-EVANGELICALISM, AND BLACK FAMILY PATHOLOGY

Although the emergence of neo-evangelicalism in the 1970s and 1980s (most notably the Moral Majority as a visible and outspoken arm of the Christian Right) is often understood as the moral branch of conservatism, neo-evangelicalism is not conservatism's only voice. The Silent Majority—working and middle-class white Americans who did not participate in the dissident countercultures of the 1960s—who fed the resurgence of conservatism in the 1970s subscribed to meritocratic notions of individualism and race-neutral language that opposed liberal interventions precipitated by the civil rights movement such as busing, quotas, and welfare (Rigueur 2015, 166). Silent Majority morality held that people were supposed to uplift themselves, regardless of the structures that normalized and protected opportunities along racial and class lines. Black socioeconomic mobility was a matter of individual and familial self-reliance ameliorated by moral interventions but not a concern for the state.

The Afro-Caribbean and African American evangelicals of CBC and DBC are thus caught between racial ideas of black family pathology that write black families out of heteropatriarchal citizenship, hegemonic neo-evangelical family ideals that were constructed in relation to an archetypical morally undeserving "black family," and black engagements with class-based respectability politics. As discussed in chapter 1, the family-values discourse of the mainstream neo-evangelicalism that emerged in the 1970s was constructed in relation to white evangelical concerns about integration, welfare, deindustrialization, and miscegenation (Burlein 2002; Schäfer 2013). It was antiblack in its efforts to halt or slow the material redistributions championed by the civil rights movement and to write off black families as non-normative and undeserving of the benefits of full citizenship.

NEOLIBERALISM AND BLACK FAMILY PATHOLOGY

Both Afro-Caribbean and African American evangelicals at DBC faced an economic context shaped by neoliberalism, defined by David Harvey as a mode of capitalist accumulation by dispossession and a market rationality that advocates governmental deregulation of capitalist enterprises, individual entrepreneurialism, and the retraction and privatization of government services (2005). Randolph Hohle outlined that the neoliberal turn was also racially formulated (2012). In the context of a post-civil-rights-era South, the language of privatization emerged as a racial grammar that associated the public sphere with a degraded (and racially resented) blackness and the private sphere with a superior, self-sufficient whiteness. In the wake of the neoliberal deregulation of capitalist endeavors, decreased governmental investments in public infrastructure, and the antiblack motivations and implications of neoliberal statecraft, black families across the class spectrum carry a great degree of material and moral responsibility for their class outcomes. According to theologian Keri Day in *Religious Resistance: Womanist and Black Feminist Perspectives*, neoliberalism also poses harm to black communities through its emphasis on a possessive individualism that generates social alienation and a focus on the abstract qualities of money rather than the cultivation of a transcendent relationship with God (2016).

The bulk of my ethnographic fieldwork was conducted in 2008, at the height of the Great Recession. It was an important time in which the material and moral nexus of racial neoliberalism impacting black families coalesced. Among the most auspicious aspects of neoliberal deregulation that was affecting black middle-class families was the predatory lending of the subprime mortgage sector, which disproportionately affected black families and significantly shaped the black middle-class suburban context of the Atlanta metropolitan area. Most of the congregants I interviewed had suburban homes and were dual-income families (either working or retired) who appeared to hold the material stability associated with the middle class. No one spoke of financial problems in interviews, and except for one single mother congregant, no one spoke of financial problems during worship settings. Nonetheless, I interviewed a number of congregants who worked within the real estate sector (as either their primary or supplementary employment), and there was at least one member with a more recent mortgage who would likely have been affected by the precarity and collapse of the subprime sector. Understandably, financial and food offerings were often done in private, either in the church parking lot or beyond the watchful eyes of a participant ethnographer.

In addition to the Great Recession and the subprime collapse, which changed the material conditions navigated by black families, 2008 also witnessed the historic election of Barack Obama: the first African American president. At the time of my research, the Obama presidency was being heralded as an important symbolic victory for black communities in the US. Yet it is important to note that the Obama presidency furthered neoliberal political and economic programs (Yamahtta-Taylor 2016) and also reproduced moralized discourses of responsibility in relation to the African American community. In his second term, Obama founded the My Brother's Keeper Initiative in

2014, which was designed to create mentorship networks to help black youths, in particular black boys, navigate educational and class inequalities and to provide greater access to opportunity.[4]

Although the initiative is explicitly intended to remember racial achievement gaps, it is also couched in moral language. For instance, White House correspondence outlines My Brother's Keeper as an "initiative to help every boy and young man of color who is willing to do the hard work to get ahead."[5] Interestingly, the program parallels the focus on men and an emphasis on black male responsibility undertaken by CBC and DBC familial projects, suggesting that black evangelical and racial neoliberal discourses of black family morality focus on male responsibility (Rigueur 2017).[6]

Yet some views of black family life have illustrated that more than a corrective heteropatriarchy is needed to stem contemporary contexts of material inequality. According to Lester Spence, even black heteronormative families are not well insulated from the material insecurity and moral narratives of neoliberalism:

> The effect of the neoliberal turn on black families is *severe*. Black families forced to hustle hard are forced to be responsible for every aspect of their life while the resources required to do so in the first place are withheld from them. Even "nuclear families" with two steady "good jobs" are not immune to the stresses here, as they are required to be ever more productive and at the same time they are expected to be more and more responsible for the costs of educating their children. . . . Elites seeking to solve the problems black families face consistently adopt harsh rhetoric urging them to take more and more responsibility, harsh legislation designed to surveil and punish them if they do not make the "proper" choices, and increased charity and volunteerism. (Spence 2015, 116–19)

Thus, the *homo heteronormativus* associated with neo-evangelicalism and neo-conservatism cannot be presumed to protect DBC members and other African American and Afro-Caribbeans from the moral and material vulnerabilities of the *homo economicus* of neoliberalism.

BLACK EVANGELICALS, CORRECTIVE HETEROPATRIARCHY, AND THE NEO-EVANGELICAL FAMILY AS IDOL

Despite the hegemonic whiteness of neo-evangelicalism, the framing of family-values discourse does not take place without the participation of black evangelicals. Although hegemony promotes a dominant perspective that naturalizes, or in our case, moralizes norms of religion and family, hegemonic racial and moral narratives cannot erase the plurality of perspectives and interpretations within the evangelical subculture. All CBC and DBC members are part of an institutional setting in which patriarchal ideologies of male headship and female submission, the moralization of respectability, and an emphasis of personal responsibility, particularly on the part of men, is frequently articulated.

In the case of T. Michael Flowers and the establishment of CBC, DBC, and the broader Brethren-influenced Afro-diasporic evangelical network in which they were enmeshed, chapel and family leadership is considered to be the responsibility of men. In an interview with Wheaton College Billy Graham Center archivists, he explained, "We believe the women can do a whole lot of things. My only objection is I don't believe God has called women to be pastors. That's where I draw the line" (Wheaton College Archives Transcript 4). In establishing black Brethren-influenced chapels in the US South, Flowers encountered churched African Americans interested in a "Bible-believing Christianity." Yet by his account, he also noticed a dearth of qualified male leaders. Discussing his missionary efforts in South Carolina, Flowers explained: "I was going to say, the tragedy with Beaufort, but it isn't a tragedy. The truth is we had more qualified women than men. And my concept of the ministry, [is] that leadership in the church should be in the hands of men" (Wheaton College Archives Transcript 4). Consequently, Flowers engaged in the joint project of establishing chapel communities and forming a cadre of Afro-Caribbean and African American male leaders. The ultimate goal for Flowers was to hand over leadership to a local group of male elders.

The project of building up black male church leadership under a moral umbrella of responsibility was not just understood in religious terms by CBC and DBC members. It was also understood as something that had familial implications. During an interview, African American Elder John Hastings, who was discipled (or mentored) by an early CBC pastor in matters of faith and family to become a part of the cadre of leaders that Flowers sought to develop, outlined the problem of black male responsibility in familial terms:

> When I look at the black community, I see guys who are unproductive and who in some cases are filled with anger and a frustration of what am I supposed to be doing. And they're not being trained or equipped to do what I would call things that are productive, so there's a loss of hope of being able to achieve and that creates anger. Part of the gender differences encourage male responsibility, and if we no longer demand or make that a model, there's no drive to grow up or to expect [men have] a responsibility to provide. . . . If she has no expectation for him to provide

and support . . . then he loses that motivation and drive. If we ask where are the marriageable men, they're there. We haven't fed them the line of responsibility to assume manhood, and that enables them to walk away from responsibility and to not feel that sense of a need to grow up.

Hastings outlined male responsibility, in particular the placement of breadwinner masculinity within black households, as a corrective to a stereotypical black family of an unmarried female–headed household. Black evangelical religious participation is understood as fostering the affects (hope, motivation, drive) and social context (expectation and accountability) that foster a responsible manhood inside the church and home. Hastings's emphasis on the insertion of a black patriarchal familial presence (related to Flowers's emphasis on black male religious leadership) mirrors the corrective patriarchy prescribed by neo-evangelical and conservative discourse in relation to an essentialized trope of "the black family" and evangelical and African American religious cultures more broadly.

Black evangelicals' family perspectives do not always mirror evangelical, conservative, and neoliberal moral narratives of family. Although Flowers promoted male institutional leadership in both the church and the family, he was also suspicious that mainstream neo-evangelical centralizations of "the family" were displacing a proper prioritization of God-focused piety, salvation, and evangelism:

> The family is important to God, but the family is not as important to God as most people think. God is first, and I mean first without any close second. . . . And I am saying, "Brother, I want you to love the Lord. I want you to love your family. But be careful that the family don't become an idol." And I'm afraid in some instances the family is misplacing God. We are going to build families. You can do that without God, you know. See, that's . . . that's the fear I have, and I'm praying that it doesn't pan out. (Wheaton College Archives Transcript 5)

Echoing the relational emphasis of an Afro-diasporic evangelical movement that he helped to found, Flowers found suspect the narrowing of neo-evangelical attention on "the family," particularly as a missionary who understood evangelicalism to be a Christian project that should be perpetually focused on spreading the gospel and to be undergirded by a universalistic theology of Christian fraternalism. Moreover, adhering to notions of spiritual relatedness that pushes against identity, institutional, and interpersonal boundaries, including the structural isolation presumed by the respectable nuclear family,

Flowers's insights resound with the extra-institutional dimensions of spiritual kinship. His criticism of the family as "an idol" also refers to a misplaced devotion to family on the part of an evangelical mainstream, instead of on God. Considering the deep history of Euro-American representations of African and African-derived religious expressions in terms of fetishism—the inaccurate attribution of agency to objects and the denial of symbolic thinking to religious practitioners of African descent (Johnson 2015; Wimbush 2012)—Flowers's observation is particularly interesting. It calls out a despiritualization he ascribes to neo-evangelical Christianity that focuses on a biological nuclear family (and perhaps its interconnections with the material project of social mobility) instead of spiritual relationality with God, believers, and the evangelistic expansion of a universal Christian family. To focus on the family meant sacrificing an appropriate attention to webs of spiritual relationships that, according to ascetic Protestant Christian theology, were supposed to take precedence over genealogical relationships (Cannell 2005). To focus on the family would mean to be inwardly oriented instead of outward facing and concerned with spreading the gospel. Flowers's critique raises pointed questions about neo-evangelical family values, hegemony, and Euro-American evangelical representational dominance of a global evangelical story.

Afro-Caribbeans and African Americans at CBC and DBC partake in the universalistic relational theologies associated with the Afro-diasporic Brethren religious movement as well as a narrower mainstream neo-evangelical emphasis on heteropatriarchal families. Yet these believers do so with questions and concerns tempered by their experiences and social locations of generation, gender, and race. Whether through a critique of idolatry to neo-evangelical family values or their illustration of the very constructedness of the heteropatriarchal family, black evangelicals exhibit a thoughtful and critical positionality within and against racial and religious hierarchies rather than a simplistic assimilation of political and evangelical heteropatriarchal cultures of "the family." As Fred Moten writes in "The Case of Blackness," "This strife between normativity and the deconstruction of norms is essential not only to contemporary black academic discourse but also to the discourse of the barbershop, the beauty shop, and the bookstore" (2008, 179). Although we can insert the institutional and everyday spaces of evangelical worship and spiritual communion in his list, Moten's insights about the partial containment of black social life by pathological discourse are apropos. As I endeavor to illustrate below, black evangelicals navigate the space between norms and pathology, ideals and lived experience, and pose questions and at times even doubts about moral and racial scripts of faith and family. We see spaces in which black evangelicals generate their own social spaces not determined by pathological discourse, in which they witness, acknowledge, and even celebrate their own efforts at kincraft.

Of Arrows and Angst: The Challenges of Religious Reproduction across Generational Lines

On a March evening, a small number of DBC congregants sang an opening hymn before their weekly Tuesday-night prayer meeting and Bible study. The hymn was "Happy the Home When God Is There":

> Happy the home when God is there,
> And love fills every breast;
> When one their wish, and one their prayer,
> And one their heav'nly rest.
>
> Happy the home where Jesus's name
> Is sweet to every ear;
> Where children early speak His fame,
> And parents hold Him dear.
>
> Happy the home where prayer is heard,
> And praise is wont to rise;
> Where parents love the sacred Word
> And all its wisdom prize.
>
> Lord, let us in our homes agree
> This blessed peace to gain;
> Unite our hearts in love to Thee,
> And love to all will reign.

The lyrics paint a picture of a Christian family characterized by a mutual love of God and one another, reciprocal spiritual care, and a happiness grounded in parents together with their children sharing in prayer and in praise of the Lord. The hymn paints a happy domestic scene of Christian family life: a family iconized in mainstream US neo-evangelical culture and its affective imaginaries. Nonetheless, my work revealed that in addition to producing idyllic scenes of Christian family life, black evangelical congregants held and reproduced a number of religious messages, advice, and aspirations for family. In these instances the Christian heteropatriarchal family emerged less as an outgrowth of biogenetic kinship, the profession of Christian religious identity, or the decision to engage in familial church attendance, and more as the result of collective labor and intentionality of kincraft undertaken on the part of black evangelical family households and extended-family networks that were genealogically or spiritually defined.

"Children are a heritage of the Lord," said Brother James Avery during his special Father's Day sermon at DBC, echoing the words of the hymn.[7] Throughout his message, Brother Avery emphasized the obligations and rewards of parenthood. He repeatedly described the weighty responsibilities that come with parenting: the challenges of maintaining a Christian household headed by fathers who provide for their family and virtuous wives, the need for good models of morality that is reflected in one's own life as a parent, and the imperative of providing the care needed to help children transition to adulthood. All of these things were to be cemented by church attendance as a family. Brother Avery urged that children should be considered blessings from God because they provided parents with an opportunity for founding a legacy that extends beyond oneself: "Children are loaned to you by God to take care of. God is the archer. Parents are the bow, and children are their arrows." Parents are divinely appointed caretakers who are directly responsible for guiding the direction of their children's life courses.

This understanding of children as important carriers of parents' legacies is widespread throughout the DBC community, and church members invest significantly in church youth programs. Those black evangelicals who have two or more generations of their family represented among the chapel's ranks are important cornerstones of their respective church communities and (in the case of men) lead chapel communities as elders and deacons, or act as spiritual mothers who wield their own forms of authority. Those local church members who grew up in the Brethren tradition and who have Brethren predecessors in their family (widely referred to as "born Brethren") often possess a somewhat more elevated status than those who found their way to Brethrenism as adults.

This intergenerational transmission of religious identity is no easy task. As outlined by David Hempton in *Evangelical Disenchantment: Nine Portraits of Faith and Doubt*, "The passing of the baton of evangelical faith from parents to children is one of the most highly prized aspirations of the tradition" (2008, 16). In his analysis of the parent-child dynamic between British literary figure Edmund Gosse and his Plymouth Brethren father, Philip Henry Gosse, Hempton observes a tension between a Plymouth Brethren emphasis on "the idea of Christian brotherhood regardless of class, education, and status" and the Victorian accent of patriarchal religious authority (2008, 157). Thus, patriarchal familial culture and the democratic textual ethos of Brethren evangelicalism are fundamentally at odds. In our current case, this relational paradigm is compounded by the anxieties that attend the reproduction of religious identity associated with the Millennial generation in the US and the challenges of transmitting middle-class identity across generations in black immigrant and African American families.

FAMILY FAITHFULNESS: THE INTERGENERATIONAL TRANSMISSION OF RELIGIOUS IDENTITY

The CBC and DBC congregants also associate religious fidelity with the maintenance of intergenerational connection in the realm of everyday experience. In the fall of 2008 I conducted an interview with Sister Judene Cleary, an octogenarian church member from Jamaica. After the formal interview was over, we continued our conversation about family as we sat in her daughter's living room. She told me about how happy she was to have such a dutiful, caring daughter and to be surrounded by her grandchildren and great-grandchildren. She told me that she had always prayed to God for a loving daughter who would be a nurse who would love the Lord, and that God blessed her with such a daughter. For Sister Cleary, her piety and faith positively affected her relationship with her daughter and was transferred into her sustained connection with the following two generations of her family. For her, faith and family, faithfulness and intergenerational familial connection, went hand in hand.

Yet for some CBC and DBC members, concerns about their children's identities remain paramount. Early in my fieldwork, I conversed after Sunday service with Sister Yvette Goode, an African American mother in her twenties with two young children. As we talked about family relationships, she responded by leaning in and quietly confessing her concerns about her children's future life choices: "The Bible tells parents to train up a child in the ways they should go and when they are old, they will not depart from it. But I never want them to depart from it, whether they're young or old." Her concern that her children might even temporarily depart from the values she had patiently instilled in them revealed not only her strong desire for intergenerational religious transmission; it also reflected her anxieties about her capacity to shape her children's future religious commitments. Only a few months later, I had a remarkably similar conversation with Sister Goode's husband, Jacob, during an annual church conference about his own apprehensions for his children, his commitment to raising them in the faith, and his worries about their future life choices. Unbeknownst to each other, they had separately confided their worries about their children and their parenting in very similar terms and exhibited an uncertainty that undoubtedly many parents have about their children inside and outside of chapel walls.

After a sermon about youth given at the Family Bible Conference, Sister Janet Long lamented to me that she wanted to do more work with the church's youth group but felt limited as the mother of small children. A senior church sister promptly replied, "In this phase, you should focus on raising your children." The interaction revealed that contributing to religious and familial reproduction generated a heavy sense of responsibility on the part of women, who often had to prioritize their commitments within the home and who were often mentored by senior church people to do so.

I return to my interactions with the Goodes because they reveal most poignantly the anxieties that attend parents' efforts to transmit religious values across generations. Black evangelical anxiety about religious identity production stems from overlapping evangelical, black immigrant/diasporic, and neoliberal moral scripts that make parents responsible or culpable for children's outcomes. Moreover, the impromptu acts of confiding engaged in by Sister Yvette and Brother Jacob are acts of confessional intimacy that occurred in the interior spaces of conversations between spiritual kin and between church members and me in ethnographic settings inside and outside of interview narratives—that existed as spaces where church members could air different emotions, reflections, and criticisms about familial ideology and their kincraft endeavors.

Although evangelical Christian notions of salvation tend to focus on individual religious subjects, the intergenerational anxieties of CBC and DBC evangelicals instigate a consideration of collective notions of salvation. As observed by Fenella Cannell in her ethnographic study of Mormon understandings and motivations for conversion, Latter Day Saints "did their utmost not to convert alone. Many converts were explicit about the fact that they had been looking for a church that would be good for their children or other family members, and would support family relationships both practically and doctrinally" (2017, 159). Evangelicals and Mormons hold different theologies, yet the concept of collective salvation and the familial piety of black evangelicals at least raise questions about the hyper-individualism of evangelical religious subjectivity. These expanded perspectives cue our attention not only to the social context of evangelical faith but also to the various kinds of intersubjectivity generated by evangelicals' shared desires for collective fates and futures.

If a broad observance of family piety in CBC and DBC settings provides a context in which church members understand themselves to be responsible for their children's life outcomes in matters of faith and life, and if the reproduction of intergenerational family closeness and religious identity is taken as an indication of parents' religious commitment, then the converse may also be true. In this schema, parents who raised children from whom they are now alienated or who do not identify as Christians assume responsibility for their nontransmission of religious identity. As might be expected, this equation of faithfulness and religious transmission, of culpability and nontransmission, generates anxiety on the part of parents. Whereas children's religious accomplishments are heralded by their parents during interviews and displayed during church-wide gatherings, children's transgressions against familial religious continuity (including renunciations of faith, decisions no longer to attend church, and rejection of church moral codes) were often silenced.

BLACK EVANGELICAL MILLENNIAL DISENCHANTMENT

One Afro-Jamaican church member in his thirties asked me if I had heard about Calvin Drummond, the son of a senior church member at DBC and his longtime friend. When I replied in the negative, he supplied a story about how Drummond decided, after attending church his whole life, that he no longer believed in God. By Drummond's account, his parents did not like to discuss their son's change in religious status, and his wife's family was also perturbed that their daughter had married a man of faith who eventually turned away from it. Brother and Sister Drummond never mentioned their son's lapse in faith during our interviews. They also did not request prayer for him in church settings. Yet Drummond's childhood friend sustained a solidarity with him inside and outside of his Christian religious devotion.

A number of young adults who grew up in CBC and DBC attend other congregations in the Atlanta metropolitan area. One DBC member, Sister Ramia Butler, the twenty-five-year-old daughter of an Afro-Jamaican member, told me after I had completed my year of intensive fieldwork that she had begun to attend a local Baptist church. She took issue with older church members' constant criticisms of the young adult ministries and programming: "We [youths and young adults] have a lot to offer and need an outlet to use those skills. At college, I get to participate in campus Christian events, and it is cool to be surrounded by people of your own age. But with youth Sundays, things may be looking up." Sister Butler ended her observations on a positive note, but had already sought out another mode of fellowship that made more space for young adult perspectives.

Certainly, there are instances when church members insisted that space should be made for younger church members. For example, during a time of testimony a senior church sister used one of the only church-wide speaking platforms to express her sentiments that more young adult men should be preaching in the pulpits on Sundays. In another setting a visiting pastor admonished older church members to follow the example of Paul, Timothy, Moses, and Aaron by stepping down and training their replacements. During the course of my fieldwork, it appeared that CBC and DBC congregations did a better job of creating an environment that catered to the doctrinal sensibilities of older members and the pragmatic needs of members with young and school-aged children rather than unmarried young adults without families. The age gaps visible in church leadership and Butler's accompanying observation that young church members tended to leave after college and after getting married do compel a consideration that patriarchal evangelical religious subculture could generate intergenerational estrangements among CBC and DBC evangelicals.

Church members' testimonies of family piety were just as significant as the silences of intergenerational ruptures in religious identity and Brethren moral standards. Both the testimonies and silences affirm heteronormative family ideology. Although I never encountered someone directly implicating a parent for a child's life choices, the silences and expressed anxieties suggest parents' own self-implications in their children's life choices. Prayers for children's struggles in faith and life were shared among spiritual kin stoically and steadily in Tuesday-night prayer meetings. For example, during a Bible study an Afro-Trinidadian church brother rejoiced that while on a trip to Trinidad, he was able to lead his son and his son's wife to Christ.

It is important to note that despite the moral imperatives and technologies that evangelical subcultures place on familial reproduction of religious identity, there are a number of social, economic, and religious forces that can inhibit the intergenerational transmission of black evangelical religious identity. Research has suggested that generational differences in religious observance in the United States are growing. According to the 2014 Religious Landscape Study conducted by the Pew Research Center on Religion and Public Life, 28 percent of evangelicals are from Generation X (ages 30 to 49), and 35 percent are from the Baby Boomer generation (ages 50 to 64).[8] By contrast, 23 percent of evangelicals are Millennials (ages 18 to 29). Beyond figures that capture declining numbers of evangelical religious observance are studies that examine the disidentification of Millennials with institutionalized religion (in other words, the increasing numbers of Millennial "nones") and seek to understand the reasons for Millennial identification as spiritual rather than religious. However, it is important to insert the caveat that figures for black evangelicals differ from the general figures of evangelical generational divides. So 59 percent of black evangelicals are from Generation X (29 percent) or the Baby Boomer generation (30 percent) in comparison to 31 percent of evangelical Millennials.[9] Although black evangelicals are a smaller subset of the evangelical population (6 percent),[10] the percentage of black Millennial evangelicals is higher than Millennial evangelicals as a whole.[11]

The intergenerational transmission of religion, particularly to Millennials, is understood by Bengston, Putney, and Harris (2013) as fraught. In *Families and Faith: How Religion Is Passed Down across Generations*, they write that "in the eyes of many, families have lost a disturbing amount of their moral and religious influence, seemingly a consequence of parental divorce, excessive individualism, and a breakdown in traditional social structures. From this perspective, if parents are passing religion on to their children, they are not doing it very often or very well" (11).

Instead of affirming a meta-narrative that links a presumably impending secularism with a decline of family morality (the very clarion call around which the Moral Majority coalesced), Bengston, Putney, and Harris found in their longitudinal study that there was a high degree of intergenerational transmission of religious identity between 1970 and 2005, despite increasing individualism and changing familial forms and roles (2013, 66). They also found that for evangelical Protestants, the rate of parent-child similarities (e.g., religious affiliation, intensity, participation, literal and conservative biblical interpretation, and understanding of the significance of religion in public life) remained remarkably high between 1970 and 2005 (2013, 66), mainly because of their participation in a distinctive religious culture that exhibits the traits of minoritized cultures and because "group religious practices are highly interconnected with family activities, and there is a high value placed on families and family continuity" (2013, 166). Given the high degree of evangelical transmission of religious identity across generations, it may be that evangelical claims of secularism and its attending decline in family stability are less a statement of reality than an evangelical bulwark against intergenerational religious change.[12]

BLACK EVANGELICAL PARENTS, CHILDREN, AND THE (DE)MORALIZATIONS OF RACE AND CLASS

In addition to ideas about intergenerational religious connections that are conditioned by an evangelical subcultural emphasis of endemic religious and familial entropy, CBC and DBC parents' expression of concerns about their children's future religious identities also reflects embedded concerns about the reproduction of class identities. As a predominantly black, middle-class constituency, CBC and DBC members have anxieties about material conditions and intergenerational relationships that are shaped by moral scripts that typically go hand in hand with immigration and racial neoliberalism. According to evangelical studies scholars (see Gallagher and Smith 1999), the same concerns are associated with the framing of the Moral Majority and a subsequent white mainstream neo-evangelical focus on the family amid the changing material conditions instigated by racial integration and deindustrialization.

If transferring evangelical identity across generations is understood to defend against the tides of a looming secularism, then the preservation of Afro-Caribbean and African American intergenerational church attendance can also be conceptualized not only as a mode of religious transmission, a spiritual form of collective salvation, but also as a defense against downward mobility. Scholars understand the process of immigration and the separation from communities and cultures of origin as producing distinct generational experiences that are sites of difference and, at times, conflict between first-generation migrants and their second-generation children born away from the family's place of origin. First-generation parents are burdened with the pressure to instill in their children cultural norms without the assistance of natal social, familial, and religious networks. First-generation parents are also tasked with the project of upward social mobility, which may be reflected in their own maintenance or improved class positions after immigration or in the class outcomes of their children. Nonetheless, the familial project of immigrant social mobility, which is a highly moralized project with class and religious implications in the Caribbean, is challenged by the downward mobility associated with blackness on the part of US-born and immigrant blacks alike.

Scholars of Afro-Caribbean immigration such as Mary Waters (2001) and Milton Vickerman (2016) have debated whether second-generation children of Caribbean migrants will identify more closely with Caribbean or African American culture as a result of the top-down forces of racialization that can flatten black ethnic distinctions into an undifferentiated landscape of blackness. The moralization of black ethnic distinctions vis-à-vis essentialized notions of black immigrant success and African American class stagnation has prompted debates among race and ethnicity scholars. Researchers have examined how black ethnic identity distinctions affect black diasporic solidarities and how narratives of black immigrant success invoked by scholars and black immigrants in relation to African Americans illustrate the declining significance of race in shaping socioeconomic outcomes in the post–civil rights era. Within such schemas, identification with Caribbean familial networks and the interconnected value systems of social mobility and respectability are understood to help Afro-Caribbean migrants and their children to navigate, and potentially sidestep, the downward mobility associated with blackness in

US contexts (Olwig 2007). Given the long-standing history of Afro-Caribbean Christian churches as institutions that foster bourgeois respectability (Besson 1993, 2002; Wilson 1973), Afro-Caribbean intergenerational connections and church attendance can then be understood as a means of buttressing Caribbean immigrant social mobility.[13]

According to the 2014 Pew Religious Landscape Study statistics, there is an observable difference between first- and second-generation black evangelical religious observance. A total of 14 percent of first-generation black immigrants identify as evangelicals in contrast to 8 percent of second-generation black immigrants.[14] Such intergenerational differences in Afro-Caribbean religious observance might be seen as a result of a decreasing pull of Caribbean migrant family influence and a drift away from interconnected religious and familial traditions that are believed to help shape the second generation's ascent to Heaven and up the US class hierarchy.

Although many of the African American evangelicals whom I interviewed were domestic migrants (and not international immigrants), their concerns for their children paralleled that of Afro-Caribbean members. On the part of African Americans, scholars have depicted black church attendance as a means to instill the values of respectability and a strong sense of racial subjectivity and self-esteem, values that can help black congregants navigate the physical, spiritual, and identity assaults of antiblack racism and social mobility. According to Andrea Abrams in *God and Blackness: Race, Gender, and Identity in a Middle Class Afrocentric Church*, African American church members at First Afrikan Presbyterian church in Lithonia, Georgia, construct black religious identities, vis-à-vis modes of Afrocentric blackness and black liberation theology, that they understand to be more culturally authentic and generative than that produced by working-class blacks. Thus, even within African American contexts that foreground intentional and positive constructions and valuations of black religious identities, intra-ethnic reckonings of class also generate a sense of otherness and cultural hierarchies of value. In her study of Afro-anglophone Caribbean immigrants in Cuba, Andrea Queeley observes that self-making grounded in respectability "simultaneously challenges and reinscribes the racial hierarchy and Black marginality" through its ability to create moralized modes of intraracial distinction (2015, 5). Like ethno-racial distinctions, narratives of respectability generate their own "otherness."

I cannot venture a clear-cut reading of the distinctions between Afro-Caribbean and African American practices and anxieties about intergenerational identity transmission. I also have no record of Afro-Caribbean and African American congregants making ethnic distinctions in their approaches to parenting or family values. This may be an outgrowth of my ethnic identity as African American (and a subsequent bracketing of such discourse along ethnic lines), of the complex and myriad identity positions taken by second-generation Caribbean congregants (who may alternately identify as Caribbean, Caribbean American, or African American), of the potentially multiethnic character of congregant families, or of the shared labor and witnessing of child rearing of Afro-Caribbean and African American congregants over the years. Although many African American Brethren tend to have converted from other Christian traditions to Brethrenism, they often have less extensive Brethren intergenerational histories than their Afro-Caribbean counterparts. This may fuel a specific set of anxieties on the part of African American evangelicals who may be first-generation evangelicals themselves, who are trying to reproduce a religious identity across generations that is not widely associated with African Americans, and who have inhabited a US context shaped by a pathologization of black family systems longer than their Caribbean coreligionists (though, as mentioned above, Caribbean family systems have been implicated in colonial and postcolonial schemas of color and class).[15]

BLACK EVANGELICAL PARENTS AND CONFESSIONAL INTIMACY

As parents, both Afro-Caribbean and African American evangelicals of CBC and DBC inhabit a US racio-religious milieu that makes black families morally and materially responsible for their class outcomes. Black evangelicals inhabit a moralized racial and religious territory between evangelical family piety and a political cult of black parental blame conditioned by (conservative and neoliberal) governmental discourses of black family pathology and an evangelical family-values discourse that was written in relation to the presumed pathology of black family systems. Church youths and young adults navigate the interconnected moral pulls of religious beliefs, family obligations, and patriarchal/parental hierarchies from below. Thus, black evangelical parents raise, hope, and fear for their children amid the idealizations of intergenerational transfer of religious identity as a marker of parental faithfulness and the ethno-racial, generational, and class processes that make black parenting challenging. Together, the experiences of black evangelical parents and youths illuminate the moral intersections of race, religion, and heteropatriarchal citizenship that fuel CBC and DBC parental anxieties and the utility of confessional intimacy to air concerns that attend to raising children while attempting to transmit evangelical religious identities to them.

Black Evangelicals and the Ideals, Ordeals, and Intimacies of Marriage

If, as the popular saying claims, "It takes a village to raise a child," then the evangelicals of DBC could respond that it takes a vigilant community to sustain a marriage. Socioreligiously speaking, marriage is a central signifier of respectability. Moreover, sustaining heterosexual marriage, particular in an environment in which marriage is understood in terms of its fragility within contemporary US society on the part of evangelicals, becomes a significant marker of faithfulness.

Sister Sharon Winston, the wife of the Afro-Jamaican Brethren minister, spoke at the annual United Bible Conference in Lake Junalaska, North Carolina, in 2008, a conference attended by DBC members, CBC members, and other black Brethren evangelicals. She painted a picture of the fragility of marriage during a conference breakout session:

> The Barna survey, which is updated through yearly tracking studies, confirm[s] that born-again Christians have the same likelihood of divorce as do non-Christians. Um, among married, born-again Christians, thirty-five percent—that's the—the—that's in the update report, five-fourteen um—the five fourteen two oh eight—thirty-five percent have experienced a divorce. Now look at the bottom. That thirty-five percent figure is identical—is *identical* to the outcome among those who are not born-again Christians.[16]

As Winston put it in another portion of her presentation, the challenges and frustrations of marriage and the context of marital dissolutions can generate a comical yet common perspective about marriage that people can cultivate. She described this as "When I got married, I was looking for an ideal. Then it became an ordeal. And now I want a new deal."

Just as parents raise their children in contexts that are shaped by a deep history of black family pathology, intergenerational dynamics, and religious and political moral narratives, black evangelical marriages are located in a similarly troubled ideological field. The ideals and ordeals of marriage are shaped by prevailing notions of black nonheteronormativity, Brethren perspectives on marriage, neo-evangelical marriage ideologies and practices, and neoliberal ideological imprints. Yet in these overlapping social forces shaping black evangelical marriages one can also find spaces of reflection crafted by black evangelicals and most often mediated by spiritual kinship relationships in which church members raise questions and share experiential insights and dissident perspectives.

THE "IDEALS" OF MARRIAGE: ONE FLESH, MALE HEADSHIP, AND FEMALE SUBMISSION

Similar to their creation of a religious culture that values youth religious instruction, the black evangelicals with whom I interacted constructed environments in which marriages are valued and supported institutionally. Wedding celebrations were big church affairs with multiple members contributing to different aspects of the wedding experience, including planning, hosting bridal showers, participating in the bridal party retinue or the service itself, and preparing reception food. In addition to helping to create and participate in marriage celebrations, the chapel communities created a celebratory and supportive environment for marriages. As might be expected in an environment in which heteronormative relationships are not only institutionally centered but fervently celebrated, the numbers of single adult church members were few (except for the unmarried sons and daughters of longtime members who grew up in the church). Moreover, during the time of my fieldwork there were no openly professing gay members attending the church, which demonstrates that the heteronormative religious culture fostered a context in which LGBTQ members and identifications would be silenced and marginalized.

As a religious movement influenced by Plymouth Brethrenism and the practices of Afro-Caribbean religious cultures, the Afro-Caribbean and African American evangelicals of DBC and CBC hold strong theological views about the sanctity of marriage. Church members construct marriage as a sacred relationship that is distinctive, that is enduring, and that produces a special type of intersubjectivity: the creation of wives and husbands as "one flesh."[17] In a sermon about the "biblical model of family authority"—built upon wifely submission to male headship and children's obedience to parental authority—the brother preaching observed "a supernatural union created by God that must be undertaken with supernatural strength given by God." Marriage, in making two become one, reflects the mystery of the Trinity. Marriage is an example of the mysteries of unity in diversity.

Church members' spiritualization of marriage emerges also in terms of marriage's existence as an analogue of the relationship between Jesus Christ ("the bridegroom") and the Christian Church ("the bride"). In the words of Brethren theologian Norman W. Crawford, "The bride [of Christ] is kept in spotless purity through the virtue of Christ's blood" (1997, 43). As the bride of Christ, the universal Christian Church (and Christians as constituents of that Church by extension) is viewed as ideally being submissive to Christ, much as all wives are enjoined to submit to their husbands. At the same time, congregants personify the Church as Christ's beloved, an entity for which Christ (as an ideal husband) rightfully sacrifices his body.[18] Thus, marital intimacy evokes the spiritual relationship between Christians and Christ. Put another way, Plymouth Brethren theology locates marriage at the heart of the most significant relationship of Christian identity. Yet if husbands are analogized with Christ the bridegroom, even if couched within a language of sacrifice, the creation of "one flesh" and "oneness" must also be understood to be hierarchical in terms of patriarchal gender norms. This familial patriarchy resounds with broader neo-evangelical ideologies of "the family" and religious and secular interventions for black family pathology prescribed by secular and religious racial and moral scripts.

"ORDEALS" OF MARRIAGE: CBC AND DBC EVANGELICALISM AND THERAPEUTIC MARRIAGE CULTURE

Given the ways in which marriage emerges as a special kind of sacred intersubjectivity between men and women, between Christ and Church, and among the members of the Trinity in Brethren theology, congregants' emphasis on sustaining marriage is not surprising. Divorce is frowned upon. A popular adage used by Afro-Caribbean members that references Brethren marriage ideals is "One wife. One life." The phrase was a definitive statement about lifelong heterosexual monogamy, albeit from a masculine perspective. My interactions with congregants also revealed that marriage was discussed in terms of a contrast between frail romantic love versus a solid intentional love. Sister Sharon Winston voiced these sentiments in the context of the Bible conference minisession in North Carolina mentioned previously:

> So when you marry because of romantic love, you are going to marry somebody who is going to hurt you as you were hurt in your childhood. You are going to have the most *horrific* nightmare when you marry for *romantic* love. We are taught—now if you marry, and when the scales fall off your eyes, and you say, "What am I doing here? I don't want to be with this woman. I don't want to be with this man, and you hang in there, and you work it through to mature love, *that* is what we're talking about. Mature love. OK, so love is a *choice*.

As an Afro-Jamaican church sister put it during an interview with her husband, "Love is an act of the *will*." Thus, congregants insisted on marriage as a matter of intentional commitment rather than the outgrowth of romance. And this discussion of the labor of marital love illustrates that members understand the very constructedness of "the family." Even if "the family" is naturalized as an outgrowth of biology, socialized through cultural scripts of normativity, and spiritualized as God-ordained, black evangelicals understand kinship as the product of intention. Kincraft in its nuclear and more extended manifestations emerges, in part, from a commitment to seeing things through.

The emphasis on marital commitment was not just reinforced through the public celebration of marriage ceremonies and anniversaries, colloquial wisdom, or personal experiences. It was also reinforced at the level of institutional practices of discipline.[19] The DBC community understand corrective discipline to be the duty of a loving church community toward its "brothers and sisters in Christ" and as a preemptive measure that ensures the health of the church community. Sin is understood as a contagion that can spread through the church, to which, in addition to familial metaphors, church members often refer as the body of Christ. Consequently, the bodies of church members—as a site of potential sin, and in particular the sexual sin of marital infidelity—are a significant focus of community attention and collective discipline. As noted by Brother Littlefield at the opening of this chapter, theoretically all sin is condemned. Practically, however, in Littlefield's words, "Adultery is a big sin." The big sin of adultery also attests to the foundational significance of marriage within CBC and DBC communities theologically and institutionally, and as a sign of Christian faithfulness and endurance. Yet I propose that the "big sin" of adultery (and the big win of successful long-term monogamous marriages) within these black evangelical settings also signals the significance of marriage in the broader society, in particular in relation to "the unholy bundle" of antiblack moral narratives of black family life propagated by conservative, evangelical, and neoliberal discourse.[20]

Yet even with marriage's foundational significance inside and outside of chapel walls, and the interconnected network of *oughts* and *shoulds* intended to produce conformity to heteropatriarchal norms, there are two gender-based tensions that make marriages, like parenting, a difficult enterprise. The egalitarian ethos of Brethrenism (undergirded by ideologies of spiritual brotherhood and sisterhood, critical views of clerical hierarchy, and a belief in the priesthood of believers) is in tension with the patriarchal hierarchy of Victorian family norms. The tension between egalitarianism and patriarchy affects not only the intergenerational relationships between parents and children and older and younger congregants; it also affects understandings and enactments of marriage relationships. This is compounded by the tension between evangelical notions of oneness/mutual love and God-ordained hierarchy that emerged in DBC marriage ideology. In their study of evangelical family norms, Sally Gallagher and Christian Smith found that evangelical gender projects were characterized less by schemas of male dominance and female obedience and more by notions of symbolic traditionalism and pragmatic egalitarianism (Gallagher and Smith 1999).

The topic of male headship and female submission inside of the home and church was an active subject of exegesis, conversation, and contemplation. For instance, in a Bible study setting, the question of male headship and female submission was debated by attendees, a few of whom were not DBC congregants. In particular, attendees questioned the prohibition of women's church leadership and the practice of women's use of head coverings in worship settings.[21]

Much of the conversation centered around whether head coverings and female submission were a matter of biblical imperative or cultural tradition. A few church brothers were emphatic that the Bible was true down to the very letter, even in response to the issue of head coverings. One outspoken church brother held that not observing the truth of every biblical command meant undermining the truth of the Bible as whole. A calmer, older DBC church sister replied that the practice of female submission through the wearing of the head covering could be an act of conforming to the faith community of which you were a part, regardless of one's personal belief. She also dissented from a strict critique of women's leadership by making the pragmatic observation that given the demographic majority of women in many churches, most churches would be empty without women's interventions as leaders.

I could not help but wonder if her words, which were carefully and thoughtfully spoken, were the product of her own sustained contemplation of the boundaries between herself and community and of her place in her home and church and that of women more generally. Moreover, her statement attests to a thoughtful piety in relation to evangelical institutional religious norms around gender. If the members of this black evangelical constituency demonstrate their thoughtful engagement with evangelical Christianity—a religion with a worldview that has been conscripted into racial, imperial, and geopolitical hierarchies—then this is all the more the case for black evangelical women who participate in a Brethren-informed religious movement. In terms of gender Brethren emphasize a corrective heteropatriarchy that is intended to build the capacity of men and to promote women's recognition and acceptance of their leadership.

Located in an economic context that is shaped by the social disruptions of migration, which can disrupt marriages through spatial separation or the economic and social stressors of downward mobility, married churchmen and churchwomen participating in this black evangelical fellowship must also deal with the challenges of neoliberalism. Black evangelical men navigate secular and religious responsibilization as leaders and providers in the church and home, and face the combined weight of such pressures. Within the moral field of black evangelical family values, black women are called upon to do the converse and to distance themselves from archetypes like the female household head iconized in the Moynihan Report for her emasculation and marginalization of male providers. Differing from their black male coreligionists, who navigate evangelical and neoliberal moral demands that call for their material and spiritual leadership in the overlapping domain of church and home, black evangelical women navigate neoliberal market demands that celebrate entrepreneurial success in the workplace (associated with competitive, risk-taking, individualistic proclivities) and religious ideologies that idealize women's submission in the home. It is a paradoxical field of moral discourse that calls for moves in opposite directions. Women are enjoined to assert themselves as dominant in the public sphere of work and submissive in the private sphere.[22]

Therefore, the challenges for black evangelical married women located amid the moral paradigms of racism and neoliberalism are not only material and are not only expressed in the intersectional race, gender, and class oppressions that shape women's inequitable access to material resources. The challenges they navigate are also conceptual, and the black women of the CBC and DBC communities are in good company. In *The Promise of Patriarchy: Women and the Nation of Islam*, Ula Taylor discusses the complex choices that African American women made to invest in the patriarchy family and religious projects organized by the Nation of Islam (NOI) that promised "protection, financial stability, and loving husbands" to black women (2017, 4). Rather than painting an image of rank-and-file submission, Taylor illustrates the appeal of NOI patriarchy to a wide range of African American women, including civil rights activists and even artists like Sonia Sanchez. In so doing, Taylor illustrates that African American women's complex negotiations of gender, familial, religious, and racial solidarities generated an informed consent to patriarchal formations and the modes of prosperity and steadiness that it was thought to promote, especially against the racist and sexist precarity engendered in white supremacist social structures and its material, environmental, and symbolic impact on black family lives.

In *Raising the Race: Black Women Redefine Marriage, Motherhood, and Community*, anthropologist Riché Barnes examines contemporary African American middle-class women in Atlanta and their thoughtful practices of strategic mothering. She finds that black women generate flexible approaches that combine work, family, and community commitments and conceptualize marriage in terms of submission that, at times, contrast with socializing influences that emphasize women's independence. Barnes examines what she terms a neo-politics of respectability that emerges in relation to women's "desire[s] to maintain their marriages and find ways to be successful wives and mothers. They rely on their religious views, their families and friends, and their own resolve to rationalize why they work so hard toward maintaining their unions, despite the difficulties" (2016, 133–34).

In *Entrepreneurial Selves: Neoliberal Respectability and the Making of a Caribbean Middle Class*, Carla Freeman notes that middle-class entrepreneurs in Barbados—though often navigating tensions between work and familial obligations—apply the entrepreneurial and innovative ethos fostered by neoliberal organizations of class to create flexible family arrangements (2014). They also experiment with cultivating modes of familial communion and intimacy. Thus, African American and Afro-Caribbean religious and middle-class women enter into their familial arrangements contemplatively. They meet the moral and material demands of middle-class respectable family expectations inside and outside of religious spaces through the creation of emergent networks of support and intimacy.

MARRIAGE AND CONFESSIONAL INTIMACY

What do church members do when marriages are failing, especially in an institutional context where heteronormative marriage is so heavily celebrated? As outlined by the senior elder who was a certified marriage counselor and who conducted weekly marriage enrichment courses during the DBC Sunday-school time slot, "By the time couples seek out advice, it's almost too late. They need to hear this stuff before the rough times come." My discussions with Afro-Caribbean and African American evangelicals about their family practices and experiences inside and outside of church spaces revealed their use of the reflective spaces mediated by spiritual kinship, technologies of self-revelation encoded in testimonial practices, and interview and research conversations as spaces for what I call a *confessional intimacy*. Although intimacy is often privatized, and popularly relegated to the confines of the marriage relationship itself, confessional intimacy emerges in the conversational realm of the spiritual or extra-institutional spaces of lived religious experience between close kin, whether familial or spiritual. Like many modes of kinship that are not biogenetically defined or organized, modes of intimacy that emerge outside of the genealogical grid are often understudied. In their study of care and intimacy, Sasha Roseneil and Shelley Budgeon examine intimacies that occur outside of heterosexual and heterorelational relationships, which include friendships and nonsexual relationships (2004). Although their analysis is pitted in opposition to dominant heteronormative definitions of intimacy, they call for studies of "affective life" that "can register a fuller range of practices of intimacy and care" (Roseneil and Budgeon 2004, 154).

Elder John Hastings and his wife, Sister Alana, mentioned that they shared their personal experiences with sexuality and marriage with their children and Christian audiences:

> ELDER JOHN HASTINGS: We have had to share some of our history [around teenaged pregnancy] with our children. And there is a balance. And some people will say you're sharing gory details. But there's a balance in showing enough details to let them know that your Christian life has not been a perfect walk. And in some ways that gives them a realness.
>
> SISTER ALANA HASTINGS: There was an article we did for a mission magazine, and we talked about marriage counseling. And a woman said, why are you airing your dirty laundry? People are going to read this, and they're gonna know that ya'll had problems. And I said that we had problems, but what they're gonna see is that there's hope. And she kept saying, I hope so-and-so don't see this. And that's the feeling you get from believers even. Some said, do ya'll wanna share that much? But I don't have time to play games. Behind my doors I want there to be honest truth and not having to mask what's going on. It got to me that people were feeling like, oh, you and him had problems?

Although Elder and Sister Hastings subscribed to the patriarchal gender arrangements associated with "the family," they also shared with their children, church community, and broader religious audiences their struggles with approximating those family norms.

In a small-group Bible study setting, Sister Rita Bivins shared her critical insights on evangelical gender ideology. From her perspective, lessons about women's submission have been distorted by clergy who do not mention that such submission is conditional upon men's committed demonstration of love to their wives. Similarly, she noted that teachings about women's silence and submission in the face of male leadership that failed to teach about believers' mutual submission were inaccurate. As a result of these teachings, she argued, women have been encouraged to stay with abusive and cheating husbands. She told the story of a woman beaten to the point of hospitalization when she tried to make her marriage last because of her exposure to the frequent teaching "God hates divorce." She also told her own story about how she divorced her husband, who pretended to become a Christian after her conversion. Although she also endured physical abuse, her discovery of his infidelity and his deception about his own conversion was what motivated her decision to file for divorce.

In generating these scenes of confessional intimacy, the Hastings and Sister Bivins disturbed the decorum and bounding of family business within the nuclear family household and illustrated the very constructedness of heteronormative family life. They also posed significant challenges to the institutionalization of gender ideologies and the privatization of familial challenges.

In other instances, church members used the reflective spaces of evangelical spirituality to question the centrality of "the family" to evangelical moral landscapes. Doctor Selah Carrington, an Afro-Jamaican woman dentist, resident of Lithonia, and sister member of DBC, shared the following reflections:

> I hear people talking about . . . sometimes they'll say . . . they'll talk about a woman who didn't get married and have kids as her life not being complete or [as being] less . . . than. And they are so wrong. If she has Jesus in her life, that's what it's all about. It's more than ten kids. It's more than the best marriage in the world. That's what it's all about. God didn't intend for us all to get married. The people that we read about in the Bible. There are a lot of dysfunctional . . . there are not many good families in the Bible. They're all pretty dysfunctional [laughing]. Heavily dysfunctional!!! So I mean the Bible itself shows us that the marriage and the children is not where it's at. It is just . . . it's all about God, and it's all about Jesus. If you ask me about the relationship with the people at church, most times when you're talking to somebody at church you're already talking to a Christian. None of us know who's saved and who's not saved. But if they are saved, and the Holy Spirit is talking to the Holy Spirit in them, I think that that is one of the most fulfilling forms of communication that there is.

Sister Carrington's observations illustrate the ways in which black evangelicals can use the reflective spaces and contemplative practices mediated by evangelical religiosity, like Bible study, to query popular evangelical emphases of the family as a central signifier of evangelical identity. She also illustrates the particular ways that black evangelicals can use evangelical spirituality to produce therapeutic spaces for confessional intimacy. Confessional intimacy provides spaces for revelation, nonjudgmental support, and contexts for a subjective and intersubjective coherence that Anna Strhan attributes to contemporary modes of urban evangelicalism in England (2015). In particular, the location of these intimate discussions and critical contemplations outside of congregational spaces illustrates the power of the spiritual to govern modes of sociality that are not always beholden to institutional ideologies.

If "the black family" is the cause of and cure for black socioeconomic stability, according to scholars, policy makers, citizens, and Christians alike, we might be persuaded to think of "the black heteronormative family" as a secular and sacred sign of black moral worthiness. Those who form and sustain heteronormative marriages are understood to fulfill the political model of heteropatriarchal citizenship emphasized by conservatives and liberals alike as well as evangelical outlines of a God-ordained familial design. To fall short of this particular model of morality is to open up a potential wellspring of guilt and other effects, as Brother Littlefield's testimony illustrates. To attain this model is to earn congregational and societal prestige. Families are work. But most members create and maintain their families amid a neoliberal racio-religious context shaped by endemic antiblack racialization, an economic recession, and an ensuing moral discourse that increases the apportionment of responsibility and blame for black citizens. That requires a great deal more physical and reflective labor. And the ethnographic portraits of DBC members' collective labor around family life illustrate that. Although the weight of pathological discourse is heavy, black evangelicals are still able to create spaces of reflexivity and intimacy in which to navigate the anxieties, criticisms, and marginalizations of family moral discourse via spiritual relationships. We are left with two views of family. The heteronormative family is sanctified through racial and religious discourses of normativity and divine ordination. The church family is spiritualized through the relating capacity of embodied Holy Spirit, theological and biblical discourse of fraternalism, and ritualized and close everyday relationships of trust and intimacy that are seasoned through time. The coexistence, and at times overlap, of those modes of family in black evangelical religiosity and lived experience illumines the counter-hegemonic implications of black evangelical constructions of spiritual kinship within moral orders of race, kinship, and religion as well as the need for different analytical mappings of family and religious sociality.

The conclusion ends this book by outlining a set of lessons that derive from attention to DBC and CBC members' constructions of spiritual kinship and how a narration of US moral orders of religion, race, and family from the social location of black evangelicals raises important insights about the US social landscape.

Conclusion

Five and a half years after I left Atlanta and the site of my research, I received a phone call from my spiritual parents, Brother and Sister Stewart. They told me that after their morning Bible study, Sister Susan Stewart said my name crossed her mind. Brother Bernard Stewart marveled that he, too, had been wondering how I was getting along. It was the kind of serendipity that this Brethren community understands to be significant—and that it takes as a spiritual call to affirm connection. Their phone call found me in Vermont rushing from my Caribbean religions class to the campus day-care center to pick up my then two-year-old son. Their name appeared on my cell phone screen. I paused before I answered. Guilt washed over me. I had not done a great job of keeping in touch with them. They had opened their home to me. They had been so generous in their nurturance of me, so forthright in sharing their experiences with me, so genuine in providing me company. Fear and embarrassment engulfed me. My life had changed substantially since we had last spoken. How would they interpret the choices I had made? And what would this mean for our relationship? An abbreviated recounting of our conversation follows.

> BROTHER BERNARD: Sister Todne, you came across our minds today. It's been a long time. How are you doing?
>
> TT: I'm sorry. I know it's been a long time. I'm OK. How are you?
>
> BROTHER BERNARD: We're doing good. Where are you now? Are you still in Virginia?
>
> TT: No, I'm living in Vermont. I got a job here, and I'm teaching.

BROTHER BERNARD: That's good. How's your son doing?

TT: He's doing great. Growing fast. He's two now.

BROTHER BERNARD: And your husband?

TT: . . . I have no husband.

BROTHER BERNARD: Explain.

TT: We got a divorce. Things got complicated. He moved to another city to pursue a job opportunity, and then with the distance and all the pressures, things got really hard.

BROTHER BERNARD: So he moved away from you and the baby?

TT: Yeah.

BROTHER BERNARD: Then you must let him go. Sister Tabitha wants to talk to you.

SISTER TABITHA: What happened?

TT: I got a divorce. Things became complicated.

SISTER TABITHA: Was adultery an issue? Because if so, adultery is grounds for divorce. Matthew 19 discusses it. That's biblical.

I answered them. We talked a bit more about their health and about my life in Vermont. I apologized profusely for being so haphazard about keeping in touch and promised to do a better job. We said our good-byes and ended our call.

My conversation with Brother and Sister Bernard about the end of my marriage initially astounded me. We shared a spiritual kinship with one another. Their house was the place I knew I could go if I needed a warm welcome. It was their mentorship of me in life and faith: our mutual, deep confiding about marriage, family, and life that fostered our deep sense of kinship. They had attended my wedding in Tennessee. And although we had a spiritual relatedness that we developed over time that extended beyond the formal parameters of my fieldwork, I had hidden myself and my life circumstances from them. I assumed that the heteronormative religious culture of the CBC and DBC communities would necessarily mean they would frown on my decision to get a divorce. Even though I was writing a book that examined the ways in which black evangelicals produced family beyond "the family," even though I had experienced what it meant to be accepted by this community, I still fell into the assumption that our relationship would be contingent upon my successful maintenance of a heteronormative marriage.

My association of evangelicalism with judgment was not accidental or benign. Ideas come from a place. Evangelical Christianity is, and has been, composed of many (and, at times, conflicting) ideologies about social membership. Evangelicalism is premised on a number of ideals about a born-again conversion, engagement with an authoritative scripture, an emphasis on evangelism, and the outward expression of faith through works. It calls for a Christianity that transforms the person but that is made visible through demonstrating one's personal piety and reverential interactions with text. Evangelicalism is also a religion definitively associated with social context. Consequently, an attention to a born-again salvific concept and a representation of personal piety is not quite enough. CBC and DBC evangelicals demonstrate their Christian faithfulness through their imagination and investment in their relationships with others through genealogical, theological, congregational, biblical, quotidian, and confessional processes of kincraft.

As shaped by the movement of Plymouth Brethrenism, believers understand that social context expansively to include a universal body of believers that consists of Christians who have existed across space and time, and who will reunite at the time of Christ's second coming. Plymouth Brethren also hold a strong idea of the local community, how it should model the familial community of New Testament predecessors, how that community should engage the Bible, and where the boundaries of fellowship should be set. Neoevangelicalism was created by religious founders who wanted to engage the world more than their fundamentalist predecessors did. Yet these engagements by and large turned to entrenchments when faced with racial desegregation and the calls for inclusion proposed by women and LGBTQ members in the 1960s. The heteronormative family became a religious icon and a sanctified enclosure. Calls for ongoing social activism and material redistribution authored by an evangelical Left and racial reconciliation–oriented evangelicals of color would not be widely heard until the 1990s.

The evangelicalism that many of us have come to know in the US, either by personal experience or via the workings of racial hegemony and popular culture, is an evangelicalism that defines and embraces true believers as those who belong, in contrast to moral outsiders who are often disowned. Racial and conservative religious identities tend to be understood as fixed social positionings. The same can be said of evangelical constructions of heteronormative family life that often generate hardened moral positions on what kind of family counts, and who is included or excluded from the ranks of fellowship as a result. And this evangelicalism, in tandem with heteropatriarchy and the institutionalized boundaries it has erected since the 1970s, has done harm. This has to be acknowledged. People have been marginalized for LGBTQ sexuality and gender identity and expressions, marital infidelity, for having children out of wedlock, and for asking questions about institutionalized biblical interpretations and their Christian faith. I admit that this was the evangelicalism that first came to mind when I unexpectedly found myself speaking with my church parents.

My church parents reminded me that the evangelicalism in my mind has its shortcomings, that I was reducing black evangelical religiosity to ideology at the cost of more complex, emergent views of practice. As an Afro-Caribbean migrant, my church father reminded me that family togetherness, when possible, should be prioritized. As a woman, my church mother reminded me that even with the endemic patriarchy of evangelical religious subculture, the Bible provided recourse for married persons in cases of infidelity.

I had also forgotten or not fully believed for myself in my own situation that, amid the popular moralities associated with religion, race, and family in the US that are plotted around axes of Right and Left, inside and outside, normativity and pathology, black evangelicals had demonstrated to me on many occasions that people can show up for each other. I equated the borders of black evangelical sociality with "the family."

I also almost enclosed the borders of the "field" of my fieldwork to my time of local face-to-face community interactions. In reality, the coproduction of ethnographic knowledge is ongoing, and comes in fits and starts, in the drawing of conclusions, misestimations, and revisions. And just as my interactions with my church parents during my time in Atlanta taught me much about the contents of spiritual kinship, my conversation with them about my changed familial conditions also illustrated the salience of my argument. My framing of their religious project as a set of processes of community self-fashioning could not be reduced to the boundaries of heteronormativity. My familial experiences interfaced with the myriad familial experiences that DBC and CBC evangelicals narrated and allowed me to witness. This demonstrated to me that we create, study, theorize, and write kinship in part through our familial locations. Family interaction and experiences are not only modes of belonging but also sites of ethnographic learning and knowing.

Although my spiritual parents had shared a generous transparency about their life experiences with me over the years, I almost returned that transparency with opacity about my own life circumstances. This was not reciprocity.

In falling into a common practice of privatizing my heteronormative family business, I almost missed my blessing. I almost foreclosed the opportunity to have my spiritual parents "come alongside" me. Locally, "coming alongside" is a praxis of showing up across the boundaries of nuclear family life or of congregational settings to meet people where they are, in good times and bad. This is the practice of the spiritual and extra-institutional mode of communion that provides spaces of spiritual and material support, care, confiding, and intimacy. The work of their collective kincraft—the means by which church members make themselves into kin through received ideologies and practices of intention—is an important aesthetic product of black evangelical religiosity. When posing the question of why members would participate in a religious movement that insisted that its members follow challenging moral orthodoxies, it is this practice of "coming alongside," this central and valued process of kincraft, of engaging in the shared labor and benefits of community fashioning and belonging, that constitutes a very important motivation for membership.

In a conversation with Sister Amanda Morrison, an African American woman in her thirties who used to attend DBC and who had gone through a divorce, she mentioned that she had received a great deal of support from her black evangelical in-laws. I asked her how she was received by the church after news of her divorce spread. She responded, "There are some personalities, but people are mostly just happy to see you." "Personalities" can say one thing. Hands, eyes, smiles, greetings, welcomes, check-ins, offerings, prayers, head nods, understandings can do another. So most members extended to Sister Morrison the offer and continuation of community that were welcomed by her, even amid the heavily heteronormative population of the church's membership. Despite the presence of a few strong critics of her decision to divorce, she was not cut off; she still belonged.

This raises important questions about the nature of conservative and orthodox religious movements and the ways in which the rank and file, the people in pews who participate in these movements, may also tend to be read in terms of the "personalities" or the dominant voices who frame evangelical family moral discourse. The social position and experiences of the framers of evangelical family morality, inside the DBC and CBC communities and beyond, may not tell the stories we most need to hear about evangelical Christianity.

This book has captured the stories of *kincraft* in which black evangelicals engage, people who are rarely protected by various forms of racial, ethnic, gendered, class, and interpretive privilege associated with the framers of heteropatriarchal family discourse and the founders of hegemonic white neo-evangelicalism. Instead, these black evangelicals inhabit a space in which they have to translate evangelical religious ideals into the uncertain terrain of lived religious experience, where the connections of moral ideals and social outcomes are tentative, experimental, and contemplated.

In fact, the spiritual kin who were nearest and dearest to the hearts of DBC and CBC members were the ones who showed up for one another with acceptance rather than moral prescription. By voicing their support (or at least their nonjudgment) of my divorce, Brother and Sister Bernard emphasized our enduring relatedness as spiritual kin. They reminded me that the relationship the three of us had and continue to have is also the point of our spiritual kinship, that our bond does not break even though a marriage bond might. They affirmed my value as a person and even searched for a potentially biblical basis on which to authenticate my divorce. They reminded me that they were still with me, beyond the temporal and spatial boundaries of my local fieldwork in Atlanta and the dissolvable bonds of marriage. They demonstrated that kincraft was a technology of kin-making, one that wed spiritual definitions of Christians as a family of God to material concerns. Spiritual kinship endures, even amid the mobilities and marginalizations of diaspora and race. Their kincraft wed conventional family ethics, institutional memberships, spiritual lexicons of relationship, and extra-institutional acts of communion and care. This technology could shape everyday life and meet emergent concerns such as migration, job loss, illness, death, and divorce. The Bernards showed me that there are multiple possibilities for connection and opportunities for collective faith in black evangelical religious communities.

BLACK EVANGELICAL KINCRAFT: CONCEPTS AND PRACTICE

This book has demonstrated that the study of black evangelical kincraft requires twin processes of learning and unlearning. Racial and conservative religious identities tend to be understood as fixed social positionings. The same can be said of evangelical constructions of heteronormative family life. It can be understood as generating hardened moral positions on what kind of family counts, and thus who is included or excluded from the ranks of fellowship.

In viewing how black evangelicals make themselves into a family beyond the family, our attention is drawn to the language and rituals of spiritual kinship produced among DBC members as "brothers and sisters in Christ," "spiritual mothers," "spiritual fathers," "spiritual children," and "prayer partners." We are also beckoned to see how the moral and categorical enclosures of religion, race, and kinship can be balanced by counter-hegemonic, boundary-crossing alterities that reproduce and push beyond the boundaries of nuclear religious fellowship and community life.

As we saw in the first half of the book, kinship creates genres of relationships and ways of relating. The conceptual and performative labors of DBC and CBC members help us to envisage the social phenomenon of black evangelical *kincraft* and its attendant processes of making, bridging, and revising. The first half of the book illustrates how DBC and CBC members co-constitute one another as spiritual kin by using spiritual kinship as a frame beyond the frames of ethno-national genealogy, racial segregation, and ethno-congregationalism. Influenced by diasporic consciousness and the antisectarianism and primitivism of Plymouth Brethrenism, church members understand their religious membership in transcendent, familial terms as an alternative to denominational boundaries. Church members construct a sense of belonging to broad kinship collectives (e.g., transnational diasporized family networks, family of God) through imaginaries that are not just distant and aspirational but also deeply meaningful and personal. Church members understand themselves to be part of trans-local networks of sister churches that are linked by their own migration histories. This is far from just a profession of communal ideology; it shapes how they imagine and map Christian community beyond a face-to-face local community. Their broad understandings of Christian relatedness determine to whom church members talk, whom they mourn, for whom they pray, and whom they visit, how they reproduce the communion and care they receive locally, and what they expect to receive in turn.

Church members also construct themselves as spiritual kin through a familial model of congregational belonging referred to locally as "church family." They do so in a US religious landscape in which congregational membership is frequently determined by racial and ethnic boundaries. Although black Christianity is often read through the particular framework of "the Black Church," black evangelicals imagine their location in the church in universal terms. To be a Christian, they insist, is to be part of a transcendent "body of Christ" and to push against and to rebuke the racial enclosures that were deposited by twentieth-century evangelicalism. Thus, DBC and CBC evangelists and church members conceptualize familial theology so that it is a critique of racio-religious color lines, a call for reformation of exclusionary boundaries, a reminder of shared diasporic and intraracial kinship in a religious movement that foregrounds salvation and biblicism rather than racial or ethnic membership as a signifier of religious identity. Paradoxically, even as the family endeavors to create a more inclusive, lateral institutional field of Christian practice, through its encoding of inside and outside, recognition and nonrecognition, it also contains the seeds of hierarchy and alienation deposited by racial and colonial structures and is reproduced by CBC and DBC evangelicals. Even with their antisectarian and kinship orientations, it is important to note that church members create intra-religious cleavages between African Americans and Afro-Caribbeans, as well as moral hierarchies of belonging and authority that divide founders versus converts, Bible believers versus nonbiblical literalists, respectable versus nonrespectable religious subjects, and Christians versus non-Christians. This sense of black racial kinship, which has long been important and politically significant in the US, has become punctuated with religious and ethnic differences that are not only variously expressed but that unfortunately also silence those perceived as other in urban, congregational, and interpersonal contexts.

The book has also explored how church members animate one another as spiritual kin through religious and spiritual practice. It has depicted some of the collective processes that mediate black evangelical kincraft, which includes two of the most common religious rituals of Bible study and prayer, as well as feeding, mentorship, care, and talking. Through Bible study and the breaking-of-bread Communion service, church members make themselves into an interpretive community by building consensus and interweaving experiential scripts of biblical contemplation. They also endeavor to close the gaps between themselves and biblical narratives and interlocutors through a literalist hermeneutic that attempts to collapse the spaces between Christian religious practitioners across space and time, and between moral ideals and enactments. Although Bible study and exegesis occur in gendered, fraternal spaces that foreground male voices via institutional practices of male leadership, it is particularly (but not exclusively) in extra-institutional spaces that we see churchwomen's contributions. Through everyday extra-institutional practices of prayer, everyday shared practices of chatting, daily prayer, discipling, encouragement, and nurturance that take place in and between church members' homes, not just at church, the community is knit together. In addition to these everyday contexts where the pleasures and joys of fellowship are made visible, church members turn to their close spiritual kin to air their anxieties about marriage and child rearing. In the safe spaces spiritual kinship can provide, black evangelicals can express their critiques and contradictions of heteronormative family morality. Thus, spiritual kinship hosts spaces and processes of confessional intimacy between church members, and the heteronormative family sits within a plurality of kinship ties and contemplations.

VISTAS OF UNLEARNING: BLACK EVANGELICALISM AND "THE FAMILY"

And even though I knew full well about these processes of confessional intimacy, I made assumptions about the contingent loyalties of my own spiritual kin. Since then, my error has been an instrument. I learned that in the United States, religion, race, and kinship in triplicate can operate as hypercharged mechanisms for generating alienation and difference. In particular, social schemas generated by hegemonically white US neo-evangelicalism (religion), antiblack skepticisms of black institutional conformity (race), and heteronormative definitions of kinship (family) generate strong tendencies to render and, at times, misinterpret social groups in terms of their ascription to dominant normativities.

Thus, exploring black evangelicals' social and spiritual worlds also requires us to *unlearn* some of our understandings about religion, race, and kinship. Racial hegemony experienced by those on the underside of power who do not own the representational means of producing religious or kinship norms does not necessarily mean the full-scale assimilation of minoritized subjects. Thoughtful and nuanced habitations occur. Religion is not just a repository for orthodoxy. Religion is also a vector for imagining and enacting different kinds of transcendent and immediate forms of sociality. And black kin-making, particularly when conducted in forms beyond the heteronormative family, is perhaps not a series of problems to be solved but a set of overlapping phenomena to be witnessed and experienced in future work.

Regardless of the common sanctification of "traditional" heteropatriarchal family arrangements, "the family" is not the only form of kinship observed by evangelical Christians such as DBC and CBC congregants. The heteronormative family does not contain the universal aspirations for Christian relatedness that emerge from black evangelicals' imagination of "the family of God." "The family" also does not include the relatedness that emerges when congregants—"brothers and sisters in Christ," "spiritual mothers," "spiritual fathers," and "spiritual children"—construct, perceive, and treat one another as spiritual kin related through their mutual embodiment of the Holy Spirit as believers. Taken together, this collection of relationships generates a network of social ties that greatly and more amply shapes members' experiences and commitments. Therefore, "the family" is not a social entity unto itself, but one of many units responsible for transmitting, hosting, and conceptualizing evangelical religious identity, one of many benchmarks—like neighborliness and everyday reciprocity—used as signifiers of evangelical faithfulness.

Certainly, DBC evangelicals construct the heteronormative family as "God's design" for family life and invest considerable energy into creating and sustaining patriarchal nuclear families, which emerge as the norm rather than the exception within the DBC congregational community. The reproduction of family life is a labor undertaken by households, congregations, and the network of spiritual kinship relationships in which church members are enmeshed. "The family" is not a self-replicating entity unto itself. Rather, household members receive institutional moral instruction from worship services and marriage-enrichment classes and mentorship from other congregants; access opportunities for more intensive advice, support, and confiding from spiritual mothers and fathers; and call down divine assistance to fortify marriages, to keep children on the right path, and to commit or recommit to the labor and love of family.

Producing this "family" requires the labor of a larger kinship network. As congregants and spiritual kin, church members offer one another financial assistance through love and personal offerings of money, groceries, cooked food, other much-needed material items, connections for employment opportunities, and help with child care. It is through all of these modes of kinship devotion—genealogical and spiritual—that congregants understand themselves as embodying and exhibiting God's love for humanity and the universal church. To use "the family" as a gauge to test the evangelicalism of black evangelical religiosity would be to use a hypercharged symbol that often negatively invokes black family pathology—and non-normativity. To use "the family"—with its historical ties to Anglo-American Victorian bourgeois family kinship and its more-contemporary entanglements with whiteness and neoliberal processes of privatization—misses the other cultural and structural influences that shape CBC and DBC family values. This book has outlined many of these other cultural and structural influences, including an Africana sociality that infuses the broader landscape of Afro-diasporic religious movements, the material conditions of racialization and diaspora, and the communal religio-familial ethos that emerges from CBC and DBC interpretations of evangelical Christianity.

Finally, to use the heteronormative family as a lens to understand the form, motivations, or "success" of black evangelical religiosity would be to presume that "the family" is a (even *the*) natural and normal unit of social life. To do so would be to miss how this book's ethnographic portraits of black evangelical community life reveal that "the family"—constituted and maintained by the collective labor of household members, congregants, and spiritual kin—is very much an entity that is socially produced. It is an outgrowth of collective labor. The boundaries, workings, and stability of "the family" cannot be taken for granted, even "the family" as a dominant model for kinship in the US social landscape and a social unit moralized by evangelicals as divinely sanctioned and foundational to producing a stable socio-moral order. The very existence of spiritual kin illustrates that the boundaries of the family are not institutionally discrete. Rather, there exist enduring religious-family linkages that connect relatives and congregants morally, institutionally, and through the labor of kinwork, at the level of lived religious experience. Moreover, DBC and CBC evangelicals understand religious and family lives to be co-constituted. They have ideas about the intersections of genealogical and spiritual kinship. They raise questions about the presumed institutional isolation and autonomy associated with the respectable nuclear family.

The book's local exploration of a black Atlantic evangelical church association in the Atlanta area suggests a broader need to de-essentialize cultural scripts of religion, race, and kinship in a US social landscape. We must make room for black evangelicals' long-standing and critical habitations of evangelical Christianity. This means redressing a popular categorical captivity of evangelicalism by a moralized and representationally dominant whiteness. This book demonstrates that we must acknowledge the diverse array of religious expressions that fall under the rubric of African American Christianity and the work that congregants conduct to make intentional religious communities across ethnic, national, and ideological and theological lines. Black evangelicals show us that there is much left to explore about the myriad reckonings of family that coexist within contemporary religious milieus.

This book requires that we resist the urge to conceptualize more-conservative religious identities, like evangelicalism, in the same manner in which we construct race—as immutable or reproductive of fixed schemas of classification. Although "the evangelical" exists within various regional, popular cultural, political, statistical, and religious imaginations, it is also a trope that upon deeper scrutiny breaks down and begs to be questioned. This work demonstrates that discursive hegemony might obscure, but does not preclude, the existence of multiplicity. There are myriad expressions of evangelicalism in the United States, some of which derive from outside the North American context. There are black Christian communities in the US that exist beyond an Afro-Protestant mainline and an African American majority, and there is no singular way to be black. There is no singular definition of family. Heteropatriarchy coexists with more-flexible, horizontal kinship networks. Acknowledging the existence of these religious, intraracial, and familial pluralities allows us to move from a conceptualization of black evangelicals as illegible religious subjects or as interstitial religious participants located between a white evangelicalism and a

Black Church to making space for a religious movement that operates in and on its own terms.

This book has also demonstrated that the spaces between the boundaries and contents of institutionalized identities can be opened up by religious practitioners who attend to the emergent demands of everyday life and who notice the coexistence of diverse grammars and methods of relationality. There are many types of family and ways to make family. The variety of stories of kincraft and association authored by the DBC and CBC communities are those that we can learn from and read through and into our own lives.

Coda

As I have completed my revisions on this manuscript over the past two weeks, I have inhabited a social milieu that has been decisively affected by the COVID-19 pandemic. I have observed two models of sociality that have emerged in the wake of recommended forms of social distancing and self-quarantine practices, and the closing of major public institutions, including churches, universities, and primary schools. The first is a project of heteropatriarchal family enclosure and resource concentration that in some instances has led to hoarding and shortages of vital supplies. The second model of preparation is one of mutual aid, of collaborative resource and information sharing across local households. I expect that DBC and CBC members are tending to their homes and to one another, tying together the models of sociality they have already created and mobilizing them in this moment.

I cannot help but think that the spiritual kinship networks created by DBC and CBC members that extend an Afro-diasporic ethos, in which the making of kinship was a survival praxis, were made for such a time as this. Therefore, there is much we can learn from them. This might mean foregrounding an ethos of care and broader reckonings of our human family and experimental modes of sociality. It might mean tapping into preexisting praxes of connection or experimenting with new practices of showing up for one another virtually and materially, of creating broader lines of emotional and material reciprocity versus the privileging of individualistic wellness or nuclear family well-being. It might mean asking reflexive questions of our own social locations especially during social events (like this pandemic) that rupture the veil of enclosure and normativity.

Among these questions are these: What must we learn and unlearn about religion, race, and kinship and their received boundaries? Who is your family? Who is your community? How do you know? How do you make yourselves into family and community? How do you reveal yourselves to one another? How do you show up for one another? How can we all create emergent forms of sociality by which we can come alongside one another? Black evangelicals provide important views of socialities that meet people where they are, that attend to precarities, that provide spiritual support, and that provide belonging—and even joy—from which we can all learn.

Notes

INTRODUCTION

1 To preserve the confidentiality of research collaborators, I use pseudonyms for actual church and respondent names. I use the actual name of T. Michael Flowers for historical purposes.
2 Although I use the term *African American* to identify the US-born children of Afro-Caribbean immigrants, scholars have also examined the complex identifications of second-generation Caribbeans who can identify alternately as Afro-Caribbean, Caribbean American, and African American depending on the racial, ethnic, and class contexts in which they are situated (Foner 2018; Lorick-Wilmot 2018).
3 In addition to emerging in my own research interactions with black evangelicals, the term *Bible-believing* has been discussed by black evangelical theologians such as William Bentley (1975, 110) as an emic term that denotes evangelical orientations among African American Christians.
4 Although CBC and DBC evangelicals have historical and genealogical connections to black Bible camps and schools that were established by fundamentalists from the early to mid-twentieth century and Plymouth Brethrenism—which propagated a predispensational millennialism that was foundational to fundamentalist worldviews—I propose that contemporary CBC and DBC evangelicals are best characterized as evangelicals because of their born-again soteriology, literalist biblical hermeneutic, and their moral orthodoxy. In contrast to the insularity associated with fundamentalism, I argue that CBC and DBC members are evangelicals because of their emphasis on missions as an endeavor deserving financial support, as a religious activity in which members participate, or as an aspirational marker of Christian commitment.
5 In "African American Evangelicals," Soong-Chan Rah identifies four threads of black evangelicalism. The first is a fundamentalist thread associated with the Nottage brothers and Plymouth Brethrenism, which directly implicates the DBC

and CBC communities. The second thread refers to African American Pentecostals, in particular the Church of God in Christ, founded by William H. Bentley. The third and fourth are black evangelicals with ties to evangelical educational institutions and para-church organizations (2019, 76–77).

6 In "The Church in African American Theology," R. Drew Smith makes the compelling observation that African American churches hold different meanings for scholars than for congregants and clergy, who emphasize black churches' deep and long-standing material and social sustenance of black communities: "Black church life has been constructed, deconstructed, celebrated, and criticized from many vantage points. Black churches may be much of what scholars say they are, but they are undoubtedly much more than that as well—especially as viewed by the many congregants and clergy who have sustained and been sustained by these institutions over the centuries and who may bring fewer social presuppositions than scholars sometimes do in their perspectives on churches" (2014, 237).

7 In *American Evangelical Christianity*, Mark Noll defines evangelicals as the "heirs to Anglo-American religious revivals" that occurred from the eighteenth century through the twentieth century. Evangelicals exhibit "a consistent pattern of convictions and attitudes," including an emphasis on conversion as a life-changing experience, an understanding of the Bible as the fundamental source of truth, a desire to spread the Christian faith, and a concentration on the salvation offered through the redemptive figure of Christ (2001, 13). Yet although black evangelicals such as Rebecca Protten, Moses Bakker, and George Lisle are important participants in the trans-Atlantic proliferation of evangelicalism since the eighteenth century (Frey and Wood 1998; Pulis 1999b; Sensbach 2006), Noll concedes that "the relationship of African-American churches to evangelical traditions is complex" (2001, 14). In other words, the location of black evangelicalism, rather than the historical narratives of black evangelists, exists as a still-active site of contemporary scholarly excavation.

8 The variable definitions of *evangelicalism* stem from its differential linguistic uses. The term *evangelical* captures a Christian religious orientation that can be professed by individuals or assigned by scholars in relation to a set of identified characteristics. Evangelicalism is also often tied to a set of religious revivals, movements, and organizations that emerge during established historical epochs—a set of contexts that is constantly and productively expanding with emergent scholarship.

9 Because Flowers professed his own ambivalence regarding the aims of the racial reconciliation movement as a religious project that did not properly centralize Christ, it is difficult to identify Flowers as an evangelist officially associated with the racial reconciliation movement.

10 "Religious Landscape Study," Pew Research Center, Religion and Public Life, 2014, http://www.pewforum.org/religious-landscape-study/religious-tradition/evangelical-protestant.

11 I apply Antonio Gramsci's concept of hegemony here as the intellectual and moral undertones of supremacy that validate the common sense of a majority

population. I also draw on Gramsci's observation that confessional religion can contribute to the common sense of hegemony to understand how popular evangelical Christianity consolidates and normalizes white racial identity (Grelle 2017).

12 Eddie Glaude Jr. (2010) echoes Evans's sentiments, discussing the differentiation of African American identities, the routinization of prophetic discourses, and the decentralization of black church attendance against the broader landscape of African American social life, and has proclaimed that "the Black Church is dead."

13 Studies of black Christian voting practices have noted the ways in which religious and racial affinities may shape but cannot predict political partisanship. In their study of black and white Protestants, Jason Shelton and Michael Emerson find that black Protestants across a variety of traditions (though none who fall under the auspices of the black evangelicalism defined above) tend to prioritize structural and experiential dimensions of race as a shared basis for group identity and voting over the religious differences that distinguish them (2012). In her investigations of the voting practices of black evangelicals influenced by neo-evangelical fundamentalist theologies and black Christians who are influenced by black liberation theology, Allison Calhoun-Brown finds that theological affinities cannot predict the political participation of black Christians (1998; 1999). Caryn Robinson (2006) also observes that many black Christians identified with the moral principles of the Christian Coalition, but socially conservative principles do not necessarily generate an ascription to Republican or conservative political platforms (although black born-again believers, black Christians who reported frequent Bible reading, and black Christian women were a bit more likely to support the political programs of the Christian Coalition). Moreover, similar to the observation made by Leah Rigueur (2015) in her study of black Republicans that there is no such thing as a black Republican, my ethnographic engagements with a black evangelical constituency also compel me to conclude analogically that there is no such thing as a black evangelical just as there is no singular way to be or inhabit a black identity.

14 In her study "Whither Fictive Kin? Or, What's in a Name?," Margaret K. Nelson conducts a rhetorical analysis of social scientific research on fictive kinship from the 1970s through the early 2000s and finds that 34 percent of fictive kinship references were attributed to African American research participants, 16 percent of kinship references were associated with immigrant respondents, and 2 percent were associated with white research participants. She concludes that fictive kinship is discursively racialized in social scientific research. She explains that by defining fictive kinship as "consensus without real obligation" and associating it with racially minoritized communities, the actions of certain groups are represented as "being more problematic than those of others" (2014, 217). In addition to contemplating the racial and representational implications of identifying African American constructions of kinship as "fictive," Nelson's conclusions also demonstrate the need for projects like this one that explore the myriad grammars of sociality created by African Americans.

15 As outlined by Orlando Patterson (1982) in *Slavery and Social Death*, the master/ slave relationship was primary in the context of slavery. All other relationships, including familial ties, held no social or juridical consequence.
16 I also conducted five pilot interviews with Afro-Caribbean and African American migrants in the Atlanta metropolitan area during my preliminary fieldwork research in the summer of 2006.
17 Other Afro-Caribbean congregants whom I engaged were from St. Kitts and Guyana.
18 The lion's share of my ethnographic research was conducted with the members of Dixon Bible Chapel. Therefore, a great deal of my ethnographic analysis from the second half of the book emerges from my extended engagements with the DBC community.

CHAPTER 1. ON "GODLY FAMILY" AND "FAMILY ROOTS"

1 DBC and CBC members were significantly influenced by Plymouth Brethrenism and its strong anticlerical positions. As a result, church members were often ambivalent about the institutionalization of a church pastor. At DBC church members conceded that a "full-time worker" was a necessary, pragmatic compromise, for that person could be available to current and prospective members throughout the week. At the time of my research, the "full-time worker" had also pursued graduate theological training. At CBC, there was a different pastoral worker, but congregants did not seem to express the same concern about the institutionalization of the pastoral role as DBC members.
2 The transcript of this Bible study is a verbatim depiction of the discussion. In order to allow the nuances of congregant perspectives to appear as they were expressed in real time, the transcript has not been edited for grammar.
3 Acts 17 describes the conversion of Berean Jews and Greeks as a result of Silas and Paul's preaching in Berea.
4 Both CBC and DBC members also use the grammar and imaginary of family to create close-knit local assemblies of worship and imagine a transcendent Christianity community. Brethren thought of themselves in communal terms as assemblies that were gathered within a universal family of God in addition to being a part of the "body of Christ." The discourse of family, as an antidenominational option, is directly encoded in the term "Brethren," which derives from a biblical source.
5 Carter argues that the construction of the modern citizen is the outgrowth of a theology of whiteness, articulated by Kant, that rests upon "'the euthanasia of Judaism' which Kant figures as coeval with the realization of the coming ethical community, [which] only brings to completion a rational theology of atonement in which the death of Christ is a dying away from Judaism and from all that makes one a 'son of earth' rather than a son of God. In short, it is a dying away from all that holds one 'fettered to earthly life to the detriment of morality'" (2008, 120).
6 According to Bernard Ineichen, Edmund Gosse's *Father and Son: A Study of Two Temperaments* has been in print almost continuously since 1907, marking it as a

significant work of apostasic memoir (2019). Rebecca Stott's book *In the Days of Rain: A Daughter, a Father, a Cult* describes graphically how Brethren and former Brethren harmed themselves as a result of a schism that emerged in Aberdeen in the wake of elder misconduct that tore congregants and families apart. She writes that "the Exclusive Brethren had turned into a cult and played out their torments *in plain sight*" (2017, 215).

7   Scholars of American evangelicalism have recently contextualized the ascendant neo-evangelical perspective within many streams of evangelical thought (including an evangelical Left that was partly populated by a contingency of liberally oriented black evangelicals) and have demonstrated that the evangelical Right partook of mainstream political and cultural discourses and institutions rather than constituting an isolated countermovement (Swartz 2012).

8   According to Susan Greenbaum, the embedded morality of conservative notions about black families and poverty can be traced to Protestant religious worldviews (2015). Recapitulating Max Weber's idea that capitalist accumulation was moralized by Calvinist associations of material acquisitions as a sign of divine favor, Greenbaum draws attention to a string of religious morality embedded in the presumably secular ideological apparatus of conservatism.

9   In 2004, George W. Bush ceded $1.5 billion in federal funds in marriage promotion programs, including premarital education and marriage counseling, that were designed to raise marriage rates in "poor neighborhoods" (Pear and Kirkpatrick 2004). Though there was pressure to establish a marriage amendment that would define marriage in strictly heterosexual terms, the marriage promotion program was directed toward inner-city sites and black churches as mediating organizations. Therefore, there were class and racial implications of the marriage promotion initiative. Robert Pear and David D. Kirkpatrick. "Bush Plans $1.5 Billion Drive on Marriage," *New York Times*, January 14, 2004.

10 Because it is part of this book's goal to demonstrate the ways in which racial and religious categories and identities are essentialized, I must note that the label of *conservatism*, like *evangelicalism*, also reflects a great deal of social and ideological variability. As Leah Rigueur illuminates in *The Loneliness of the Black Republican: Pragmatic Politics and the Pursuit of Power*, black Republicans in the 1960s also identified with a conservative emphasis on the individual work ethic, respectability, free market enterprise, race-blind discourse, and valorization of upward mobility (2014). Black Republicans working in local, national, and federal venues also saw their engagement with Republican Party electoral politics and administrations not as a form of exceptionalism but as an outgrowth of a broader African American cultural adherence to the values of respectability—and even as an economic approach to civil rights (Rigueur 2014, 166, 154). Yet the strands of black Republicanism illuminated by Rigueur focused on the specific political and economic interests of the black middle class.

Michael Javen Fortner also destabilizes the equation of conservatism with whiteness in his controversially received *Black Silent Majority: The Rockefeller Drug Laws and the Politics of Punishment*. Specifically, Fortner makes the claim that working-class and middle-class African Americans in the 1960s and 1970s who experienced the Harlem heroin epidemic became disaffected with liberalism, "which they believed had disregarded their striving and pain and had come to the defense of a minority of malcontents" (2015, 264). In the wake of crime and safety concerns, they opted for a conservative moral view that emphasized personal responsibility and underscored the need for more-punitive carceral measures. Thus, Fortner draws attention to the contextual factors, such as class, that motivated black ideological dispositions. Therefore, the common racialization of political ideological positions, in particular the kinds of reductionism that attend categorizations of blackness in religious and political terms, must be de-essentialized. If—contrary to a racially hegemonic view of the US socioreligious landscape—all evangelicals are not white, it stands to reason that neither are all of the conservatives. We are left then with a view of black conservatives as participants in a broader ideological context shaped by African Americans' long engagement with respectability worldviews and shifting alignments of class and moral outlook that were precipitated by the civil rights movement, urbanization, migration, social mobility, and conservative governance. An examination of Afro-Caribbean and African American evangelical engagements with neo-evangelical conservative family values also prevents a simple mapping of black evangelicals onto a conservative ideological grid.

11 In the Latin American context, the word *evangelical* is used to denote Protestantism more broadly. In many instances, this Protestantism is a result of Pentecostal missions that arose with increasing frequency in the 1970s and beyond.

12 Plymouth Brethrenism existed in many Caribbean landscapes prior to the missionization of Pentecostalism and neo-Pentecostal prosperity televangelism.

13 Although my research is grounded in black evangelical communities, I suspect that this is the case for other contemporary evangelical communities as well.

14 Incest prohibitions have often been considered central to demarcating kinship systems cross-culturally.

15 Smallwood writes that "the social fabric of African communities was rent by the disappearance of kinfolk. And on the ocean's horizon the captives encountered only the social world of the slave ship, a similarly mutilated assemblage that was not a functioning whole but rather an arbitrary collective of isolated and alienated persons" (2008, 121).

16 By denoting an *elsewhere* of kinship, I build on the insights of Jacqueline Nassy Brown in *Dropping Anchor, Setting Sail: Geographies of Race in Black Liverpool*, stating that kinship can be understood in various ways. According to Brown, black Liverpudlians use the term *kinship* to invoke racial and multiracial genealogies of blackness and to invoke a claim to place or *"hereness"* (2005, 81). In the case of the black evangelicals of DBC and CBC, I identify an *elsewhere* of kinship that emerges from a kinship sensibility that is authenticated outside the boundaries of US biological genealogical categories and Christian congregational life in relation to an Afro-diasporic spiritual (extra-institutional) imaginary of connection, the Afro-Caribbean provenance of the black Atlantic movement of which

CBC and DBC are a part, and the religious emphasis of New Testament familial church communities so important to Plymouth Brethren.

17 According to Karen McCarthy Brown, "First, healing is the *primary* business of these [Afro-Caribbean] religious systems. . . . Second, the understanding of personhood operative within these Afro-Caribbean healing traditions is fundamentally a relational one. The individual is defined by a web of relationships that includes not only the extended family but also the ancestors and the spirits and the saints" (2006, 2).

18 Scholars such as Diane Austin-Broos (1997) and Katrina Hazzard-Donald (2012) have examined the syncretic quality of Jamaican Revivalism (as a mixture of Afro-Baptist and indigenous spiritual expressions such as Myal) and the black Sanctified Church in the US South (as an assemblage of charismatic Protestant Christianity and Hoodoo).

19 The question can be raised of whether DBC members' missionary activities constitute a medium of Afro-Atlantic connection, especially considering the colonial implications of Christians missions even among African and African-descended populations. Certainly, the small group of Dixon congregants who engaged in missionary activity at the time of my research understood their connections to Africa in religious as well as deeply personal and sentimental terms. Africa intermittently emerged as a meta-symbol of community. Church missionaries expressed the impression that Kenyans really understood the significance of community. Nonetheless, contemplations of African connections were not commonly expressed church-wide.

CHAPTER 2. MOVING AGAINST THE GRAIN

1 In other publication venues I have referred to T. Michael Flowers (1920–2015) under the pseudonym of Aaron Powell. I use his given name here so that the provenance of the CBC and DBC religious movements can be more easily ascertained. I am now writing about Flowers posthumously, motivated by the conviction that his story and its relationship to the CBC and DBC religious complex, as well as to the US religious landscape, should be told and attributed to him, not couched in a pseudonym.

2 This chapter's recounting of that story emerges from my firsthand exposure to Flowers's recollections of his evangelistic ministry during my weekly Bible study discussions with him in the warm kitchen of his home in Decatur, Georgia. I combine those ethno-historical accounts with an oral history of Flowers's life collected by archivists of Wheaton College's Billy Graham Center in 1990 and 1995. See Wheaton College Archives, "Collection 431: Oral History Interviews with T. Michael Flowers," https://archives.wheaton.edu/repositories/4/resources/1112.

3 The Macedonian call references Acts 16:9–10, in which the Apostle Paul had a vision of a Macedonian man begging for the gospel, a vision that Paul believed was divinely ordained. According to the biblical record, Paul headed to Macedonia promptly thereafter.

4   Academics subject oral histories to particular scrutiny because of their subjective character. Nonetheless, an oral reconstruction of the organization's founding provides an origin story via local voices and can flatten some of the representational hierarchies found in conventional historical narratives. Moreover, for an evangelical subgroup in the US that has received minimal attention, an oral reconstruction of black evangelical history will hopefully be supplemented by future scholarship. I have endeavored to supplement the oral historical record with other source materials. The Glasgow Bible Institute, a school to which Flowers matriculated to take coursework on biblical studies, is closed, and the records are minimal, so there are no records available for the time at which Flowers was there. The administration of Cedine Bible Camp in Spring City, Tennessee, has confirmed that T. Michael Flowers and Ella Flowers worked for the organization in the 1950s.
5   According to Winston G. Litchmore in "Christian Brethren Assemblies in Jamaica, 1923–2003," Plymouth Brethrenism first came to Jamaica in 1850 by way of J. N. Darby and G. V. Wigram (2006, 191–92). Although two Closed Brethren communities were founded shortly thereafter, the 1920s witnessed a split between the traditional Closed Plymouth Brethren community and a new strain of Brethrenism locally referred to as Christian Brethrenism that was fed by North American missionaries. Thus, Jamaicans also took part in evangelistic Brethren enterprises in the early twentieth century around the time of Flowers's own conversion in a gospel hall meeting. Moreover, Afro-Jamaican Brethrenism is a complex composite that is influenced by, but not fully equivalent to, Plymouth Brethrenism.
6   Glasgow Bible Institute was a public theological school founded by the Moody Bible Institute in Chicago that provided training to laymen interested in conducting evangelistic work. It was thus a part of a transatlantic network of learning, knowledge production, and dissemination (personal correspondence with David Bebbington, December 30, 2019).
7   According to a *Power for Living* periodical published by Moody Bible Institute, B. M., T. B., and Whitfield Nottage were "ministers of the Brethren movement known unofficially as the Plymouth Brethren" who migrated to the United States from the Bahamas in 1905, 1909, and 1910, respectively, and spent the remainder of their lives engaged in active ministry (Mathers, 1965). All three of the brothers worked as co-ministers of Grace Gospel Chapel in Harlem for twenty years. B. M. went on to found Bethany Tabernacle in Detroit in 1932, where he likely encountered Flowers. Whitfield ministered at Ebenezer Community Tabernacle in Philadelphia for more than thirty years. T. B. ministered at Elim Gospel Chapel for a similar time span in Cleveland. B. M. also appeared as a speaker for Moody Bible Institute events and radio broadcasts.
8   Matthews's analysis focuses on denominational publications, so we should be cautious about equating these institutional perspectives framed by high-ranking denominational officials with those of rank-and-file participants. Moreover, because Baptist ecclesiology allows for a great deal of local autonomy in the operation of congregations, considerable variation in African American Baptist religious practice existed in the mid-twentieth-century United States.

9 In Trinidad the Spiritual Baptist Church, which is believed to have emerged from the religious influence of African American Baptists and former soldiers who moved to Trinidad after the War of 1812, was banned in Trinidad from 1917 to 1951 (Duncan 2008). N. Fadeke Castor notes that Spiritual Baptists and Orisha practitioners who were referred to inaccurately via the conglomerate "Shouter Baptists" had their religious practices (such as shouting, bell ringing, drumming, and dancing) targeted by the Shouter Prohibition Ordinance but were also "subject to criminalization and discrimination, losing homes, jobs and at times their freedom" (2017, 33).

10 Incidentally, one of the first Afro-Baptist churches in North America was founded in 1773 in Savannah, Georgia, the site where Flowers began his own black Atlantic missionary project almost two hundred years later with his first church.

11 The notable exception is the Peace Mission, in which Father Divine prescribed celibacy and a break from heteronormative marriages and blood relationships.

12 Genesis 1:27 reads, "So God created mankind in his own image, in the image of God he created them, male and female he created them" (NIV). Flowers's use of scripture and his application of a literal reading of the Bible underscore a transracial point of human origins.

13 Additionally, the black evangelical understanding of humanity as fallen man reifies an androcentric religious discourse.

14 Gilbreath summarizes a sermon on reconciliation given by Rev. Russell Knight during a chapel service at the predominantly white evangelical campus of Judson College: "This was not a preacher who demanded a lot of 'amens' or 'hallelujahs' from his listeners. Instead, he quietly but deliberately laid out his thesis. America is a racist nation by nature, and the American church is complicit in this sin if it continues to remain silent. *What's going on here?* I thought to myself, nervously looking around to check the comfort level of the mostly white congregation. *Is it okay to say stuff like that . . . here?* 'Who will speak for justice and risk his own life?' Knight asked us, sounding both literal and rhetorical. 'Will you speak for brotherhood if there's a chance that you may lose your own popularity? Will you speak for equality if suffering is in sight? Will you speak for liberation if all other voices are silent?'" (Gilbreath 2006, 46–47)

15 As Curtis Evans (2009) notes in "White Evangelical Responses to the Civil Rights Movement," white neo-evangelicals often emphasized spiritual and evangelistic solutions rather than systemic solutions to the problem of race during the civil rights era. Yet as Delroy A. Reid-Salmon notes, Flowers's nonadherence to a civil rights politics could also be the result of his diasporic locations. In *Home away from Home: The Caribbean Diasporan Church in the Black Atlantic Tradition*, Reid-Salmon writes that although the "Caribbean diasporan church is a contributory factor in the changing character in American society and religion, its primary concern was geared towards personal aspects of religion including personal salvation, social services, and church planting. This emphasis is noticeable in the church's lack of involvement in social justice" (2009, 126).

CHAPTER 3. BLACK LIKE ME? OR CHRISTIAN LIKE ME?

1 In spite of the many celebratory narratives of the black Atlanta elite in the early twentieth century, the gains made by Atlanta's black middle class must be weighed against the politics of segregation and the racial stratifications that shape American social class. In his study of black middle-class life, Frazier concludes that the entrepreneurial efforts of the black middle class were small when compared with similar white business ventures (1957). Along the same lines, Goldfield observes that many black businesses in the area were family ventures in retail and service industries, and that many local black settlements (regardless of inhabitants' class backgrounds) were in poorly serviced urban areas, primarily consisting of rental properties that were often in need of repair (1982).

2 As the Americans of the 1960s and 1970s saw the deindustrialization of northern industrial centers into the Rust Belt, they also witnessed the emergence of the Sun Belt South—a collection of southern economic urban centers (e.g., Atlanta, Dallas, and Charlotte) that were home to national and international investments, regional corporate headquarters, indigenous banking enterprises, and expansions in minor industrial and service-job sectors.

3 The 1906 race riot and a 1913 zoning ordinance intensified Jim Crow distinctions and motivated the drawing of sharper lines between local black and white communities in Atlanta. As civil rights activists fought to have federal rulings on the desegregation of public spaces and facilities enforced in the 1950s and 1960s, white residents protested these changes by relocating to the city's suburbs. According to Kevin Kruse, white flight to the suburbs drew even sharper racial residential lines that resulted in an impoverished black inner-city core and wealthier, almost exclusively white suburbs (2005).

4 According to the 2000 US Census Fact Finder, 50.1 percent of Atlanta city's population identified as black or African American. The 2000 US Census County and City Data Book lists a higher percentage of 61.4 percent for the city's black and African American population, which made it the city with the seventh-largest black population in the United States.

5 A 1972 *Atlanta Journal-Constitution* article billed Atlanta as "a Mecca for Black Businessmen." Since that time, Atlanta has also been dubbed a "New Mecca for Young Blacks" (*Ebony* magazine, September 1973), a "mecca" and a "hub" for "black gays" (*Atlanta Journal-Constitution*, 2004), and more generally as a "Black Mecca" (Atlanta.net). Marketed as a city for young urban professionals, 45.7 percent of the city's population are residents who hold a bachelor's or higher degree (in contrast with a national average of 27.5 percent) ("Atlanta City, Georgia Fact Sheet," accessed March 1, 2011, http://quickfacts.census.gov /qfd/states/13/1304000.html). Forty-seven percent of the city's population is employed in "management, professional, and related occupations," and 48 percent of Atlanta's residents are age 44 or younger (http://factfinder.census.gov/servlet /NPTable?_bm=y&-geo_id=16000US1304000&-qr_name=ACS_2009_5YR_G00 _NP01&-ds_name=&-redoLog=false).

6 According to the 2014 "Religious Landscape Study" conducted by the Pew Research Center, Atlanta had the second-highest concentration of affiliated Christians of any major metropolis in the United States. Specifically, 76 percent of Atlanta's residents are Christians, with 33 percent attending evangelical congregations, 12 percent attending mainline Protestant congregations, and 18 percent attending "historically black" Protestant churches. Plymouth Brethrenism, the British evangelical movement that informs CBC and DBC evangelical worldviews, is not mentioned in the evangelical traditions listed by the Pew study.

7 I do not intend to displace onto white evangelicals the racial essentialisms that are written onto black populations. In short, the study of white evangelical hegemony is not intended to suppress the variations of Euro-American evangelical racial and religious orientations. As discussed in the introduction, evangelicalism in the United States is a multiracial, multicultural religious movement. White evangelicals in the United States are a diverse constituency that is shaped by significant regional, political, and, I would conjecture, much less discussed ethnic affinities.

8 Notions of post-blackness—an individualistic construct of blackness that reinforces the representational and geopolitical privileges of an African American elite as well as US neoliberal and neocolonial paradigms of personhood and global inequality (Russell 2015; Simmons 2015; Thomas 2015)—can be seen as narrowing the use of blackness as a strategic essentialism for Afro-Caribbean and African American evangelicals and black populations more broadly. Thus, CBC and DBC members navigate the intersections of religion, race, and ethnicity within a context in which blackness is being differentially mapped along the axis of the public and the private spheres. As Treitler (2013) suggests, it may be that ethnicity rather than blackness becomes a new language of difference for Afro-descended communities in the US.

9 The Hart-Cellar Act of 1965, for instance, changed many of the immigration quotas that greatly expanded the reception of migrants from the Caribbean and Africa to the United States.

10 Moreover, academic representations themselves can also be conscripted into the discourse of ethnic projects (Matory 2015) and contribute to "an increasing unproductively balkanized racial landscape in both the academy and in public discourse" (Russell 2015, 114).

11 Coleman shared this reflection during the closing collaborative panel at the "Christianity, Politics, and Social Activism in Africa and the African Diaspora" Colloquium at the University of North Carolina, Chapel Hill, March 4–5, 2016.

CHAPTER 4. BIBLE STUDY, FRATERNALISM, AND THE
MAKING OF INTERPRETIVE COMMUNITY

1 The DBC members often referred to 1 Peter 2:9 to establish what they term "the priesthood of all believers." The verse reads, "But you are a chosen people, a royal priesthood, a holy nation, God's special possession, that you may declare the praises of him who called you out of darkness into his wonderful light" (NIV).

2   The DBC members refer to the churches in their Brethren network as "sister" churches, which evokes an image of the church's relatedness, shared descent from Flowers's evangelistic work, and the same laterality invoked by the churches' model of lateral fraternal governance. However, because church members understand the church as an entity that is conceptually female (the bride of Christ), religious participants refer to the church's kinship in similarly gendered terms through the language of sisterhood.

3   Afro-Caribbean and African American men have been depicted as economically and spatially marginalized from the families they create (Barroteau 2003; Moynihan 1965). Working-class and unemployed black men have been depicted in terms of male peer groups (Liebow 2003 [1967]). In some instances, these streetcorner peer groups were associated with competing with family and churches for male presence and contributions (Wilson 1973). Nonetheless, some scholars of Afro-diasporic family systems have encouraged a closer look at the ways in which men from the African diaspora contribute to families as fathers, husbands, uncles, and cousins (Chamberlain 2006; Stack 1974, 1996).

4   Church members cite Acts 2:44–45 as a motivation for church-wide giving: "All the believers were together and had everything in common. Selling their possessions and goods, they gave to anyone as he had need" (NIV).

5   In the year after my fieldwork, Brother Samuel Andrews took a position with a church in Antigua in which he used his specialization in family ministry and counseling. Since then, DBC has returned to the traditional Brethren model of elder governance.

6   This biblical excerpt is taken from 1 Corinthians 14:34–35 (NIV).

7   Women engage in biblical teaching at women's conferences or in women's meetings at chapel conferences and demonstrate their substantial biblical knowledge and prowess in biblical interpretation.

8   Elsewhere, Wimbush proposes that scripturalization—"a social-psychological-political structure establishing its own reality"—is established through narrative processes by which an "unreflective and unmarked whiteness . . . claims to be universal" (2012, 19, 169). This universalization of white Christian cultural locations contributes to Euro-Christian cultural hegemony and makes the cultural decontextualizing impetus he associates with biblical literalism a project of black cultural dispossession.

9   The DBC members repeatedly referenced Acts 2:42–47 and Acts 4:32–37 in their discussion of foundational New Testament models of Christian communalism.

10 The Bereans were a New Testament community noted in the Apostle Paul's letter to the Thessalonians for their eagerness to hear biblical messages and to study the scriptures.

11 Brethren cite Acts 2:42 in their usage of "breaking bread," which reads, "They devoted themselves to the apostles' teaching and to the fellowship, to the breaking of bread and to prayer" (NIV). Their citation of a scriptural term to identify this important weekly ritual once again reveals the ways in which literalism operates in their everyday lives.

CHAPTER 5. CHURCHWOMEN AND THE INCORPORATION
OF CHURCH AND HOME

1 In *Religion in the Kitchen: Cooking, Talking, and the Making of Black Atlantic Traditions*, Elizabeth Pérez argues that "cooking and talking are at the very quick of Black Atlantic religions" and that "such material and discursive acts get under the skin of practitioners, equipping them with the repertoire of skills, dispositions, and habits necessary for religious norms to be internalized, then reproduced" (2016, 8–9). In other words, cooking and the conversations that attend food preparation are vital pathways by which black religious subjectivities are produced through feeding practices. Bodies, the Holy Spirit inside of them, and the relationships connecting them are nourished.

2 During my fieldwork, I was adopted as a spiritual daughter by two married couples. Sister Francine and Delroy Marshall were one such couple. Our relationship began after Sister Francine invited me over for an impromptu dinner at her house during the second week of my fieldwork. These meal invitations, casual visits, and kitchen-table talk—at times with Sister Marshall and at times with both her and her husband—continued over the course of my fieldwork. Their home was also a site in which I interacted with church members between weekly worship and scheduled church programs.

CHAPTER 6. BLACK EVANGELICALS, "THE FAMILY,"
AND CONFESSIONAL INTIMACY

1 The hegemonic heterosexuality of the DBC and CBC communities is evident in congregants' rendering of homosexuality as a sin that exists beyond the sexual sin of heterosexual adultery.

2 For instance, both Karen Fog Olwig (1999a) and Carol Stack (1996) have examined the ways in which Afro-Caribbeans and African Americans from the rural South participate in institutions of family land: collective land ownership by the descendants within a given familial generation. Such practices of collective extended-family land ownership run contrary to the popular association of private property with nuclear family units.

3 In *Aberrations in Black: Toward a Queer of Color Critique*, Roderick Ferguson argues that political and social scientific discourses (however situated in a presumably secular public sphere) demoralized black familial and cultural difference as pathological and displaced the blame of black family difference onto black families themselves, "making African American intimate relations the site of material struggle" (2004, 37).

4 Information outlining the objectives of the My Brother's Keeper program can be found by visiting the following websites: https://obamawhitehouse.archives.gov/node/279811#section-about-my-brothers-keeper and https://obamawhitehouse.archives.gov/the-press-office/2014/02/27/fact-sheet-opportunity-all-president-obama-launches-my-brother-s-keeper-.

5 "FACTSHEET: Opportunity for All: President Obama Launches My Brother's Keeper Initiative to Build Ladders of Opportunity for Boys and Young

Men of Color," The White House, President Barack Obama, 2014, https://obamawhitehouse.archives.gov/the-press-office/2014/02/27/fact-sheet-opportunity-all-president-obama-launches-my-brother-s-keeper-.

6 In "Neoliberal Social Justice: From Ed Brooke to Barack Obama," Leah Rigueur (2017) outlines a genealogical connection between Barack Obama's advocacy of a neoliberal justice program focused on using free market solutions to address the country's economic and racial ills and black Republican Ed Brooks's progressive conservatism. In doing so, Rigueur illustrates the overlap between conservative and neoliberal notions of respectability, self-reliance, and capitalism and the permeable boundaries between liberalism and conservatism. For our purposes, Rigueur's discussion also illustrates the ways in which neoliberal and conservative moral discourses about black family pathology and corrective heteropatriarchy exist as overlapping moral discourse. "Neoliberal Social Justice: From Ed Brooke to Barack Obama," Social Science Research Council, May 30, 2017, http://items.ssrc.org/neoliberal-social-justice-from-ed-brooke-to-barack-obama.

7 This verse is taken from Psalm 127:3: "Children are a heritage from the Lord, offspring a reward from him" (NIV).

8 "Religious Landscape Study: Evangelical Protestants," Pew Research Center, Religion and Public Life, 2014, http://www.pewforum.org/religious-landscape-study/religious-tradition/evangelical-protestant.

9 "Religious Landscape Study: Evangelical Protestants Who Identify as Black," Pew Research Center, Religion and Public Life, 2014, http://www.pewforum.org/religious-landscape-study/racial-and-ethnic-composition/black/religious-tradition/evangelical-protestant.

10 "Religious Landscape Study: Evangelical Protestants," Pew Research Center, Religion and Public Life, 2014, http://www.pewforum.org/religious-landscape-study/religious-tradition/evangelical-protestant.

11 These statistics provide only a broad contextual picture. As previously discussed, mapping a concise definition of black evangelicalism is challenging for a number of reasons. The statistics do not illustrate ethnic variation; neither do they provide a simple explanation for the racial variation of black Millennial evangelical observance. We do well to be cautious about explaining the higher rates of Millennial black evangelical religious observance (in comparison to a white or disaggregated figure that generates an essentialist view of black populations as inherently religious).

12 However, scholars of religion might attribute these intergenerational differences to different causes, such as intergenerational changes in religious culture or the dynamics of religious landscapes. For these scholars, there are instances in which evangelical Christians from minoritized backgrounds are introduced in participating in nonethnic or multiethnic evangelical congregations (discussed in chapter 3). And if not following a Millennial emphasis of spirituality over religion or a Millennial tendency to buck the religious conventions of previous generations (challenged by scholars like Bengston, Putney, and Harris [2013]), the emerging adults raised in and/or attending CBC and DBC would have access to

a broad number of voluntary associations in which churches would be included. In particular, young adult Afro-Caribbean and African American evangelicals located in the Atlanta metropolitan area live in a southern US urban religious marketplace where mainline Protestant, evangelical, and other Christian movements are numerous.

13   *Caribbean Journeys: An Ethnography of Migration and Home in Three Family Networks* by Karen Fog Olwig illustrates the ways in which younger generations understand their Caribbean identities in familial terms and as a sense of belonging that is positively reinforced when meeting certain measures of social mobility and that might give way when younger relatives do not meet expectations of educational, professional, and class advancement. In short, Olwig examines the ways in which Caribbean transnational and intergenerational networks have their own morality that cannot be confined to host society cultural norms (2007, 265–66). Olwig's findings challenge the notion that generational and spatial distance may automatically generate Caribbean familial alienation or disidentification and, for our present purposes, a subsequent rejection of familial religious patterns or familial morality and values, which may be interpolated with religious and/or class-based values of respectability.

14   "Religious Landscape Study: Evangelical Protestants Who Identify as Black," Pew Research Center, Religion and Public Life, 2014, http://www.pewforum.org/religious-landscape-study/racial-and-ethnic-composition/black/religious-tradition/evangelical-protestant.

15   According to the Pew Forum, foreign-born black immigrant marriage rates (48 percent) are higher than that of US-born blacks (28 percent). Explanations for this difference are not forthcoming. "Chapter 1: Statistical Portrait of the U.S. Black Immigrant Population," Pew Research Center, Social and Demographic Trends, April 9, 2015, http://www.pewsocialtrends.org/2015/04/09/chapter-1-statistical-portrait-of-the-u-s-black-immigrant-population.

16   I did not have access to the particular study cited in this presentation. The Barna group seems to be a faith-focused research firm whose research is commonly cited in sermonic and religious settings. See "What is Barna?" at https://www.barna.com/about.

17   The language of "one flesh" that congregants use echoes the biblical language of marriage used in Mark 10:8, which reads: "For this reason a man will leave his father and mother and be united to his wife and the two will become one flesh" (NIV).

18   The scriptural reference that church members mobilize in their interconnected discussions of marriage in terms of "one flesh" and the church as "the bride of Christ" is found in Ephesians 5:25–32: "Husbands, love your wives, as Christ loved the church and gave himself up for her, that he might sanctify her, having cleansed her by the washing of water with the word, so that he might present the church to himself in splendor, without spot or wrinkle or any such thing, that she might be holy and without blemish. In the same way husbands should love their wives as their own bodies. He who loves his wife loves himself. For no

one ever hated his own flesh, but nourishes and cherishes, just as Christ does the church, because we are members of his body. 'Therefore a man shall leave his father and mother and hold fast to his wife, and the two shall become one flesh.' This mystery is profound, and I am saying that it refers to Christ and the church" (NIV).

19 Although there are few to no ethnographic explorations of Caribbean Brethrenism, Diane Austin-Broos makes reference to Afro-Jamaican Brethren's strong views on marriage in *Jamaica Genesis: Religion and the Politics of Moral Orders* via a research respondent (and Pentecostal convert) who characterized the Brethren congregation she attended as "strict and stern" in demeanor after her marriage began to unravel.

20 I am indebted to Cori Hayden for conceptualizing the tangle of racial and moral narratives navigated by African American and Afro-Caribbean evangelicals as an "unholy bundle" in her responses to my 2017 American Anthropological Association Meeting paper "(Ir)ration(aliz)ing African American Kinship: Neoliberal Moral Orders of Family and Race."

21 Some CBC and DBC women wore small black circular lace head coverings on their heads to conform to the Pauline injunction that women should cover their heads during worship (1 Corinthians 11:2–16).

22 This moral paradox of workplace assertion and domestic submission is also explored by Judith Casselberry (2017) in *The Labor of Faith: Gender and Power in Black Apostolic Pentecostalism*.

References

Abrahams, Roger D. 1983. *The Man-of-Words in the West Indies: Performance and the Emergence of Creole Culture*. Baltimore, MD: Johns Hopkins University Press.
Abrams, Andrea C. 2014. *God and Blackness: Race, Gender, and Identity in a Middle Class Afrocentric Church*. New York: New York University Press.
Akenson, Donald Harman. 2018. *Exporting the Rapture: John Nelson Darby and the Victorian Conquest of North American Evangelicalism*. Montreal: McGill-Queen's University Press.
Alexander, Elizabeth. 2004. *The Black Interior: Essays*. Minneapolis, MN: Graywolf.
Alexander, M. Jacqui. 2005. *Pedagogies of Crossing: Meditations on Feminism, Sexual Politics, Memory, and the Sacred*. Durham, NC: Duke University Press.
Alumkal, Antony W. 2004. "American Evangelicalism in the Post–Civil Rights Era: A Racial Formation Theory Analysis." *Sociology of Religion* 65, no. 3: 195–213.
Ammerman, Nancy Tatom. 1997. *Congregation and Community*. New Brunswick, NJ: Rutgers University Press.
Appadurai, Arjun. 1996. *Modernity at Large: Cultural Dimensions of Globalization*. Minneapolis: University of Minnesota Press.
Austin-Broos, Diane J. 1997. *Jamaica Genesis: Religion and the Politics of Moral Orders*. Chicago: University of Chicago Press.
Aymer, Paula L. 2016. *Evangelical Awakenings in the Anglophone Caribbean: Studies from Grenada and Barbados*. New York: Palgrave Macmillan.
Barnes, Riché J. Daniel. 2016. *Raising the Race: Black Career Women Redefine Marriage, Motherhood, and Community*. New Brunswick, NJ: Rutgers University Press.
Baroucki, Alex. 2015. *From Shipmates to Soldiers: Emerging Black Identities in the Rio de la Plata*. Albuquerque: University of New Mexico Press.
Barriteau, Eudine. 2003. "Requiem for the Male Marginalization Thesis in the Caribbean: Death of a Non-Theory." In *Confronting Power, Theorizing Gender: Interdisciplinary Perspectives in the Caribbean,* edited by Eudine Barriteau, 324–55. Kingston, Jamaica: University of the West Indies Press.

Barrow, Christine. 1996. *Family in the Caribbean: Themes and Perspectives*. Kingston, Jamaica: Ian Randle.

Barrow, Christine, ed. 1998. *Caribbean Portraits: Essays on Gender Ideologies and Identities*. Kingston, Jamaica: Ian Randle.

Barth, Frederick. 1998. "Introduction." *Ethnic Groups and Boundaries*. Long Grove, IL: Waveland.

Bartkowski, John P. 2004. *The Promise Keepers: Servants, Soldiers, and Godly Men*. New Brunswick, NJ: Rutgers University Press.

Bashi, Vilna Francine. 2007. *Survival of the Knitted: Immigrant Social Networks in a Stratified World*. Stanford, CA: Stanford University Press.

Bashi Treitler, Vilna. 2013. *The Ethnic Project: Transforming Racial Fiction into Ethnic Factions*. Stanford, CA: Stanford University Press.

Baumann, Gerd, and Thijl Sunier, eds. 1995. *Post-migration Ethnicity: De-essentializing Cohesion, Commitments, and Comparison*. Amsterdam: Het Spinhuis.

Bayor, Ronald H. 1996. *Race and the Shaping of Twentieth-Century Atlanta*. Chapel Hill: University of North Carolina Press.

Bebbington, David W. 1989. *Evangelicalism in Modern Britain: A History from the 1730s to the 1980s*. London: Routledge.

Becker, Peggy. 1999. *Congregations in Conflict: Cultural Models of Local Religious Life*. Ithaca, NY: Cornell University Press.

Beidelman, T. O. 1982. *Colonial Evangelism: A Socio-historical Study of an East African Mission at the Grassroots*. Bloomington: Indiana University Press.

Beliso-De Jesús, Aisha M. 2015. *Electric Santería: Racial and Sexual Assemblages of Transnational Religion*. New York: Columbia University Press.

Bengtson, Vern L., Norella M. Putney, and Susan Harris. 2013. *Families and Faith: How Religion Is Passed Down across Generations*. New York: Oxford University Press.

Bentley, Nancy. 2009. "Kinlessness and African American Narrative." *Critical Inquiry* 35, no. 2 (Winter): 270–92.

Bentley, William H. 1975. "Bible Believers in the Black Community." In *The Evangelicals: What They Believe, Who They Are, Where They Are Changing*, edited by David F. Wells and John D. Woodbridge, 108–21. Nashville, TN: Abingdon.

Besson, Jean. 1993. "Reputation and Respectability Reconsidered: A New Perspective on the Afro-Caribbean Peasant Woman." In *Women and Change in the Caribbean: A Pan-Caribbean Perspective*, edited by Janet Momsen, 15–37. Bloomington: Indiana University Press.

Besson, Jean. 1995. "The Creolization of African-American Slave Kinship in Jamaican Free Village and Maroon Communities." In *Slave Cultures and the Cultures of Slavery*, edited by Stephan Palmié, 187–209. Knoxville: University of Tennessee Press.

Besson, Jean. 2002. *Martha Brae's Two Histories: European Expansion and Caribbean Culture Building in Jamaica*. Chapel Hill: University of North Carolina Press.

Best, Wallace D. 2005. *Passionately Human, No Less Divine: Religion and Culture in Black Chicago, 1915–1952*. Princeton, NJ: Princeton University Press.

Bialecki, Jon, Naomi Haynes, and Joel Robbins. 2008. "The Anthropology of Christianity." *Religion Compass* 2, no. 6: 1139–58.

Bialecki, Jon, and Girish Daswani. 2015. "Introduction: What Is an Individual? The View from Christianity." *HAU: Journal of Ethnographic Theory* 5, no. 1 (Spring): 271–94.

Bielo, James S. 2009. *Words upon the Word: An Ethnography of Evangelical Group Bible Study.* New York: New York University Press.

Bielo, James S. 2011. *Emerging Evangelicals: Faith, Modernity, and the Desire for Authenticity.* New York: New York University Press.

Billingsley, Andrew, and Barbara Morrison-Rodriguez. 1998. "The Black Family in the 21st Century and the Church as an Action System: A Macro Perspective." *Journal of Human Behavior in Social Sciences* 1, nos. 2–3: 31–47.

Blackwood, Evelyn. 2005. "Wedding Bell Blues: Marriage, Missing Men, and Matrifocal Follies." *American Ethnologist* 32, no. 1: 3–19.

Blum, Edward J. 2014. "Beyond Body Counts: Sex, Individualism, and the Segregated Shape of Twentieth-Century Evangelicalism." In *Christians and the Color Line: Race and Religion after Divided by Faith*, edited by J. Russell Hawkins and Philip Luke Sinitiere, 161–77. New York: Oxford University Press.

Bonilla-Silva, Eduardo. 2006. *Racism without Racists: Color-Blind Racism and the Persistence of Racial Inequality in the United States.* Lanham, MD: Rowman and Littlefield.

Brown, Audrey Lawson. 1995. "Afro-Baptist Women's Church and Family Roles: Transmitting Afrocentric Cultural Values." *Anthropological Quarterly* 67, no. 4: 173–86.

Brown, Jacqueline Nassy. 2005. *Dropping Anchor, Setting Sail: Geographies of Race in Black Liverpool.* Princeton, NJ: Princeton University Press.

Brown, Karen McCarthy. 2006. "Afro-Caribbean Spirituality: A Haitian Case Study." In *Vodou in Haitian Life and Culture: Invisible Powers*, edited by Claudine Michel and Patrick Bellegarde-Smith, 1–26. New York: Palgrave Macmillan.

Brusco, Elizabeth E. 1995. *The Reformation of Machismo: Evangelical Conversion and Gender in Colombia.* Austin: University of Texas Press.

Burdick, John. 2013. *The Color of Sound: Race, Religion, and Music in Brazil.* New York: New York University Press.

Burlein, Ann. 2002. *Lift High the Cross: Where White Supremacy and the Christian Right Converge.* Durham, NC: Duke University Press.

Buss, Doris, and Didi Herman. 2003. *Globalizing Family Values: The Christian Right in International Politics.* Minneapolis: University of Minnesota Press.

Butchart, Ronald E. 2010. *Schooling the Freed People: Teaching, Learning, and the Struggle for Black Freedom, 1861–1876.* Chapel Hill: University of North Carolina Press.

Butler, Judith. 2002. "Is Kinship Always Already Heterosexual?" *differences* 13, no. 1: 14–44.

Calhoun-Brown, Allison. 1998. "The Politics of Black Evangelicals: 'What Hinders Diversity in the Christian Right?'" *American Politics Quarterly* 26, no. 1: 89–109.

Calhoun-Brown, Allison. 1999. "The Image of God: Black Theology and Racial Empowerment in the African American Community." *Review of Religious Research* 40, no. 3: 197–212.

Callahan, James Patrick. 1996. *Primitivist Piety: The Ecclesiology of the Early Plymouth Brethren.* Lanham, MD: Scarecrow.

Cannell, Fenella. 2005. "The Christianity of Anthropology." *Journal of the Royal Anthropological Institute* 11, no. 2: 335–56.

Cannell, Fenella. 2017. "'Forever Families': Christian Individualism, Mormonism and Collective Salvation." In *New Directions in Spiritual Kinship: Sacred Ties across the Abrahamic Traditions*, edited by Todne Thomas, Asiya Malik, and Rose Wellman, 151–69. Cham, Switzerland: Palgrave Macmillan.

Carby, Hazel. 1997. "White Woman Listen! Black Feminism and the Boundaries of Sisterhood." In *Black British Feminism: A Reader*. London: Routledge.

Carsten, Janet. 2000. *Cultures of Relatedness: New Approaches to the Study of Kinship*. Cambridge: Cambridge University Press.

Carter, J. Cameron. 2008. *Race: A Theological Account*. New York: Oxford University Press.

Casselberry, Judith. 2017. *The Labor of Faith: Gender and Power in Black Apostolic Pentecostalism*. Durham, NC: Duke University Press.

Castor, N. Fadeke. 2017. *Spiritual Citizenship: Transnational Pathways from Black Power to Ifá in Trinidad*. Durham, NC: Duke University Press.

Catwell, Sylvan. 1995. *The Brethren in Barbados: Gospel Hall Assemblies, 1889-1994*. St. George, Barbados: S. R. Catwell.

Chamberlain, Mary. 1999a. "Brothers and Sisters, Uncles and Aunts: A Lateral Perspective on Caribbean Families." In *The New Family*, edited by Elizabeth B. Silva and Carol Smart. London: Sage.

Chamberlain, Mary. 1999b. "The Family as Model and Metaphor in Caribbean Migration to Britain." *Journal of Ethnic and Migration Studies* 25, no. 2: 251–66.

Chamberlain, Mary. 2000. "'Praise Songs' of the Family: Lineage and Kinship in the Caribbean Diaspora. *History Workshop Journal* 50: 114–28.

Chamberlain, Mary. 2006. *Family Love in the Diaspora: Migration and the Anglo-Caribbean Experience*. New Brunswick. NJ: Transaction.

Chatters, Linda, Robert Taylor, and Rukmalie Jayakody. 1994. "Fictive Kinship Relations in Black Extended Families." *Journal of Comparative Family Studies* 25, no. 3: 297–312.

Chatters, Linda M., Robert Joseph Taylor, Kai McKeever Bullard, and James S. Jackson. 2009. "Race and Ethnic Differences in Religious Involvement: African Americans, Caribbean Blacks and Non-Hispanic Whites." *Ethnic and Racial Studies* 32, no 7: 1143–63.

Chevannes, Barry. 2001. *Learning to Be a Man: Culture, Socialization and Gender Identity in Five Caribbean Communities*. Barbados: University of the West Indies Press.

Chevannes, Barry Estate. 1997. *Rastafari: Roots and Ideology*. Syracuse, NY: Syracuse University Press.

Chow, Rey. 2002. *The Protestant Ethnic and the Spirit of Capitalism*. New York: Columbia University Press.

Clarke, Edith. 1966. *My Mother Who Fathered Me: A Study of Family in Three Selected Communities in Jamaica*. London: Ruskin House.

Clarke, Kamari M. 2013. "Notes on Cultural Citizenship in the Black Atlantic World." *Cultural Anthropology* 23, no. 3: 464–74.

Collins, Patricia Hill. 1998. "It's All in the Family: Intersections of Gender, Race, and Nation." *Hypatia* 13, no. 3: 62–82.

Crapanzano, Vincent. 2000. "Transfiguring Translation." *Semiotica* 128, nos. 1–2: 113–36.

Crawford, Norman. 1997. *Gathering Unto His Name*. Glasgow, UK: Gospel Tract Publications.

Crosson, Brent J. 2014. "Own People: Race, 'Altered Solidarities,' and the Limits of Culture in Trinidad." *Small Axe* 18, no. 3 (November): 18–34.

Csordas, Thomas. 2004. "Asymptote of the Ineffable: Embodiment, Alterity, and the Theory of Religion." *Current Anthropology* 45, no. 2: 163–85.

Csordas, Thomas. 2007. "Introduction: Modalities of Transnational Transcendence." *Anthropological Theory* 7, no. 3: 259–72.

Cumming, Elaine, and David M. Schneider. 1961. "Sibling Solidarity: 'A Property of American Kinship 1.'" *American Anthropologist* 63, no. 3 (June): 498–507.

Curtis, Edward E., IV, and Danielle Brune Sigler. 2009. *The New Black Gods: Arthur Huff Fauset and the Study of African American Religions*. Bloomington: Indiana University Press.

Dameron, Rebecca J., and Arthur D. Murphy. 1997. "An International City Too Busy to Hate? Social and Cultural Change in Atlanta: 1970–1995." *Urban Anthropology and Studies of Cultural Systems and World Economic Development* 26, no. 1 (Spring): 43–69.

Davies, Carole Boyce, and Monica Jardine. 2003. "Imperial Geographies and Caribbean Nationalism: At the Border between 'A Dying Colonialism' and U.S. Hegemony." *CR: The New Centennial Review* 3, no. 3 (Fall): 151–74.

Day, Keri. 2016. *Religious Resistance to Neoliberalism: Womanist and Black Feminist Perspectives*. New York: Palgrave Macmillan.

Delgado, Gary. 2012. "Kill the Messengers: Can We Achieve Racial Justice without Mentioning Race?" In *Racial Formation in the Twenty-First Century*, edited by Daniel Martinez HoSang, Oneka LaBennett, and Laura Pulido, 162–82. Berkeley: University of California Press.

Desmangles, Leslie G., Stephen D. Glazier, and Joseph M. Murphy. 2003. "Religion in the Caribbean." In *Understanding the Caribbean*, edited by Richard S. Hillman and Thomas J. D'Agostino, 263–304. Boulder, CO: Lynne Rienner.

Diakité, Dianne M. Stewart, and Tracey E. Hucks. 2013. "Africana Religious Studies: Toward a Transdisciplinary Agenda in an Emerging Field." *Journal of Africana Religions* 1, no. 1: 28–77.

Dill, Bonnie Thornton. 1993. "Fictive Kin, Paper Sons, and *Compadrazgo*: Women of Color and the Struggle for Family Survival." In *Women of Color in U.S. Society*, edited by Maxine Baca Zinn, 149–69. Philadelphia: Temple University Press.

Dixon, Lorraine. 2007. "The Nature of Black Presence in England before the Abolition of Slavery." *Black Theology* 5, no. 2: 171–83.

Douglass, Lisa. 1992. *The Power of Sentiment: Love, Hierarchy, and the Jamaican Family Elite*. Boulder, CO: Westview.

Drake, St. Clair, and Horace R. Cayton. 2015 (1945). *Black Metropolis: A Study of Negro Life in a Northern City*. Chicago: University of Chicago Press.

Du Bois, W. E. B. 1995 (1899). *The Philadelphia Negro: A Social Study*. Philadelphia: University of Philadelphia Press.

Duncan, Carol B. 2008. *This Spot of Ground: Spiritual Baptists in Toronto*. Waterloo, ON: Wilfrid Laurier University Press.

Ebaugh, Helen Rose, and Mary Curry. 2000. "Fictive Kin as Social Capital in New Immigrant Communities." *Sociological Perspectives* 43, no. 2: 189–209.

Edwards, Korie L. 2014. "Much Ado about Nothing? Rethinking the Efficacy of Multiracial Churches for Racial Reconciliation." In *Christians and the Color Line: Race and Religion after Divided by Faith*, edited by J. Russell Hawkins and Philip Luke Sinitiere, 231–54. New York: Oxford University Press.

Elisha, Omri. 2008. "Faith beyond Belief: Evangelical Protestant Conceptions of Faith and the Resonance of Anti-humanism." *Social Analysis* 52, no. 1 (April): 56–78.

Elisha, Omri. 2011. *Moral Ambition: Mobilization and Social Outreach in Evangelical Megachurches*. Berkeley: University of California Press.

Elisha, Omri. 2015. "Personhood: Sin, Sociality, and the Unbuffered Self in US Evangelicalism." In *The Anthropology of Global Pentecostalism and Evangelicalism*, edited by Simon Coleman and Rosalind I. J. Hackett, 41–56. New York: New York University Press.

Emerson, Michael O., and Christian Smith. 2000. *Divided by Faith: Evangelical Religion and the Problem of Race in America*. Oxford: Oxford University Press.

Engelke, Matthew. 2007. *A Problem of Presence: Beyond Scripture in an African Church*. Berkeley: University of California Press.

Erzen, Tanya. 2006. *Straight to Jesus: Sexual and Christian Conversions in the Ex-gay Movement*. Berkeley: University of California Press.

Evans, Curtis J. 2008. *The Burden of Black Religion*. Oxford: Oxford University Press.

Evans, Curtis J. 2009. "White Evangelical Protestant Responses to the Civil Rights Movement." *Harvard Theological Review* 102, no. 2 (April): 245–73.

Feeley-Harnik, Gillian. 1981. *The Lord's Table: Eucharist and Passover in Early Christianity*. Philadelphia: University of Pennsylvania Press.

Ferguson, Roderick A. 2004. *Aberrations in Black: Toward a Queer of Color Critique*. Minneapolis: University of Minnesota Press.

Foner, Nancy. 2001. *New Immigrants in New York*. New York: Columbia University Press.

Foner, Nancy. 2011. "Black Identities and the Second Generation: Afro Caribbeans in Britain and the United States." In *The Next Generation: Immigrant Youth in a Comparative Perspective*, edited by Mary C. Waters and Richard Alba, 251–68. New York: New York University Press.

Fortner, Michael Javen. 2015. *Black Silent Majority: The Rockefeller Drug Laws and the Politics of Punishment*. Cambridge, MA: Harvard University Press.

Franklin, Sarah, and Susan McKinnon, eds. 2002. *Relative Values: Reconfiguring Kinship Studies*. Durham, NC: Duke University Press.

Frazier, E. Franklin. 1939. *The Negro Family in the United States*. Chicago: University of Chicago Press.

Frazier, E. Franklin. 1957. *Black Bourgeoisie*. New York: Free Press.

Frazier, E. Franklin. 1964. *The Negro Church in America*. New York: Schocken.

Frederick, Marla F. 2003. *Between Sundays: Black Women and Everyday Struggles of Faith.* Berkeley: University of California Press.

Frederick, Marla F. 2015. "Mediated Missions: The Gospel According to Women." *Missiology* 43, no. 2 (April): 121–36.

Frederick, Marla F. 2016. *Colored Television: American Religion Gone Global.* Stanford, CA: Stanford University Press.

Freeman, Carla. 2014. *Entrepreneurial Selves: Neoliberal Respectability and the Making of a Caribbean Middle Class.* Durham, NC: Duke University Press.

Frey, Sylvia R., and Betty Wood. 1998. *Come Shouting to Zion: African American Protestantism in the American South and British Caribbean to 1830.* Chapel Hill: University of North Carolina Press.

Frishkopf, Michael. 2003. "Spiritual Kinship and Globalization." *Religious Studies and Theology* 22, no. 1: 1–25.

Gadsby, Meredith. 2006. *Sucking Salt: Caribbean Women Writers, Migration, and Survival.* Columbia: University of Missouri Press.

Gaither, Bill, and Gloria Gaither. 2005. "Family of God." In *The Greatest Songs of Bill and Gloria Gaither.* Milwaukee, WI: Hal Leonard.

Gallagher, Sally, and Christian Smith. 1999. "Symbolic Traditionalism and Pragmatic Egalitarianism: Contemporary Evangelicals, Family, and Gender." *Gender and Society* 13, no. 2 (April): 211–33.

Gallagher, Sally K. 2003. *Evangelical Identity and Gendered Family Life.* New Brunswick, NJ: Rutgers University Press.

Gasaway, Brantley W. 2014. "'Glimmers of Hope': Progressive Evangelicals and Racism, 1965–2000." In *Christians and the Color Line: Race and Religion after* Divided by Faith, edited by J. Russell Hawkins and Philip Luke Sinitiere, 72–99. New York: Oxford University Press.

Geary, Daniel. 2015. *Beyond Civil Rights: The Moynihan Report and Its Legacy.* Philadelphia: University of Pennsylvania Press.

Gilbreath, Edward. 2006. *Reconciliation Blues: A Black Evangelical's Inside View of White Christianity.* Downers Grove, IL: IVP Books.

Gilkes, Cheryl. 2001. *"If It Wasn't for the Women . . .": Black Women's Experience and Womanist Culture in Church and Community.* Maryknoll, NY: Orbis.

Gilroy, Paul. 1993. "It's a Family Affair: Black Culture and the Trope of Kinship." In *Small Acts: Thoughts on the Politics of Black Cultures.* London: Serpent's Tail.

Gilroy, Paul. 1994. "'After the Love Has Gone': Bio-politics and Etho-poetics in the Black Public Sphere." *Public Culture* 7, no. 1: 49–76.

Gilroy, Paul. 1995. *The Black Atlantic: Modernity and Double Consciousness.* Cambridge, MA: Harvard University Press.

Gilroy, Paul. 2004. *Between Camps: Nations, Cultures and the Allure of Race.* London: Routledge.

Glaude, Eddie S., Jr. 2000. *Exodus! Religion, Race, and Nation in Early Nineteenth-Century Black America.* Chicago: University of Chicago Press.

Glaude, Eddie S., Jr. 2003. "Of the Black Church and the Making of a Black Public." In *African American Religious Thought: An Anthology,* edited by Cornel West and Eddie S. Glaude, 341–65. Louisville, KY: Westminster John Knox.

Glaude, Eddie S., Jr. 2010. "The Black Church Is Dead." *Huffington Post*, April 26.
Gmelch, George. 1992. *Double Passage: The Lives of Caribbean Migrants Abroad and Back Home*. Ann Arbor: University of Michigan Press.
Goldfield, David R. 1982. *Cotton Fields and Skyscrapers: Southern City and Region, 1607–1980*. Baton Rouge: Louisiana State University Press.
Goldschmidt, Henry, and Elizabeth McAlister. 2004. "Introduction." In *Race, Nation, and Religion in the Americas*, edited by Henry Goldschmidt, 3–23. Oxford: Oxford University Press.
Gosse, Edmund. 1990 (1905). *Father and Son: A Study of Two Temperaments*. Warwickshire, UK: Pantianos Classics.
Goulbourne, Harry. 1999. "The Transnational Character of Caribbean Kinship in Britain." In *Changing Britain: Families and Households in the 1990's*, edited by Susan McRae, 176–98. Oxford: Oxford University Press.
Greenbaum, Susan D. 2015. *Blaming the Poor: The Long Shadow of the Moynihan Report on Cruel Images about Poverty*. New Brunswick, NJ: Rutgers University Press.
Gregory, James Noble. 2005. *The Southern Diaspora: How the Great Migrations of Black and White Southerners Transformed America*. Chapel Hill: University of North Carolina Press.
Grelle, Bruce. 2017. *Antonio Gramsci and the Question of Religion: Ideology, Ethics, and Hegemony*. London: Routledge, Taylor and Francis.
Griffith, R. Marie. 1997. *God's Daughters: Evangelical Women and the Power of Submission*. Berkeley: University of California Press.
Griffith, R. Marie. 2000. *God's Daughters: Evangelical Women and the Power of Submission*. Berkeley: University of California Press.
Guadeloupe, Francio. 2009. *Chanting Down the New Jerusalem: Calypso, Christianity, and Capitalism in the Caribbean*. Berkeley: University of California Press.
Guridy, Frank Andre. 2010. *Forging Diaspora: Afro-Cubans and African Americans in a World Empire and Jim Crow*. Chapel Hill: University of North Carolina Press.
Handman, Courtney. 2014. *Critical Christianity: Translation and Denominational Conflict in Papua New Guinea*. Berkeley: University of California Press.
Harding, Susan Friend. 2000. *The Book of Jerry Falwell: Fundamentalist Language and Politics*. Princeton, NJ: Princeton University Press.
Harold, Claudrena. 2007. *Rise and Fall of the Garvey Movement in the South, 1918–1942*. New York: Routledge.
Hartman, Saidiya V. 2007. *Lose Your Mother: A Journey along the Atlantic Slave Route*. New York: Farrar, Straus and Giroux.
Harvey, David. 2005. *A Brief History of Neoliberalism*. New York: Oxford University Press.
Harvey, Paul. 2005. *Freedom's Coming: Religious Culture and the Shaping of the South from the Civil War through the Civil Rights Era*. Chapel Hill: University of North Carolina Press.
Hazzard-Donald, Katrina. 2012. *Mojo Workin': The Old African American Hoodoo System*. Urbana: University of Illinois Press.
Hempton, David. 2002. "Plymouth Brethrenism." In *The Oxford Companion to Irish History*, edited by S. J. Connolly, 447. Oxford: Oxford University Press.

Hempton, David. 2008. *Evangelical Disenchantment: Nine Portraits of Faith and Doubt*. New Haven, CT: Yale University Press.

Higginbotham, Evelyn Brooks. 1993. *Righteous Discontent: The Women's Movement in the Black Baptist Church, 1880–1920*. Cambridge, MA: Harvard University Press.

Hill, Carole E., and Patricia D. Beaver, eds. 1998. *Cultural Diversity in the U.S. South: Anthropological Contributions to a Region in Transition*. Athens: University of Georgia Press.

Hills, Darius D., and Tommy J. Curry. 2015. "Cries of the Unheard: State Violence, Black Bodies, and Martin Luther King's Black Power." *Journal of Africana Religions* 3: 453–69.

Hintzen, Percy Claude. 2001. *West Indian in the West: Self-Representations in an Immigrant Community*. New York: New York University Press.

Hintzen, Percy Claude, and Jean Muteba Rahier, eds. 2003. *Problematizing Blackness: Self Ethnographies by Black Immigrants to the United States*. New York: Routledge.

Ho, Christine. 1993. *Salt-Water Trinnies: Afro-Trinidadian Immigrant Networks and Non-Assimilation in Los Angeles*. New York: AMS Press.

Ho, Christine G. T. 1992. "Internationalization of Kinship and the Feminization of Caribbean Migration: The Case of Afro-Trinidadian Immigrants in Los Angeles." *Human Organization* 52, no. 1: 32–40.

Hobson, Maurice. 2017. *The Legend of the Black Mecca: Politics and Class in the Making of Atlanta*. Chapel Hill: University of North Carolina Press.

Hohle, Randolph. 2012. "The Color of Neoliberalism: The 'Modern Southern Businessman' and Postwar Alabama's Challenge to Racial Desegregation." *Sociological Forum* 27, no. 1 (March): 142–62.

hooks, bell. 1990. *Yearning: Race, Gender, and Cultural Politics*. Boston, MA: South End.

Horst, Heather A., and Daniel Miller. 2006. *The Cell Phone: An Anthropology of Communication*. Oxford: Berg.

Hunter, Tera W. 1997. *To Joy My Freedom: Southern Black Women's Lives and Labors after the Civil War*. Cambridge, MA: Harvard University Press.

Ibsen, Charles A., and Patricia Klobus. 1972. "Fictive Kin Term Use and Social Relationships: Alternative Interpretations." *Journal of Marriage and Family* 34, no. 4: 615–20.

Ineichen, Bernard. 2019. "Losing the Rapture: Escaping from Fundamentalist Christian Belief." *Mental Health, Religion & Culture* 22, no. 7: 661–73.

Ingersoll, Julie. 2003. *Evangelical Christian Women: War Stories in the Gender Battle*. New York: New York University Press.

Introvigne, Massimo. 2018. *The Plymouth Brethren*. New York: Oxford University Press.

Jackson, John L., Jr. 2001. *Harlemworld: Doing Race and Class in Contemporary Black America*. Chicago: University of Chicago Press.

Jewell, Joseph O. 2007. *Race, Social Reform, and the Making of a Middle Class: The American Missionary Association and Black Atlanta, 1870–1900*. Lanham, MD: Rowman and Littlefield.

Jewell, K. Sue. 2003. *Survival of the African American Family: The Institutional Impact of U.S. Social Policy*. Westport, CT: Praeger.

Jill-Levine, Amy, ed. 2008. *A Feminist Companion to Patristic Literature*. London: T&T Clark.

Johnson, Colleen L. 2000. "Perspectives in American Kinship in the Latter 1990s." *Journal of Marriage and the Family* 62, no. 3: 623–39.

Johnson, Sylvester. 2004. *The Myth of Ham in Nineteenth-Century American Christianity: Race, Heathens, and the People of God*. New York: Palgrave Macmillan.

Johnson, Sylvester. 2010. "The Rise of Black Ethnics: The Ethnic Turn in African American Religions, 1916–1945." *Religion and American Culture* 20, no. 2: 125–63.

Johnson, Sylvester A. 2015. *African American Religions, 1500–2000: Colonialism, Democracy, and Freedom*. New York: Cambridge University Press.

Johnson, Violet Showers. 2006. *The Other Black Bostonians: West Indians in Boston, 1900–1950*. Bloomington: Indiana University Press.

Kaplan, Amy, and Donald E. Pease. 1993. *Cultures of United States Imperialism*. Durham, NC: Duke University Press.

Keane, Webb. 2007. *Christian Moderns: Freedom and Fetish in the Mission Encounter*. Berkeley: University of California Press.

Keel, Terence. 2018. *Divine Variations: How Christian Thought Became Racial Science*. Stanford, CA: Stanford University Press.

King, Tiffany Lethabo. 2018. "Black 'Feminisms' and Pessimism: Abolishing Moynihan's Negro Family." *Theory and Event* 21, no. 1: 68–87.

Klaits, Frederick. 2010. *Death in a Church of Life: Moral Passion during Botswana's Time of AIDS*. Berkeley: University of California Press.

Korom, Frank J. 2003. *Hosay Trinidad: Muḥarram Performances in an Indo-Caribbean Diaspora*. Philadelphia: University of Pennsylvania Press.

Kruse, Kevin Michael. 2005. *White Flight: Atlanta and the Making of Modern Conservatism*. Princeton, NJ: Princeton University Press.

Lacy, Karyn R. 2007. *Blue-Chip Black: Race, Class, and Status in the New Black Middle Class*. Berkeley: University of California Press.

Liebow, Elliot. 2003 (1967). *Tally's Corner: A Study of Negro Streetcorner Men*. Lanham, MD: Rowman and Littlefield.

Lincoln, Eric C., and Lawrence H. Mamiya. 1990. *The Black Church in the African American Experience*. Durham, NC: Duke University Press.

Litchmore, Winston G. 2006. "Christian Brethren Assemblies in Jamaica, 1923–2003." In *The Growth of the Brethren Movement: National and International Experiences*, edited by Neil T. R. Dickson and Tim Grass, 191–98. Eugene, OR: Wipf and Stock.

Logan, John, and Glenn Deane. 2003. *Black Diversity in Metropolitan America*. Albany, NY: Lewis Mumford Center for Comparative Urban and Regional Research, State University of New York at Albany.

Lorick-Wilmot, Yndia. 2017. *Stories of Identity among Black, Middle Class, Second Generation Caribbeans: We, Too, Sing America*. Cham, Switzerland: Palgrave Macmillan.

Low, Setha M., and Denise Lawrence-Zúñiga, eds. 2003. *The Anthropology of Space and Place: Locating Culture*. Malden, MA: Blackwell.

Lugones, María C., and Patt Alake Rosezelle. 1995. "Sisterhood and Friendship as Feminist Models." In *Feminism and Community*, edited by P. A. Weiss and Marilyn Friedman, 136–45. Philadelphia, PA: Temple University Press.

Marsh, Charles. 2005. *The Beloved Community: How Faith Shapes Social Justice, from the Civil Rights Movement to Today*. New York: Basic Books.

Mathers, Art. 1965. "The Nottage Brothers: 180 Years in God's Service." *Power for Living* 23, no. 1: 5–6.

Matory, J. Lorand. 2005. *Black Atlantic Religion: Tradition, Transnationalism, and Matriarchy in the Afro-Brazilian Candomble*. Princeton, NJ: Princeton University Press.

Matory, J. Lorand. 2009. "The Many Who Dance in Me: Afro-Atlantic Ontology and the Problem with 'Transnationalism.'" In *Transnational Transcendence: Essays in Religion and Globalization*, edited by Thomas J. Csordas, 231–62. Berkeley: University of California Press.

Matory, J. Lorand. 2015. *Stigma and Culture: Last-Place Anxiety in Black America*. Chicago: University of Chicago Press.

Matthews, Mary Beth Swetnam. 2017. *Doctrine and Race: African American Evangelicals and Fundamentalism between the Wars*. Tuscaloosa: University of Alabama Press.

Mauss, Marcel. 1990. *The Gift: The Form and Reason for Exchange in Archaic Societies*. New York: W. W. Norton and Company.

McAdoo, Harriette Pipes. 2007. "Religion in African American Families." In *Black Families*, edited by Harriette Pipes McAdoo, 97–100. Thousand Oaks, CA: Sage.

McGlathery, Marla Frederick, and Traci Griffin. 2007. "'Becoming Conservative, Becoming White?': Black Evangelicals and the Para-Church Movement." In *This Side of Heaven: Race, Ethnicity, and Christian Faith*, edited by Robert J. Priest and Alvaro L. Nieves, 144–63. New York: Oxford University Press.

McKinnon, Susan, and Fenella Cannell, eds. 2013. *Vital Relations: Modernity and the Persistent Life of Kinship*. Santa Fe, NM: School for Advanced Research Press.

Mentore, George. 2006. "The Triumph and Sorrow of Beauty: Comparing the Recursive, Contrapuntal, and Cellular Aesthetics of Being." *Tipiti* 4, no. 1: 295–318.

Michaels, Walter Benn. 1992. "Race into Culture: A Critical Genealogy of Cultural Identity." *Critical Inquiry* 18, no. 4: 655–85.

Miller, Albert G. 2000. "The Construction of a Black Fundamentalist Worldview: The Role of Bible Schools." In *African Americans and the Bible: Sacred Texts and Social Textures*, edited by Vincent L. Wimbush, 712–27. New York: Continuum.

Moten, Fred. 2008. "The Case of Blackness." *Criticism* 50, no. 2 (Spring): 177–218.

Moynihan, Daniel P. 1965. "The Negro Family: The Case for National Action." United States Department of Labor, Office of Policy Planning and Research. Washington, DC: Superintendent of Documents.

Mullin, Miles S., II. 2014. "Neoevangelicalism and the Problem of Race in Postwar America." In *Christians and the Color Line: Race and Religion after Divided by Faith*, edited by J. Russell Hawkins and Philip Luke Sinitiere, 15–44. New York: Oxford University Press.

Murphy, Arthur D., Colleen Blanchard, and Jennifer Hill, eds. 2001. *Latino Workers in the Contemporary South*. Athens: University of Georgia Press.

Nelson, Margaret K. 2013. "Whither Fictive Kin? Or, What's in a Name?" *Journal of Family Issues* 35, no. 2: 201–22.

Noll, Mark A. 2001. *American Evangelical Christianity: An Introduction*. Oxford: Blackwell.

Ochs, Elinor, and Lisa Capps. 2001. *Living Narrative: Creating Lives in Everyday Storytelling*. Cambridge, MA: Harvard University Press.

Olson, Dennis T. 2006. "How Lutherans Read the Bible: A North American and Global Conversation." *Dialogue* 45, no. 1 (Spring): 4–8.

Olwig, Karen Fog. 1999a. "Caribbean Place Identity: From Family Land to Region and Beyond." *Identities* 5, no. 4: 435–67.

Olwig, Karen Fog. 1999b. "Narratives of the Children Left Behind: Home and Identity in Globalised Caribbean Families." *Journal of Ethnic and Migration Studies* 25, no. 2: 267–84.

Olwig, Karen Fog. 2007. *Caribbean Journeys: An Ethnography of Migration and Home in Three Family Networks*. Durham, NC: Duke University Press.

Omi, Michael, and Howard Winant. 1994. *Racial Formation in the United States: From the 1960s to the 1990s*. New York: Routledge.

Ossman, Susan. 2004. "Studies in Serial Migration." *International Migration* 42, no. 4: 111–21.

Ownby, Ted. 2018. *Hurtin' Words: Debating Family Problems in the Twentieth-Century South*. Chapel Hill: University of North Carolina Press.

Pankhurst, Jerry G., and Sharon K. Houseknecht. 2000. "Introduction: The Religion-Family Linkage and Social Change—A Neglected Area of Study." In *Family, Religion, and Social Change in Diverse Societies*, edited by Jerry G. Pankhurst and Sharon K. Houseknecht, 1–40. New York: Oxford University Press.

Paris, Peter J. 1995. *The Spirituality of African Peoples: The Search for a Common Moral Discourse*. Minneapolis, MN: Fortress Press.

Parry, J., and M. Bloch, eds. 1989. *Money and the Morality of Exchange*. Cambridge: Cambridge University Press.

Patterson, Orlando. 1982. *Slavery and Social Death: A Comparative Study*. Cambridge, MA: Harvard University Press.

Pattillo-McCoy, Mary. 2000. *Black Picket Fences: Privilege and Peril among the Black Middle Class*. Chicago: University of Chicago Press.

Pear, Robert, and David D. Kirkpatrick. "Bush Plans $1.5 Billion Drive on Marriage 2004," *New York Times*, January 14.

Pérez, Elizabeth. 2016. *Religion in the Kitchen: Cooking, Talking, and the Making of Black Atlantic Traditions*. New York: New York University Press.

Pierre, Jemima. 2004. "Black Immigrants in the United States and the 'Cultural Narratives' of Ethnicity." *Identities* 11, no. 2: 141–70.

Pinn, Anthony B. 2010a. *Embodiment and the New Shape of Black Theological Thought*. New York: New York University Press.

Pinn, Anthony B. 2010b. *Understanding and Transforming the Black Church*. Eugene, OR: Cascade.

Pitts, Walter. 1993. *Old Ship of Zion: The Afro-Baptist Ritual in the African Diaspora*. New York: Oxford University Press.

Potter, Ronald C. 1979. "The New Black Evangelicals." In *Black Theology: A Documentary History, 1966–1979*, edited by Gayraud S. Wilmore and James H. Cone, 302–9. Maryknoll, NY: Orbis.

Prentiss, Craig R. 2003. *Religion and the Creation of Race and Ethnicity: An Introduction*. New York: New York University Press.

Priest, Robert J. 2001. "Missionary Positions: Christian, Modernist, Postmodernist." *Current Anthropology* 42, no. 1 (February): 29–68.

Pulis, John W. 1999a. "Citing [Sighting]-Up." In *Religion, Diaspora and Cultural Identity: A Reader in the Anglophone Caribbean*, edited by John W. Pulis, 357–402. Amsterdam: Gordon and Breach.

Pulis, John W. 1999b. *Moving On: Black Loyalists in the Afro-Atlantic World*. New York: Garland.

Queeley, Andrea. 2015. *Rescuing Our Roots: The African Anglo-Caribbean Diaspora in Contemporary Cuba*. Gainesville: University Press of Florida.

Raboteau, Albert J. 1978. *Slave Religion: The "Invisible Institution" in the Antebellum South*. New York: Oxford University Press.

Rah, Soong-Chan. 2019. "African American Evangelicals." In *T&T Clark Handbook of African American Theology*, edited by Antonia Michelle Daymond, Frederick L. Ware, and Eric Williams, 73–88. London: Bloomsbury.

Reid-Salmon, Delroy. 2009. *Home away from Home: The Caribbean Diasporan Church in the Black Atlantic Tradition*. New York: Routledge.

"Religious Landscape Study." 2014. Pew Research Center's Religion and Public Life Project. http://www.pewforum.org/dataset/pew-research-center 2014-u-s-religious-landscape-study.

Richardson, Riché. 2007. *Black Masculinity and the U.S. South: From Uncle Tom to Gangsta*. Athens: University of Georgia Press.

Richman, Karen E. 2008. *Migration and Vodou*. Gainesville: University Press of Florida.

Rigueur, Leah Wright. 2015. *The Loneliness of the Black Republican: Pragmatic Politics and the Pursuit of Power*. Princeton, NJ: Princeton University Press.

Rigueur, Leah Wright. 2017. "Neoliberal Social Justice: From Ed Brooke to Barack Obama." Social Science Research Council, May 30. http://items.ssrc.org/neoliberal-social-justice-from-ed-brooke-to-barack-obama.

Rivera, Mayra. 2007. *The Touch of Transcendence: A Postcolonial Theology of God*. Louisville, KY: Westminster John Knox.

Robbins, Joel. 1994. "Equality as a Value: Ideology in Dumont, Melanesia and the West." *Social Analysis* 36 (October): 21–70.

Robbins, Joel. 2007. "Continuity Thinking and the Problem of Christian Culture: Belief, Time, and the Anthropology of Christianity." *Current Anthropology* 48, no. 1 (February): 5–38.

Robbins, Joel. 2015. "Dumont's Hierarchical Dynamism: Christianity and Individualism Revisited." *HAU: Journal of Ethnographic Theory* 5, no. 1 (Spring): 173–95.

Robinson, Carin. 2006. "From Every Tribe and Nation? Blacks and the Christian Right." *Social Science Quarterly* 87, no. 3: 591–601.

Roseneil, Sasha, and Shelley Budgeon. 2004. "Cultures of Intimacy and Care beyond 'the Family': Personal Life and Social Change in the Early 21st Century." *Current Sociology* 52, no. 2 (March): 135–59.

Ross, Rosetta. 2012. "Black Theology and the History of U.S. Black Religions: Post–Civil Rights Approaches to the Study of African American Religions." *Religion Compass* 6: 249–61.

Rouse, Carolyn Moxley. 2004. *Engaged Surrender: African American Women and Islam*. Berkeley: University of California Press.

Russell, Heather D. 2015. "Post-Blackness and All of the Black Americas." In *The Trouble with Post-Blackness*, edited by Houston A. Baker Jr. and K. Merinda Simmons, 110–43. New York: Columbia University Press.

Sahlins, Marshall. 2013. *What Kinship Is—And Is Not*. Chicago: University of Chicago Press.

Sault, Nicole. 2001. "Godparenthood Ties among Zapotec Women and the Effects of Protestant Conversion." In *Holy Saints and Fiery Preachers: The Anthropology of Protestantism in Mexico*, edited by James Dow and Alan R. Sandstrom, 117–46. Westport, CT: Praeger.

Savage, Barbara Dianne. 2008. *Your Spirits Walk beside Us: The Politics of Black Religion*. Cambridge, MA: Harvard University Press.

Schäfer, Axel R. 2013. *American Evangelicals and the 1960s*. Madison: University of Wisconsin Press.

Schiller, Nina Glick, Ayse Caglar, and Thaddeus C. Gulbrandsen. 2006. "Beyond the Ethnic Lens: Locality, Globality, and Born-Again Incorporation." *American Ethnologist* 33, no. 4: 612–33.

Schneider, David, and Raymond T. Smith. 1973. *Class Differences and Sex Roles in American Kinship and Family Structure*. Edgewood Cliffs, NJ: Prentice Hall.

Schneider, David Murray. 1984. *A Critique of the Study of Kinship*. Ann Arbor: University of Michigan Press.

Scott, David. 2013. "That Event, This Memory: Notes on the Anthropology of African Diasporas in the New World." In *Caribbean Cultural Thought: From Plantation to Diaspora*, edited by Y. Hume and A. Kamugisha, 215–31. Kingston, Jamaica: Ian Randle.

Scully, Randolph Ferguson. 2007. "'I Come Here Before You Did and I Shall Not Go Away': Race, Gender, and Evangelical Community on the Eve of the Nat Turner Rebellion." *Journal of the Early Republic* 27, no. 4 (December): 661–84.

Sensbach, Jon F. 2006. *Rebecca's Revival: Creating Black Christianity in the Atlantic World*. Cambridge, MA: Harvard University Press.

Shelton, Jason E., and Michael O. Emerson. 2012. *Blacks and Whites in Christian America: How Racial Discrimination Shapes Religious Convictions*. New York: New York University Press.

Silver, Christopher, and John V. Moeser. 1995. *The Separate City: Black Communities in the Urban South, 1940–1968*. Lexington: University Press of Kentucky.

Simey, Thomas S. 1946. *Welfare and Planning in the West Indies*. Oxford: Clarendon.

Simmons, K. Merinda. 2015. "Introduction: The Dubious Stage of Post-Blackness—Performing Otherness, Conserving Dominance." In *The Trouble with Post-Blackness*, edited by Houston A. Baker Jr. and K. Merinda Simmons, 1–20. New York: Columbia University Press.

Singh, Jakeet. 2015. "Religious Agency and the Limits of Intersectionality." *Hypatia* 30, no. 4 (September): 657–74.

Skocpol, Theda, Ariane Liazos, and Marshall Ganz. 2006. *What a Mighty Power We Can Be: African American Fraternal Groups and the Struggle for Racial Equality*. Princeton, NJ: Princeton University Press.

Smallwood, Stephanie E. 2008. *Saltwater Slavery: A Middle Passage from Africa to American Diaspora*. Cambridge, MA: Harvard University Press.

Smilde, David. 2007. *Reason to Believe: Cultural Agency in Latin American Evangelicalism*. Berkeley: University of California Press.

Smith, Andrea. 2006. "'The One Who Did Not Break His Promises': Native Americans in the Evangelical Racial Reconciliation Movement." *American Behavioral Scientist* 50, no. 4: 478–509.

Smith, Candis Watts. 2014. *Black Mosaic: The Politics of Black Pan-ethnic Diversity*. New York: New York University Press.

Smith, Christian. 1998. *American Evangelicalism: Embattled and Thriving*. Chicago: University of Chicago Press.

Smith, Michael Garfield. 1965. *The Plural Society in the British West Indies*. Berkeley: University of California Press.

Smith, Raymond T. 1986. *Kinship and Class in the West Indies*. Cambridge: Cambridge University Press.

Smith, R. Drew. 2014. "The Church in African American Theology." In *The Oxford Handbook of African American Theology*, edited by Anthony B. Pinn and Katie G. Cannon, 229–38. Oxford: Oxford University Press.

Smith, Robert O. 2013. *More Desired Than Our Owne Salvation: The Roots of Christian Zionism*. New York: Oxford University Press.

Sobo, Elise. 1993. *One Blood: The Jamaican Body*. Albany: State University of New York Press.

Spence, Lester. 2015. *Knocking the Hustle: Against the Neoliberal Turn in Black Politics*. Brooklyn, NY: Punctum.

Spillers, Hortense J. 1987. "Mama's Baby, Papa's Maybe: An American Grammar Book." *Diacritics* 17, no. 2: 64–81.

Stack, Carol B. 1974. *All Our Kin: Strategies for Survival in a Black Community*. New York: Harper and Row.

Stack, Carol B. 1996. *Call to Home: African Americans Reclaim the Rural South*. New York: Basic Books.

Stephens, Michelle Ann. 2005. *Black Empire: The Masculine Global Imaginary of Caribbean Intellectuals in the United States, 1914–1962*. Durham, NC: Duke University Press.

Stewart, Dianne M. 2005. *Three Eyes for the Journey: African Dimensions of the Jamaican Religious Experience*. Oxford: Oxford University Press.

Stone, Clarence N. 1989. *Regime Politics: Governing Atlanta, 1946–1988*. Lawrence: University Press of Kansas.

Stott, Rebecca. 2017. *In the Days of Rain: A Daughter, a Father, a Cult.* New York: Spiegel and Grau.

Strhan, Anna. 2015. *Aliens and Strangers? The Struggle for Coherence in the Everyday Lives of Evangelicals.* Oxford: Oxford University Press.

Sudarkasa, Niara. 2007. "Interpreting the African Heritage in African American Family Organization." In *Black Families*, edited by Harriette Pipes McAdoo, 29–38. Thousand Oaks, CA: Sage.

Sutton, Constance R. 2004. "Celebrating Ourselves: The Family Reunion Rituals of African Caribbean Transnational Families." *Global Networks* 4, no. 3 (July): 243–57.

Swartz, David R. 2012. *Moral Minority: The Evangelical Left in an Age of Conservatism.* Philadelphia: University of Pennsylvania Press.

Taylor, Ula Yvette. 2017. *The Promise of Patriarchy: Women and the Nation of Islam.* Chapel Hill: University of North Carolina Press.

Thomas, Deborah A. 2013. "Racial Situations: Nationalist Vindication and Radical Deconstructionism." *Cultural Anthropology* 28, no. 3 (August): 519–26.

Thomas, Greg. 2015. "African Diasporic Blackness out of Line: Trouble for 'Post-Black' Americanism." In *The Trouble with Post-Blackness*, edited by Houston A. Baker and K. Merinda Simmons, 60–80. New York: Columbia University Press.

Thomas, Todne. 2016. "Strangers, Friends, and Kin: Negotiated Recognition in Ethnographic Relationships." *Anthropology and Humanism* 41, no. 1: 66–85.

Thomas, Todne, Asiya Malik, and Rose E. Wellman, eds. 2017. *New Directions in Spiritual Kinship: Sacred Ties across the Abrahamic Religions.* Cham, Switzerland: Palgrave Macmillan.

Thompson, Paul, and Elaine Bauer. 2000. "Jamaican Transnational Families: Points of Pain and Sources of Resilience." *Wadagabei* 3, no. 2 (July): 1–37.

Thornton, Brendan Jamal. 2016. *Negotiating Respect: Pentecostalism, Masculinity, and the Politics of Spiritual Authority in the Dominican Republic.* Gainesville: University Press of Florida.

Toulis, Nicole Rodriguez. 1997. *Believing Identity: Pentecostalism and the Mediation of Jamaican Ethnicity and Gender in England.* Oxford: Berg.

Tranby, Eric, and Douglas Hartmann. 2008. "Critical Whiteness Theories and the Evangelical 'Race Problem': Extending Emerson and Smith's *Divided by Faith*." *Journal for the Scientific Study of Religion* 47, no. 3: 341–59.

Turner, Victor W. 1995. *The Ritual Process: Structure and Anti-structure.* New York: Aldine de Gruyter.

Vickerman, Milton. 1999. *Crosscurrents: West Indian Immigrants and Race.* New York: Oxford University Press.

Vickerman, Milton. 2016. "Black Immigrants, Perceptions of Difference, and the Abiding Sting of Blackness." *Journal of American Ethnic History* 36, no. 1 (Fall): 71–81.

Von Germeten, Nicole. 2006. *Black Blood Brothers: Confraternities and Social Mobility for Afro-Mexicans.* Gainesville: University Press of Florida.

Wadsworth, Nancy. 2014. *Ambivalent Miracles: Evangelicals and the Politics of Racial Healing.* Charlottesville: University of Virginia Press.

Walrond, Eric. 1998. *"Winds Can Wake up the Dead": An Eric Walrond Reader*. Edited by Louis J. Paranscandola. Detroit, MI: Wayne State University Press.

Walrond, Eric. 2011 (1954). "Success Story." In *In Search of Asylum: The Later Writings of Eric Walrond*, edited by Louis J. Parascandola and Carl A. Wade, 104–40. Gainesville: University Press of Florida.

Wariboko, Waibinte E. 2007. *Ruined by "Race": Afro-Caribbean Missionaries and the Evangelization of Southern Nigeria, 1895–1925*. Trenton, NJ: Africa World.

Waters, Mary C. 2001. *Black Identities: West Indian Immigrant Dreams and American Realities*. New York: Sage.

Waters, Mary C. 2011. *The Next Generation: Immigrant Youth in a Comparative Perspective*. New York: New York University Press.

Watkins-Owens, Irma. 1996. *Blood Relations: Caribbean Immigrants and the Harlem Community, 1900–1930*. Bloomington: Indiana University Press.

Webster, Joseph. 2013. *The Anthropology of Protestantism: Faith and Crisis among Scottish Fishermen*. New York: Palgrave Macmillan.

Weisenfeld, Judith. 2017. *New World A-Coming: Black Religion and Racial Identity during the Great Migration*. New York: New York University Press.

Weston, Kath. 1991. *Families We Choose: Lesbians, Gays, Kinship*. New York: Columbia University Press.

Wheaton College Archives. 1990, 1995. "Collection 431: Oral History Interviews with T. Michael Flowers." https://archives.wheaton.edu/repositories/4/resources/1112.

Williams, Delores S. 1993. *Sisters in the Wilderness: The Challenge of Womanist God-Talk*. Maryknoll, NY: Orbis.

Wilson, Peter. 1969. "Reputation and Respectability: A Suggestion for Caribbean Ethnology." *Man* 4, no. 1: 70–84.

Wilson, Peter J. 1973. *Crab Antics: The Social Anthropology of English-Speaking Negro Societies of the Caribbean*. New Haven, CT: Yale University Press.

Wimbush, Vincent. 2003. *The Bible and African Americans: A Brief History*. Minneapolis, MN: Fortress Press.

Wimbush, Vincent L. 2012. *White Men's Magic: Scripturalization as Slavery*. New York: Oxford University Press.

Wuthnow, Robert. 1996. *Sharing the Journey: Support Groups and American's New Quest for Community*. New York: Simon and Schuster.

Yamahtta-Taylor, Keeanga. 2016. *From #BlackLivesMatter to Black Liberation*. Chicago: Haymarket.

Yanagisako, Sylvia, and Carol Delaney. 1995. *Naturalizing Power: Essays in Feminist Cultural Analysis*. New York: Routledge.

Zimmerman, Andrew. 2012. *Alabama in Africa: Booker T. Washington, the German Empire, and the Globalization of the New South*. Princeton, NJ: Princeton University Press.

Index

abolition, 19, 65
activism, 12, 81, 201, 223n11
Acts, Book of, 123
Adam (in Book of Genesis), 74, 76, 136–38
adultery, 39, 169–70, 192, 200, 225n1
African American Christianity, 11–13, 50, 59, 81–83, 92–94, 97, 100–106, 135, 209
Africana spirituality, 47–48, 52–53, 208
African Diaspora, 2, 5, 19, 46–47, 50–54, 74, 77, 208, 224n3; religious traditions, 98, 101–2, 164
Afro-Atlantic traditions, 50–51, 77, 164, 219n19, 221n10
Afro-Baptist traditions, 51, 63–67, 77, 95, 164, 219n18
Afro-Caribbean evangelicalism, 13, 70, 82–83, 97–98, 100–106, 228n20
Afro-Caribbean traditions, 94–95
Afro-Jamaican traditions, 1, 33, 52–59, 85–96, 115, 183, 189–91, 220n5, 228n19
Afro-Protestant traditions, 13, 64, 69, 79, 81, 209
American Missionary Association, 66
Andrews, Elder Samuel, 29–31, 36, 46–47, 49, 54, 112–16, 126, 224n5
Andrews, Sister Joanna, 47, 49–50
Anglican Church, 33, 60–61, 66, 81
antiblackness, 49–50, 76; material conditions and, 25; neo-evangelicalism implications and, 40–41, 173, 207; neo-liberalism and, 174, 192, 198. *See also* racism
antisectarianism, 5, 33, 164–65, 205–6

assimilation, 50–53, 92–93, 116, 178, 207
Atlanta University Center, 88
Avery, Brother James, 180

Baby Boomer generation, 184
Baker, Moses, 64
Baptist blood, 94–95
Baptist Home Mission Society, 66
Baptist Rebellion of 1831–1832, 65
Barrett, Elder Samuel, 86
Beaufort Bible Chapel, 70, 176
beloved community, 76
Berean, 120, 126, 216n3
Beverly LaHaye Institute, 42
Bible camp, 6, 63, 70, 145, 213n4
Bible school, 6, 22, 63, 145
biblicism, 19, 25, 106, 109–10, 120–22, 134, 205. *See also* fraternalism
Billy Graham Center, 58, 176, 219n2
biogenetic descent, 15, 47–49, 100, 179
Bivins, Sister Rita, 196–97
Black Church, the, 4, 6–7, 11–13, 18–21, 63, 71, 77–79; civic advancement and, 85, 88; definition of, 171–72; religious perspectives and, 93; social construction of, 102; 118, 164, 187, 205, 210, 214n6, 215n12, 217n9
black ethnic identity, 94, 97, 99, 186
Black Evangelical Association, 8, 63
black evangelicalism, 4–8, 13, 92, 100, 207–9, 213n5, 214n7, 215n13, 216n11; marriage and, 189–98; otherness and, 104

born-again, 19, 40, 48, 51–52, 62, 96, 103, 189, 213n4, 215n13; conversion, 6, 45, 60, 104, 201
born Brethren, 94–95, 180
breaking-of-bread ritual. *See* Communion
Brethrenism. *See* Plymouth Brethrenism
brotherhood, 25, 73–76, 158, 180, 192, 221n14; biblicism and, 110–11, 120; literalism and, 121–27; local meaning and, 112–20; ritual performance and, 130–34, 146. *See also* homosociality
brothers and sisters in Christ, 2–3, 45, 54, 72, 83, 133, 160, 192, 204, 207
Bush, George W., Jr., 12, 217n8
Butler, Sister Ramia, 183–84

Candomblé, 50
capitalism, 99, 173–74, 217n8, 226n6
Caribbean diaspora, 70, 94, 221n15
Carrington, Sister Selah, 197
Cedine Bible Camp, 70, 120, 150, 220n4
Chapman, Sister Evelyn, 44–46
Christianity, 20, 52, 130, 165–66; Abrahamic male authority and, 137; Afro-diasporic, 164; Bible-believing, 29, 51, 61, 70, 111, 176; binaries and, 76; black, 6, 92, 205; evangelical, 8, 10, 171, 178, 193, 201–3, 208–9, 214n11; prayer and, 127–28; Western, 7, 34
Christian Right, 8, 12, 40, 42, 80, 173. *See also* Moral Majority
Christian Zionism, 34
Church of God, 34, 139, 214n5
churchwomen. *See* Plymouth Brethrenism; sisterhood
citizenship, 41, 49, 69, 168, 172–73, 188, 198
civil rights movement, 40, 79, 81, 97, 173, 217–18n10, 221n15
Cleary, Sister Judene, 181
collectivism, 114–15, 153
colonialism, 5, 47–48, 50, 98, 101–2; racism and, 100; Western, 54, 80–81. *See also* postcolonialism
color lines, 98, 205
Columbia Bible College, 78
Commandment Keepers Ethiopian Hebrew Congregation, 68
Commission on Interracial Cooperation, 73
communalism, 124, 165, 224n9
Communion, 33–39, 54, 130–34, 146, 206
Concerned Women for America, 42

confessional intimacy, 25, 166, 171, 182, 188, 195–97, 206–7
congregational boundaries, 84, 92
congregationalism, 4, 9, 54, 82, 116
conservativism, 41, 80, 173, 203, 217n8, 217n10, 226n6
coreligionists, 37, 63, 74, 91, 98, 188, 194
Corinthians, First, 132, 137, 224n6, 228n21
Cuba, 142, 187
cult, 92, 216–17n6

Darby, John Nelson, 33–35, 220n5
Darbyites. *See* Exclusive Brethren
Davidson, Elder Jacob, 111
deindustrialization, 40, 173, 186, 222n2
denominationalism, 5–6, 33, 38, 47, 63, 205, 216n4, 220n8; Afro-Protestant, 68–69
deregulation, 173–74
desegregation, 40, 73, 79, 89, 97, 201, 222n3
diasporic blackness, 47, 104
diasporic kinship, 34, 46, 53
diasporic religious identity, 84
disenfranchisement, 13, 18–19, 39, 47, 72, 119
divorce, 39, 185, 189, 196–97, 200, 203–4
Dobson, James, 40
domesticity, 16, 106, 136, 146, 149–54. *See also* gender norms; sisterhood
Douglass, Sister Lisa, 114
Douglass, Sister Mildred, 112
Du Bois, W. E. B., 11, 66, 88

Edmondson, Brother William, 30–31, 33–34, 52–53
Edmondson, Sister Anita, 12
egalitarianism, 77, 112, 115, 118–19, 132–34, 144, 192–93
Ella's Caring Hands Day Center, 149
emotionalism, 62, 81
enslaved/enslavement, 18–19, 46–47, 50, 52, 102. *See also* slavery
entextualization, 122, 125, 129
entrepreneurialism, 173, 194–95, 222n1
Ethiopian Baptist Church, 64
ethnicity. *See* ethno-racial
ethno-congregationalism, 4, 24, 71, 78, 98, 100, 106, 205
ethno-nationalism, 5, 100, 102, 205
ethno-racial, 4–5, 20–21, 54, 59, 186; ancestry, 47; congregationalism, 20, 71, 78, 83–84, 95; friend-

248 · Index

ship, 144; genealogy, 34, 74; heteronormativity, 168; hierarchies, 76, 93, 98–99, 134; identities, 20, 90, 100, 103–6, 223n8; notions of otherness, 104, 187; parenting, 188; settings, 23, 94

ethno-religious: boundaries, 100, 106; distinctions, 97–99; identities, 5, 20, 84, 95; institutionalism, 172; membership, 105

Euro-Christian supremacy, 74, 224n8

evangelical racial reconciliation movement, 9, 76

evangelism, 6, 33, 59, 65–66, 80–87, 128–29, 162, 170, 177, 201

Eve (in Book of Genesis), 74, 136–38

Exclusive Brethren (Closed Brethren), 35–38, 216n6

exegesis, 4, 33, 74, 106, 117, 131–32, 138–41, 147, 193, 206

extended family, 25, 44, 114, 153, 171–72, 180, 219n17, 225n2

extra-institutional, 17, 73, 155, 159, 178, 195, 203–6

extramarital sex. *See* adultery

familial alterity, 84, 100, 104

Family Bible Conference, 70, 182

Family Life Community Center, 149

family of god, 1, 3, 8, 30–34, 45, 52–53, 82, 86, 112, 204–5, 216n4

Family Research Council, 42

family-values discourse, 40, 173, 175, 188

Father Divine Peace Mission, the, 68–69, 221n11

feeding, 4, 17, 135, 146–47, 155, 162–63, 206, 225n1

Fellowship of Southern Churchmen, 73

female submission, 117, 136, 139, 176, 190, 193

feminism, 16, 39–40, 136–38, 144–45, 177

fetishism, 178

fictive kinship, 15–16, 49, 110, 124–25, 134, 172, 215n14

First Great Awakening, 7–8, 64

First Missionary Baptist Church, 64

Fitzpatrick, Elder Brother Roy, 123

Flowers, Sister Ella, 57–58, 83, 148–52, 220n4

Flowers, T. Michael, 8, 24, 133, 213n1, 214n9, 219nn1–2, 221n12, 221n15, 224n2; Bible chapels and, 120, 176–78; fraternalism and, 110–12; memories of Ella and, 148–51; religious imaginaries and, 104–6

Focus on the Family, 40

Forde, Brother John, 42

Framingham, Sister Lou Ellen, 96

fraternalism, 4, 24–25, 73–76, 106–19, 124–25, 133, 177, 198. *See also* biblicism

Frazier, E. Franklin, 67, 222n11

friendship, 46, 144–45, 156–58, 195

fundamentalism, 32, 36, 40, 63, 81, 122, 201, 213nn4–5, 215n13

Garden of Eden, 136

Garvey, Marcus, 81

gender ideology, 154, 162, 192–93, 196–97, 203, 224n2; biblical teaching and, 110, 122, 128–29, 137, 206; labor and, 146; moral economy and, 43; patriarchy and, 40, 113, 117, 134, 137; sociality and, 140; spaces and, 136–38. *See also* domesticity; brotherhood; sisterhood

genealogical imaginaries, 34, 53

Generation X, 184

Genesis, Book of, 29, 58, 72, 74–75, 126, 136–38, 221n12

geopolitical hierarchies, 42, 193, 223n8

Goode, Brother Jacob, 181–82

Goode, Sister Yvette, 23, 181–82

Goodison, Brother Edwin, 89–90

Great Commission, 128–29

Great Migration, 67–69

Great Recession, 174

Halliwell, Brother David, 114

Halliwell, Sister Brenda, 149

Hamilton, Brother Moses, 115–16

Hastings, Elder John, 176–77, 196–97

Hastings, Sister Alana, 196–97

Hebrews, Epistle to the, 31, 126

heteronormativity, 2–5, 18–20, 39, 69, 190, 206; black, 172, 175, 189; displacement of, 86, 171, 221n11; evangelical constructions of, 204, 208; family and, 15, 25, 32, 41–43, 48, 167–68, 170, 184, 197; marriage and, 195–96, 198, 200–4

heteropatriarchy, 40–43, 175, 193, 202, 209, 226n6

heterosexuality, 41–42, 69, 96, 189, 191, 195, 217n9, 225n1

Hines, Samuel, 9

Holy Spirit, 1, 34, 45, 57, 112, 197–98, 207, 225n1

homosociality, 21, 46, 113. *See also* brotherhood

Howard Center, 42

human genealogy, 30, 33, 52, 74–76

humanism, 51, 76

Hutchins, Sister Wanda, 149, 158–59, 167

immigrants: Afro-Caribbean, 2, 5, 38, 48, 213n2; black, 97–99; Caribbean, 61; ethnic congregations, 90
imperialism, 52, 58–59, 61–66, 74, 80–82, 101, 193
individualism, 9, 41, 91, 96, 173–74, 182, 185
institutionalism, 164, 172–73, 202
integration, 41, 78, 82, 98, 173, 186
interracialism, 8, 10, 72, 76
Intervarsity collegiate ministries, 120–21
intraracialism, 13, 61–69, 73, 77, 101, 187, 205, 209

Jamaican Native Baptists, 64
James, C. L. R., 81
James, Lemuel, 59
Jesus Christ, 1, 14, 29–34, 37, 78, 104, 126; communion and, 129, 131–32; relationship to the Church, 190, 197
Jim Crow, 47, 55, 58, 70–71, 222n3. *See also* segregation
Johnson, Brother Cedric, 121
Johnson, Brother Winston, 30
Johnson, Sister Etta, 87
Johnson, Sister Lisa, 161
Johnson, Sister Maya, 92, 142

King, Martin Luther, Jr., 75–77, 79, 88
kin-making, 18, 45–48, 53, 152, 204, 207
kitchen table talk, 4, 157, 160–61, 225n2; Bible study and, 57, 72, 219n2; sisterhood and, 145, 152–54

Last Supper, 130–31
Latter Day Saints, 182. *See also* Mormonism
law of first mention, 123–24
Left, the, 12, 13, 80
Lewis, Sister Marsha, 30
LGBTQ, 190, 201–2
Lisle, George, 64, 214n7
literalism, 13, 25, 52, 61, 69, 110, 134, 224n8, 224n11; brotherhood and, 121–25. *See also* Word of God
Lithonia, Georgia, 2, 22, 85, 160, 168, 187, 197
Littlefield, Brother Earl, 168–70, 192
lived experience, 6, 15–16, 25, 49, 75, 103, 142, 178, 198, 204
Long, Sister Janet, 182
Lorenzo, Sister Constance, 51
Lorne, Brother Henrick, 120

male headship, 117, 137, 176, 190–93
malungo, 46–47. *See also* shipmate networks

Manchester, Sister Regina, 138–40
manhood, 113, 177
marginalization, 39, 73, 88, 90, 93, 190, 202, 224n3
Marshall, Brother Delroy, 153, 225n2
Marshall, Sister Francine, 143, 153–54, 157, 225n2
Marume, Ann, 2, 85, 152
masculinity, 42, 113–14, 177
matrifocal household, 171–72
McKay, Claude, 81
Melchizedek, 29, 31, 46–47, 126–27
mentorship, 4, 16–17, 111, 149, 175, 200, 206, 208
Methodism, 63, 95
middle-class, 117, 181, 195; black, 171, 174, 185, 194, 217–18n10, 222n1; Euro-American, 68, 119; features of, 43; white, 42, 93, 168, 173
Middle Passage, 46. *See also* transatlantic slave trade
migration, 84–85, 94, 102, 223n9; African American, 102, 216n16; Afro-Caribbean, 70, 89, 162–63; first- and second-generation, 186–87; serial; 103; southern, 67–69
Millennial generation, 184–85
miscegenation, 173
missionaries, 44, 59, 64, 66–67, 80, 219n9, 220n5
missionization, 58, 64–65, 80, 219n12
modernity, 34, 66, 68–69, 81, 89
monogamy, 169, 191–92
Moore, John, 84–85
Moorish Science Temple Movement, 68
morality/moralization, 19, 24, 41, 98, 176, 185–86, 206; Christian, 137, 159, 170, 180, 198, 216n5; conservative, 173, 217n8; evangelical, 203; familial, 171, 174, 227n13
Moral Majority, 6, 32, 113, 173, 185–86. *See also* Christian Right
Mormonism, 42, 182
Morrison, Sister Amanda, 203
Morton, Samuel George, 72
Moynihan Report, 40–41, 194
mutual aid systems, 114, 210
My Brother's Keeper Initiative, 174–75, 225nn4–5
Myers, Brother Bill, 168

National Black Evangelical Association, 8, 63
nationalism, 81–82, 99
Nation of Islam (NOI), 68, 194
Native Baptists, Jamaican, 64–65
Negro Church, 11. *See also* Black Church, the

Nelson, Brother Roger, 30
neoconservatism, 40, 175
neo-evangelicalism, 6, 8, 20, 59, 81, 83, 173, 201, 221n15; the black family and, 175–78, 191; family and, 32, 45–46, 113, 166, 186, 217n10; gender and, 42; hegemonic whiteness and, 9–10, 41; US, 32, 39–40, 43, 87, 97, 179, 203, 207; marriage and, 189; politics and, 79, 215n13, 217n7
neoliberalism, 4, 170, 173–75, 186, 193–94
New Testament, 121–24, 126, 128, 224nn9–10; Christianity, 33, 124–25, 134; Churches, 25, 69, 85, 110, 137; ecclesiology, 112; fellowship, 52, 114–15, 130–33; traditions
Newton, Benjamin Wills, 35
New World, 5; blackness, 46, 164; kinship, 50; religion, 64, 102
NOI. *See* Nation of Islam
Nott, Josiah, 72
Nottage, Berlin Martin, 62–67
Nottage, Talbot Berton, 62–67
Nottage, Whitfield, 62–67
nuclear family, 4, 7, 43, 171, 177–78, 196, 203, 209–10; heteronormative, 32, 48, 167–68; Western, 119

Obama, Barack, 12, 88, 174, 225nn4–5, 226n6
Obeah, 51
Old Testament, 34, 124, 126
Open Brethren, 35–37
original sin, 8, 75, 136
orthodoxy, 6, 19, 75, 203, 207, 213n4

Park School of Sociology, 67
paternalism, 34, 60, 73, 157
patriarchy, 16–17, 38, 73, 113; biblical practices and, 106; church leadership and, 134, 138; family and, 6, 168, 171, 177, 188, 192, 196, 208; gender and, 76, 146, 191; institutional, 176; religion and, 140, 164, 180, 184; social structures and, 118, 194
Pentecostalism, 69, 100, 147, 218nn11–12, 228n19; Afro-, 6, 22, 164, 214n5; breaking of bread and, 130
Perkins, John, 9, 57, 79
plantation regimes, 17, 47–48, 64–65, 101, 165. *See also* slavery
Plymouth Brethrenism, 5, 22, 59, 63, 72, 82, 218n12; Afro-diasporic, 79, 164, 188, 190; Bible study and, 110–12, 119–21, 125, 213nn4–5; church leader-ship and, 216n1; churchwomen, 117, 135, 147, 165; ecclesiology of, 32–38, 43, 201; heteropatriarchal norms and, 180, 192; Jamaica and, 220n5, 228n19; primitivism, 50, 53, 54, 55, 205; traditionalism, 114–18
post-colonialism, 13, 18, 66, 98, 102, 119, 168, 188. *See also* colonialism
post-racial era, 6, 88
prayer partnership, 2, 4, 25, 54, 83, 117; sociality and, 155–59, 166. *See also* sisterhood; spiritual motherhood
predatory lending, 174
premarital sex, 39
premillennialism, 63
private sphere, 17, 36, 39, 174, 194
privatization, 43, 173–74, 197, 208
Promise Keepers Movement, 9, 113
Protestantism, 5, 7, 20, 58, 147, 218n11, 219n18; Anglo-Saxon, 92; evangelical, 32, 66, 76. *See also* Afro-Protestant traditions
Psalms, Book of, 126, 226n7

racialization, 2, 10, 48, 52–54, 98, 102, 114, 186, 198, 208, 218n10
racial hegemony, 7, 9, 201, 207
racial reconciliation movement, 9, 76–79, 90–91, 201, 214n9
racio-religious systems, 10, 51, 74, 84, 89, 178, 188, 198, 205
racism, 6, 10, 54, 78, 90, 101, 194; antiblackness and, 4, 8, 13, 52–53, 71, 74, 88, 166, 171, 187; institutional, 79–80; scientific, 66, 72, 88; as sin, 76; systemic, 61; theological, 72; white evangelical, 24. *See also* antiblackness
Randall, Brother Lawrence, 44–46
rebellion, 64–65, 137
Reconstruction era, 66, 88
religious transmission, 181–83, 186
respectability politics, 18, 173
Richardson, Brother Joseph, 114
Right, the, 12, 13, 80
Robbins, Sister Pauline, 143, 160–63
Roxbury, Sister Ethel, 12

salvation, 1, 8, 17, 34, 76, 201, 205, 214n7; collective, 68, 182, 186; neo-evangelical, 177, 221n15; Protestant, 123; racial, 69, 90
Sanchez, Sonia, 194

Index · 251

Santería, 50
Saunders, Sister Andrea, 31, 46–47, 53–54
secularism, 185–86
segregation, 67, 71, 77–78, 89, 222n1; materiality of, 72; racial, 8, 20, 24, 205; religious, 91; southern, 60, 81. *See also* Jim Crow
sexual sin, 43, 169–70, 192, 225n1
SGMA. *See* Southern Gospel Mission Association
Sharpe, Samuel "Daddy," 65
shipmate networks, 46–47. *See also* enslaved; *malungo*
Silent Majority, 41, 173
sisterhood, 76, 123, 155, 164–66, 192, 224n2; feminism and, 144; material reciprocity and, 114; as religious agents, 148; social processes of, 141–43; work of feeding and, 145–47. *See also* prayer partnership; spiritual motherhood
Skinner, Tom, 9, 57, 78
slavery, 5, 65, 101, 216n1; familial loss and, 50; kinship and, 18, 46–47; polygenists and, 72. *See also* enslaved/enslavement
social gospel, 81
social mobility, 2, 6, 68, 83, 172–78, 186–87, 218n10, 227n13
Solomon, Sister Beulah, 86–87
Southern Gospel Mission Association (SGMA), 70, 121, 133
spiritual children, 2, 4, 54, 83, 160–62, 204, 207
spiritual kin, 2–3, 15–17, 72, 129, 167, 171–72, 182–84, 204–9
spiritual family, 3, 100, 162–63
spiritual fatherhood, 2, 25, 204, 207
spiritual motherhood, 2, 25, 100, 117, 160–64, 180, 204, 207–8. *See also* sisterhood; prayer partnership
Stewart, Brother Bernard, 14–16, 199–200, 204
Stewart, Sister Tabitha, 199–200, 204
subprime mortgage sector, 174
supersessionism, 33–34, 52–53
Sutton, Sister Clara, 1–2
Sweet Auburn, 88

testimony, 33, 141–43, 169, 183, 198
theology of whiteness, 34, 216n5

transatlantic slave trade, 46
transcendence, 19, 34, 58, 73, 122
transnationalism, 13, 43, 45, 106; black Christianity, 64; networks, 48, 50, 60, 205, 227n13
Trent, Sister Evelyn, 109, 134
Trent, Sister Lola, 155–57
Trinidadian Spiritual Baptist Church, 51, 64, 221n9
Turner, Nat, 65

United Bible Conference, 70, 189
United Nations, 42
universal Church, 32, 80, 208
universalism, 24, 55, 73, 84, 177–78
US evangelicalism, 4, 32, 40, 104; white, 8–10, 59, 71, 78, 81, 89–91, 223n7
US exceptionalism, 75, 217n10
US multiculturalism, 88
US South, 43, 48, 51, 55; churches and, 120, 176, 219n18; missionaries and, 64, 67, 80–81, 110–13; race and, 73, 78; segregation and, 58, 60

Victorian norms, 168, 180, 192, 208
Voice of Calvary, 79
Voodou, 50

Warrington, Edward, 1–2
Washington, Sister Claire, 117, 144
Washington, Brother Earl, 85–86
welfare, 10, 40–41, 173
Western genealogical grid, 15, 49
white Christian supremacy, 34, 89, 224n8
white privilege, 9–10
white supremacism, 75, 82, 93, 194
Whittam, Brother Earl, 162–63
Wilkerson, Brother James, 95, 100–101
Williams, Brother Alex, 105
Winston, Sister Sharon, 189, 191
Word of God, 6, 58, 62, 122–23, 147. *See also* literalism
working-class, 117, 171–72, 187, 217–18n10, 224n3
World Council of Families II, 42

yardspaces, 151–53, 162–66